Theft! A History of Music
© James Boyle and Jennifer Jenkins (2017)

This book is made available under the terms of a Creative Commons Attribution-Noncommercial-Sharealike 3.0 Unported license.

http://creativecommons.org/licenses/by-nc-sa/3.0/

This license gives you important freedoms, including the right to copy and distribute this book noncommercially without permission or fee, so long as you adhere to the terms described below.

Attribution-NonCommercial-ShareAlike 3.0 Unported (CC-BY-NC-SA 3.0)

You are free to:

- **Share** — copy and redistribute the material in any medium or format
- **Adapt** — remix, transform, and build upon the material

Under the following terms:

Attribution — You must attribute the work as: **Theft! A History of Music** by James Boyle, Jennifer Jenkins & Keith Aoki

NonCommercial — You may not use the material for commercial purposes, which we interpret to mean "to make a profit."

Share Alike — If you alter, transform, or build upon this work, you may distribute the resulting work only under a license identical to this one and you must indicate that changes have been made to the work.

- **No additional restrictions** — You may not apply legal terms or technological measures that legally restrict others from doing anything the license permits.

Any of these conditions can be waived if you get permission from the copyright holders. Your fair use and other rights are in no way affected by the above.

Credits:
Initial Sketches: Keith Aoki
Research, Writing and Graphic Design: James Boyle & Jennifer Jenkins
Art, Illustration and Inking: Ian Akin & Brian Garvey
Lettering, Coloring, Digital Publishing: Balfour Smith

About the Artists: After the tragic death of Keith Aoki, we had to find new artists to redraw the book from scratch. Those artists were Ian Akin and Brian Garvey. Veteran comic book illustrators and inkers, Ian and Brian have done work for Marvel, DC, Disney and many others. Their task was a daunting one: they had to come into a book designed and written by law professors and translate the vision of a beloved deceased artist into their own idiom. All of this in a work that was part comic book, part academic monograph. They were, quite simply, magnificent. You can see, in the pages that follow, what consummate professionals they are. They are also lovely folk to work with and we recommend them wholeheartedly. http://www.akinandgarvey.com/

Dedicated to
Keith Aoki 1955–2011

This book is dedicated to Keith Aoki: our colleague, co-author and, above all, our friend. Keith passed away, tragically young, while we were creating the comic. He told us of his illness matter-of-factly, a week before his death, as an "apology" for not completing more of the drawings Jennifer and I had designed. He also told us that he wanted us to finish the book we had begun together; in fact he told us that we had to finish the book. Those were the last words we heard him say. We later realized that he had been battling his illness through much of our work on the comic, never complaining.

Keith had told us we had to finish the book. It was only half done. We had no heart for it. In the end, it meant starting again and redrawing the book from scratch with two wonderful professional artists, Ian Akin and Brian Garvey. Every page we went through was a reminder of a conversation we had had with Keith, a joke we had made, a crazy reference to pop culture, or film noir or music or law — because Keith was an artist, a legal scholar, and a hilarious culture-jammer. And each of those reminders was a sad one. It was a deeply painful task. Still, Keith had told us we had to finish the book. Those are the kinds of commands one does not disobey.

If Keith had written this dedication, it would be unsentimental, it would redirect all the praise to others and it would be darkly funny, because Keith had a very dark sense of humor where he was the subject. The last law review "article" he published was a comic with himself as a character. If one looks closely at the T-shirt the character is wearing, it says, "You can't avoid the void." Keith knew he was dying when he drew that. No one else did.

We published a book of quotes and drawings to remember Keith — *Keith Aoki: Life as the Art of Kindness*. You can find it elsewhere. We will not rehash it here except to say: we shall not look upon his like again. Would that the rest of us could be that kind, that modest, that creative.

We finished the comic for you, man. It took us long enough. Sorry about that. But you were terrible with deadlines too, just terrible. So perhaps you'll cut us a break. You can't avoid the void. But you can make something beautiful, funny and even maybe insightful that escapes it for a little while.

James Boyle & Jennifer Jenkins
Durham, NC. 2016

Acknowledgments: We are standing on the shoulders of giants. J. Peter Burkholder's magisterial set of works on musical borrowing—he literally wrote the book(s) on the subject—was our constant guide. Professor Michael Carroll is a pioneer of the history of copyright and music and many of his insights are reflected here. Professor Olufunmilayo Arewa has written extensively about musical borrowing, appropriation and copyright. Her work was an inspiration. Our colleague and co-teacher, Dr. Anthony Kelley of the Duke Music Department provided a composer's insights more times than we can remember. But our debts go far beyond the people mentioned here. At the end of the book you will find a lengthier list of acknowledgments and further reading, while an online companion to this comic lists references for each page and every point we make. (We are geeks. So sue us.) We would also like to thank our indispensable colleague Balfour Smith, who lettered and colored the comic and wrangled the digital files over countless versions. We have been helped over the years by many research assistants: Peter Berris, Cody Duncan, Cory Fleming, Branch Furtado, Justin Greenbaum, Federico Morris, Dan Ruccia, and Michael Wolfe. Finally, we would like to acknowledge the generous support of the Ford and Rockefeller Foundations and of the Duke Law School. Errors are ours alone.

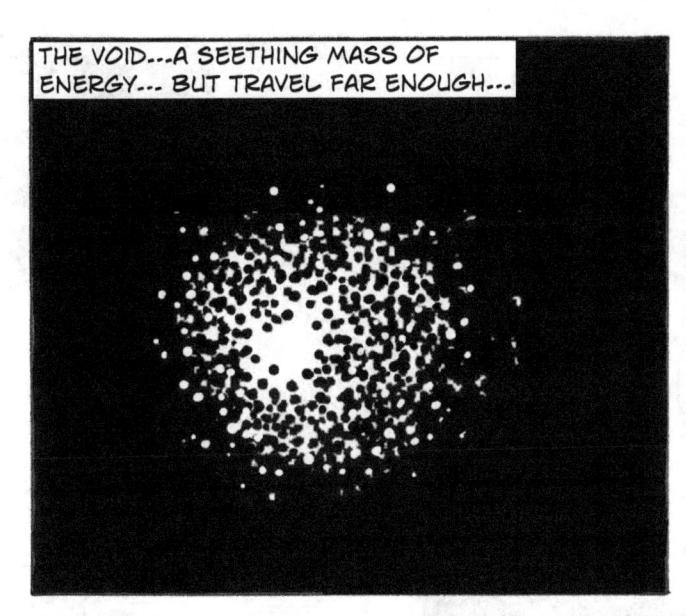

THE VOID...A SEETHING MASS OF ENERGY... BUT TRAVEL FAR ENOUGH...

AND ONE FINDS FAMILIAR FEATURES...

EXPERTS TELL US THAT MOST OF THIS GREAT UNIVERSE IS UNSEEN, INVISIBLE...

SCIENCE KNOWS LITTLE OF IT. YET IT MAKES UP 90% OF EVERYTHING AROUND US...

IS THIS STRANGE SUBSTANCE THE MISSING MASS?... DARK MATTER?

NO. IT IS THE PUBLIC DOMAIN... AND I AM THE TELLER OF ITS TALES.

COME IN, I HAVE BEEN EXPECTING YOU...

MOST OF OUR CULTURE AND SCIENCE...

PLOT LINES AND GENRES, FORMULAE AND THEORIES...

MOST OF IT COMES FROM THE PUBLIC DOMAIN, THE GREAT WELLSPRING OF CREATIVITY...

THE CHORDS AND THEMES OF OUR SONGS, OUR IDEAS...

TOGETHER WITH THE MATERIAL THAT IS OWNED — CONTROLLED BY COPYRIGHTS AND PATENTS — IT FORMS A BALANCE, AN ECOSYSTEM OF THE MIND.

NO ENTRY UNLESS AUTHORIZED

AND THAT BALANCE IS STUDIED BY THE STRANGEST PEOPLE. WHERE WILL THEY TAKE US TONIGHT?

OUR HOSTS: TWO FIGURES WHO OBSESSIVELY STUDY THIS REALM, AS THOUGH THEY HAD BEEN CURSED TO CHART THE LINE BETWEEN FREEDOM AND CONTROL IN EACH FIELD OF HUMAN CULTURE.*

HI!

HI!

WHAT ART FORM SHALL WE EXPLORE TONIGHT? MOVIES? LITERATURE?

MUSIC!!

*FOR THEIR PREVIOUS ADVENTURE, SEE BOUND BY LAW? —EDS.

WHY CAN'T I WRITE A SONG WITH THE SAME GROOVE AS ANOTHER? I FEEL LIKE THERE ARE ... BLURRED LINES!
I DIDN'T THINK YOU WERE THAT ... THICKE HEADED.
HAVEN'T MUSICIANS ALWAYS BORROWED FROM EACH OTHER?
I DON'T EVEN CONTROL THE RIGHTS TO MY OWN SONGS!!
WHY NO VIDEOS OF CATS PLAYING THE LYRE?
WHEN DID WE START THINKING THAT MUSIC WAS SOMETHING THAT COULD BE OWNED?
WHAT, YOU DON'T WANT MUSICIANS TO GET PAID?
CC

AND THUS BEGINS OUR TALE. OVER 2000 YEARS OF MUSIC AND BORROWING, FROM PLATO TO RAP...
AAAAAA!!!
OH JOY. NOW IT'S PICTURES OF DANCING ABOUT ARCHITECTURE.

AND HERE IS YOUR GUIDE ON THAT JOURNEY. COMPOSER, MUSICOLOGIST, HISTORIAN ...AND HE HAS A NICE CAR.
WOW!
MOON? VACUUM? I GUESS IT'S FOR DRAMATIC ... "ATMOSPHERE."
PLEASED TO MEET YOU. HOP IN.
WHAT KIND OF MILEAGE DO YOU GET IN THIS THING?
????
ABOUT 500 YEARS A GALLON.
WHAT DOES THIS BUTTON DO?
HEY, DON'T TOUCH THA....

DUDE DESCENDING A GRAVITY STAIRCASE

WHOOOOAH!!!

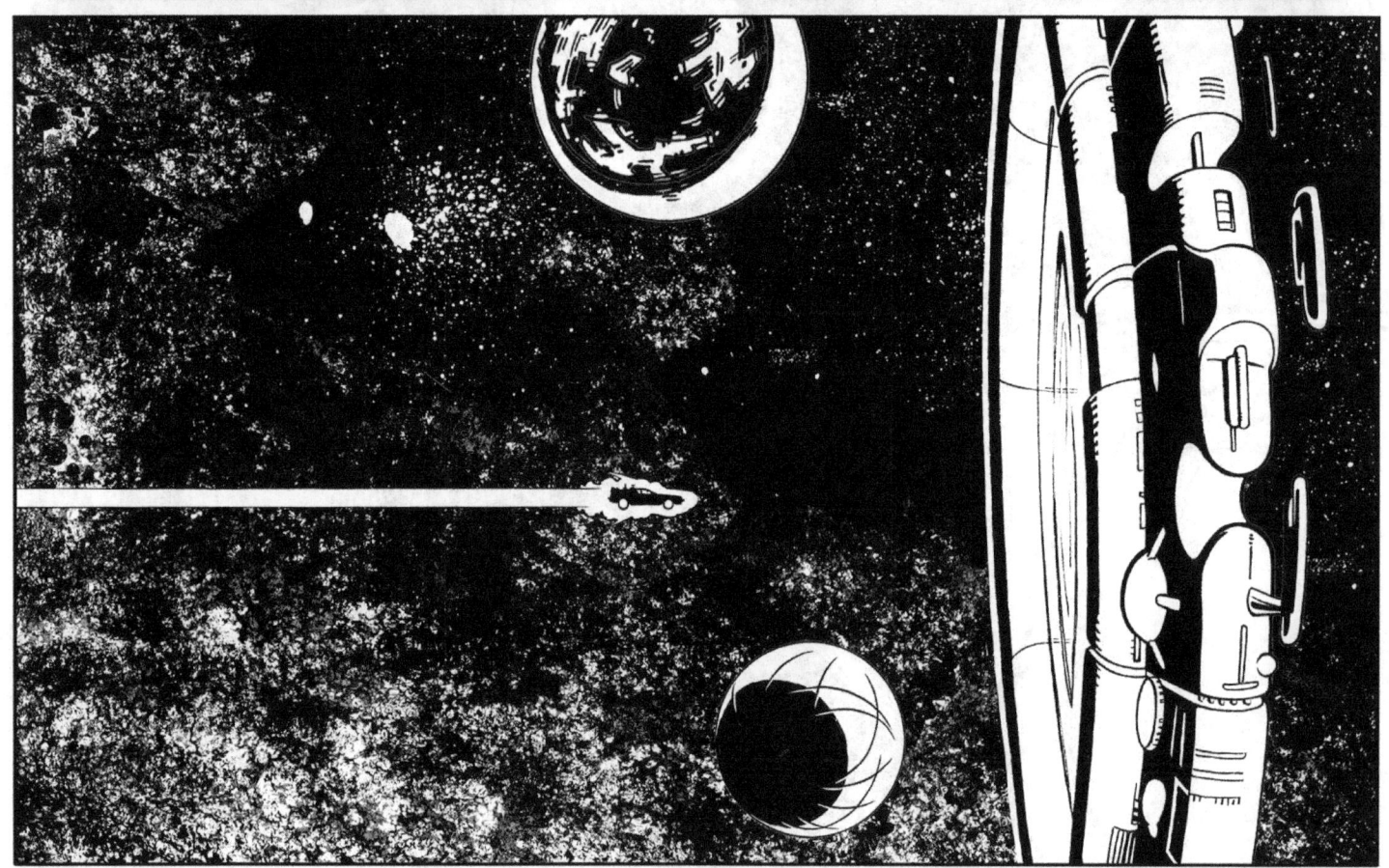

SO, THAT GUY SAID YOU WERE THE EXPERT. WHEN WAS THE FIRST TIME SOMEONE LISTENED TO A SONG AND THOUGHT IT WAS SOMETHING THAT COULD BE OWNED...?

WELL, THAT DEPENDS ON WHAT YOU MEAN BY "IT" AND WHAT YOU MEAN BY "OWNED."

IS THIS ONE OF THOSE LEGAL ANSWERS? DEPENDS WHAT THE DEFINITION OF "IS" IS?

"I DID NOT SAMPLE SONGS WITH THIS WOMAN!"

ACTUALLY, NO...

"WHEN WE THINK OF MUSIC, WE THINK OF IT AS "FROZEN." IN CDs OR MP3 FILES...

...OR TAPES, VINYL, SHELLAC... WAX CYLINDERS.

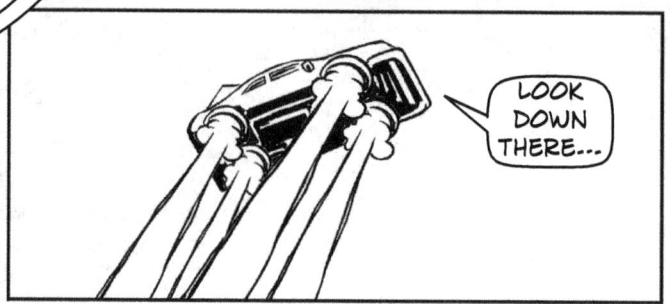

SO UNTIL MUSIC COULD BE MECHANICALLY RECORDED, IT WAS ALL JUST AN EXPERIENCE? SOMETHING THAT COULDN'T BE OWNED, ANY MORE THAN A SMELL OR A...LAUGH?

WELL, THERE ARE OTHER WAYS OF "RECORDING"... ONES THAT USE HUMANS AS THE PLAYBACK DEVICE...

TAKE SHEET MUSIC. NOTATION RECORDS MUSIC FOR LATER PLAYBACK.

A BRILLIANT IDEA — IT'S THE MUSICAL EQUIVALENT OF THE INVENTION OF WRITING! THAT'S WHERE OUR STORY BEGINS.

LOOK DOWN THERE...

EVEN THE MYTHICAL BEASTS! IT'S ALMOST JUNGIAN, THOUGH SCOTT McCLOUD WOULD ARGUE...

SOMEONE WATCHED *WAY* TOO MUCH FANTASIA...

THAT IS A COMPETITION BETWEEN DIFFERENT MUSICIANS. SCHOLARS THINK THE GREEKS SAW THEM AS A SPORTING EVENT...

YEAH, BATTLE OF THE BANDS, BC!!

HELLENIC IDOL!

DISNEY-FIED HISTORY AND HE CAN'T DRIVE...

SO ARE WE SEEING THE BIRTH OF NOTATION?

THE EARLIEST NOTATION WE KNOW OF COMES FROM LONG BEFORE THIS — 1400 BC IN MESOPOTAMIA. BUT... HOLD ON. I NEED TO LAND BY THAT STONE DOWN THERE.

THAT'S A HYMN TO APOLLO. THE MARKS ABOVE THE LETTERS INDICATE THE MELODY.

THIS IS A 2ND CENTURY CE ROMAN SCROLL OF A GREEK SONG. BUT IT GIVES US AN IDEA OF WHAT GREEK MUSIC WAS LIKE.

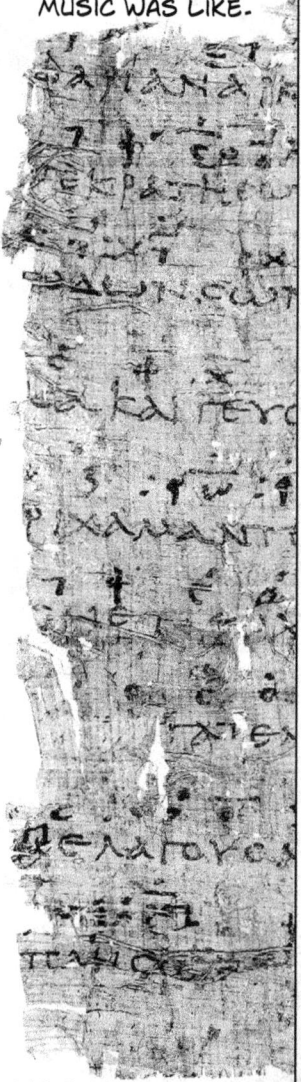

SO THE GREEKS CERTAINLY HAD NOTATION, THOUGH IT SEEMS TO HAVE BEEN USED INFREQUENTLY — AS A HISTORICAL RECORD OF SONGS, NOT SOMETHING MUSICIANS USED EVERY DAY.

WE USED TO THINK WE'D NEVER KNOW HOW THESE TUNES SOUNDED — NOW, SOME SCHOLARS THINK THEY CAN MAKE A PRETTY GOOD GUESS.

HE REALLY IS AN EXPERT! A LITTLE KNOW-IT-ALL, THOUGH...

THE SMALL SYMBOLS ABOVE THE TEXT ARE NOTES; THE LINES, THE RHYTHM.

SO SING IT FOR US, THEN.

"I WILL HOLD A BOW BEFORE YOUR FEET, AND I WILL SING THE SONG OF THE KASTALIAN NYMPHS...

I WILL TASTE OF YOUR HAIR..."

"PROBABLY A LOVE SONG...

...WRITTEN BY SOMEONE WHO HAS BEEN DUST FOR 2000 YEARS."

Panel 1:
AHEM...
COUGH
WELL...

Panel 2:
EERIE-SOUNDING. LIKE A GREGORIAN CHANT ONE MINUTE AND AN INDIAN RAGA THE NEXT... I WONDER IF I COULD USE THAT ON MY FIRST ALBUM!? "LAWYER TURNED ROCK STAR!"

Panel 3:
IT MIGHT SELL IN STARBUCKS AND WHOLE FOODS, I GUESS.

Panel 4:
SO WHAT ABOUT THE ANSWER TO OUR QUESTION? WE'VE GOT NOTATION. DID THAT MEAN PEOPLE OWNED SONGS?

Panel 5:
NOT SO FAR AS WE CAN TELL. REMEMBER, NOTATION WASN'T USED THAT MUCH...

Panel 1: "TAKE THE PLAYWRIGHT EURIPIDES..."

Panel 2: "THY BROTHER, THIS ILL-STARRED ORESTES WHO SLEW HIS MOTHER!" / "YOU THINK THAT'S BAD? THERE'S THIS GUY OEDIPUS..."

Panel 3: "...GO POUR ROUND CLYTEMENESTRA'S TOMB A MINGLED CUP OF HONEY, MILK, AND FROTHING WINE..."

Panel 4: "HE WROTE THE MUSIC FOR HIS PLAYS." / "THERE'S A FRAGMENT FROM ORESTES. BUT MUCH LESS MUSIC THAN TEXT SURVIVES."

Panel 5: "IN PRACTICE, MOST MUSIC APPEARS TO HAVE BEEN GENERATED BY IMPROVISATION AROUND COMMON THEMES..."

Panel 6: "...MAKES IT HARDER TO SAY, 'MINE!'" / "SO THERE'S NO INDICATION THAT THERE WAS ANY SENSE OF 'OWNERSHIP' OF MUSIC." / "FAME AND ATTRIBUTION, YES! PROPERTY CONTROL? NO!"

16

"THIS IS THE POINT TO WHICH, ABOVE ALL, THE ATTENTION OF OUR RULERS SHOULD BE DIRECTED, -- THAT MUSIC AND GYMNASTIC BE PRESERVED IN THEIR ORIGINAL FORM, AND NO INNOVATION MADE. THEY MUST DO THEIR UTMOST TO MAINTAIN THEM INTACT. AND WHEN ANY ONE SAYS THAT MANKIND MOST REGARD 'THE NEWEST SONG WHICH THE SINGERS HAVE,' THEY WILL BE AFRAID THAT HE MAY BE PRAISING, NOT NEW SONGS, BUT A NEW KIND OF SONG; AND THIS OUGHT NOT TO BE PRAISED, OR CONCEIVED TO BE THE MEANING OF THE POET; FOR ANY MUSICAL INNOVATION IS FULL OF DANGER TO THE WHOLE STATE, AND OUGHT TO BE PROHIBITED. SO DAMON TELLS ME, AND I CAN QUITE BELIEVE HIM; -- HE SAYS THAT WHEN MODES OF MUSIC CHANGE, THOSE OF THE STATE ALWAYS CHANGE WITH THEM."

[PLATO, THE REPUBLIC --EDS.]

18

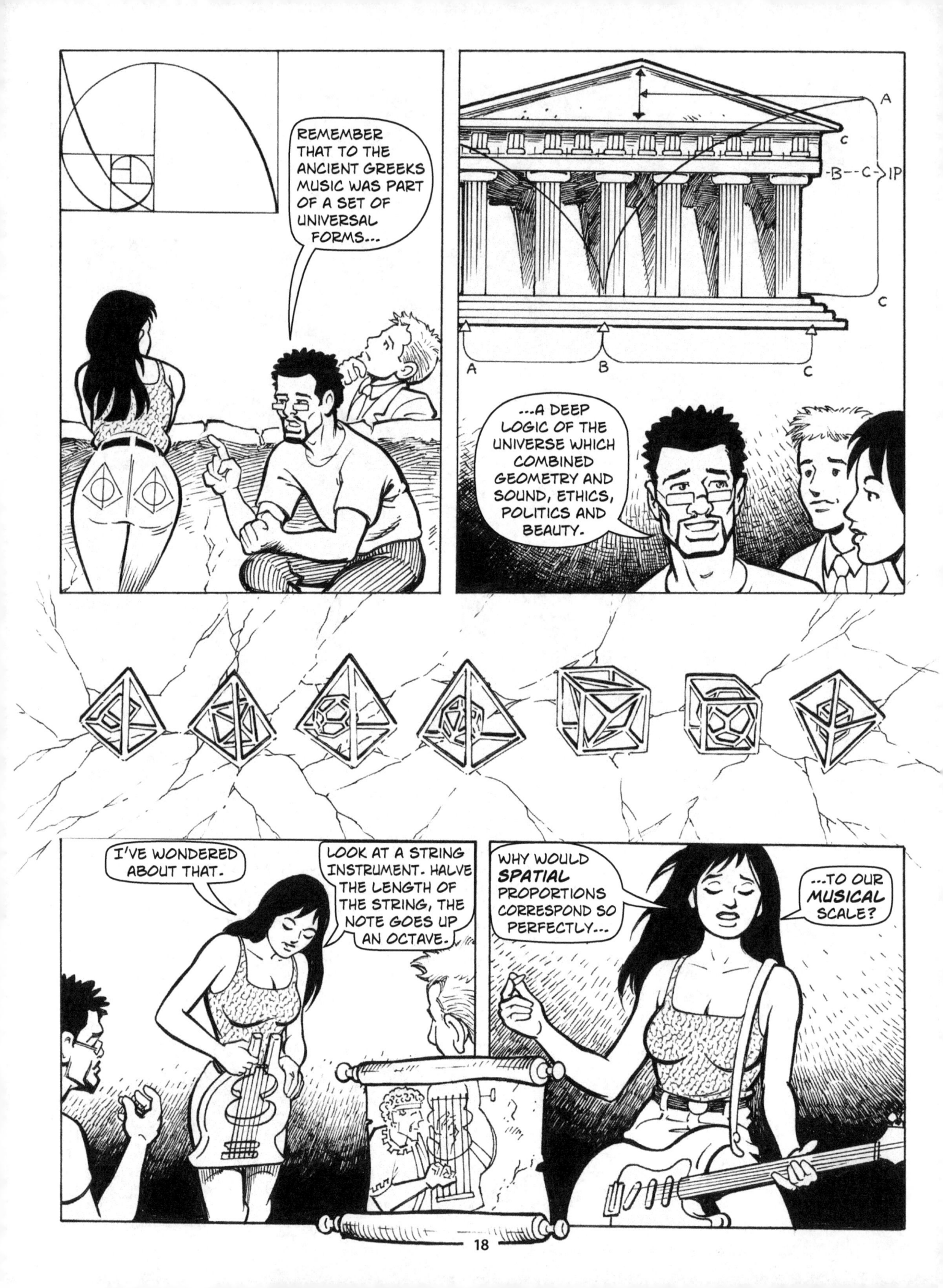

A BRIEF SNIPPET FROM GREEK MUSIC THEORY

THE GREEKS USED FAMILIAR CONCEPTS SUCH AS "NOTES" THAT CORRESPONDED TO A PARTICULAR PITCH, AND "INTERVALS" — THE SPACE BETWEEN NOTES — WHICH PYTHAGORAS DERIVED FROM MATHEMATICAL RATIOS.

IF THESE WERE VIBRATING GUITAR STRINGS, THE SECOND WOULD SOUND AN OCTAVE HIGHER THAN THE FIRST:

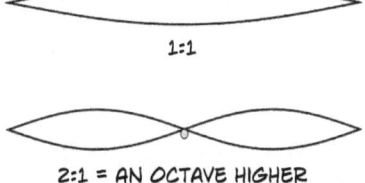

A 2:1 RATIO MAKES THE INTERVAL OF AN OCTAVE!

1:1

2:1 = AN OCTAVE HIGHER

THE GREEKS ALSO HAD UNIQUE CONCEPTS SUCH AS THE "**TETRACHORD**," WHICH WAS A BASIC MUSICAL UNIT, LIKE THE OCTAVE TODAY.

A TETRACHORD IS A GROUP OF FOUR PITCHES. THE OUTER PITCHES ARE FIXED AND ALWAYS SPAN A "PERFECT FOURTH" — THE SPACE BETWEEN THE FIRST TWO NOTES OF "HERE... COMES THE BRIDE" OR OF "AULD LANG SYNE" ("SHOULD...AULD...")

A "PERFECT FOURTH"

GREEK TETRACHORDS

DIFFERENT INNER NOTES MADE THREE KINDS OF TETRACHORDS →

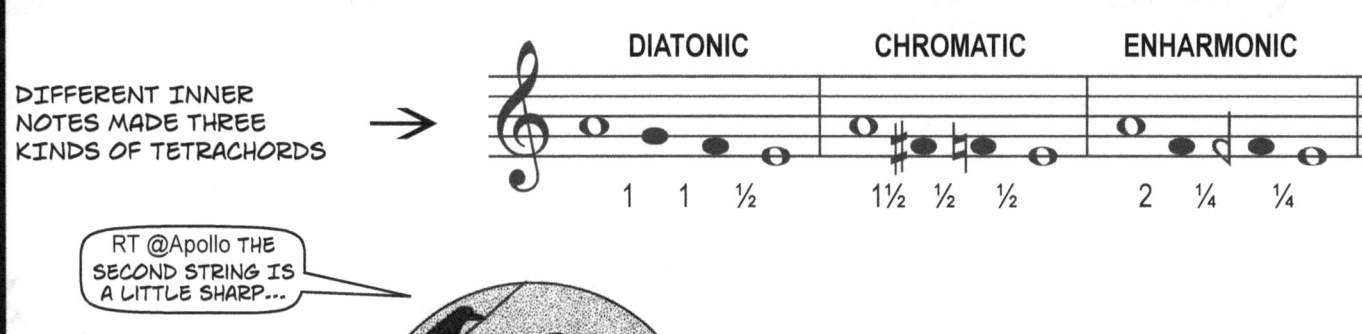

DIATONIC 1 1 ½
CHROMATIC 1½ ½ ½
ENHARMONIC 2 ¼ ¼

RT @Apollo THE SECOND STRING IS A LITTLE SHARP...

"TETRACHORD" MEANT "FOUR STRINGS," AND THEY WERE USED FOR TUNING INSTRUMENTS LIKE THE LYRE AND KITHARA.

GREEK THEORISTS COMBINED TETRACHORDS TO MAKE DIFFERENT SCALES OR MODES (THE GREEKS USED THE TERMS "HARMONIAI" AND "TONOI") THAT DETERMINED THE NOTES YOU WOULD HEAR IN A PIECE OF MUSIC.

2 DIATONIC TETRACHORDS

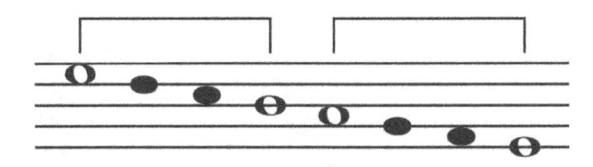

Ptolemy's Dorian Mode

MEDIEVAL CHURCH MODES BORRWED THE GREEK NAMES, BUT THEY WERE ACTUALLY DIFFERENT.

19

GREEK PHILOSOPHERS THOUGHT THE **MODES** COULD AFFECT A PERSON'S CHARACTER. PLATO ONLY APPROVED OF THE DORIAN AND PHRYGIAN MODES, WHICH WERE ASSOCIATED WITH COURAGE AND TEMPERANCE. (ARISTOTLE WAS SLIGHTLY MORE FORGIVING.)

GREEK MODES

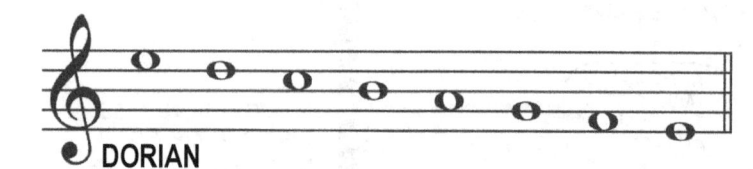

FROM PLATO'S "THE REPUBLIC"

"WARLIKE, TO SOUND THE NOTE OR ACCENT WHICH A BRAVE MAN UTTERS IN THE HOUR OF DANGER AND STERN RESOLVE"

DORIAN

FROM ARISTOTLE'S "POLITICS"

"PRODUCES A MODERATE AND SETTLED TEMPER... ALL MEN AGREE THAT THE DORIAN MUSIC IS THE GRAVEST AND MANLIEST."

"TO BE USED...IN TIMES OF PEACE AND FREEDOM OF ACTION, WHEN THERE IS NO PRESSURE OF NECESSITY... WHEN BY PRUDENT CONDUCT HE HAS ATTAINED HIS END, NOT CARRIED AWAY BY HIS SUCCESS, BUT ACTING MODERATELY AND WISELY UNDER THE CIRCUMSTANCES, AND ACQUIESCING IN THE EVENT"

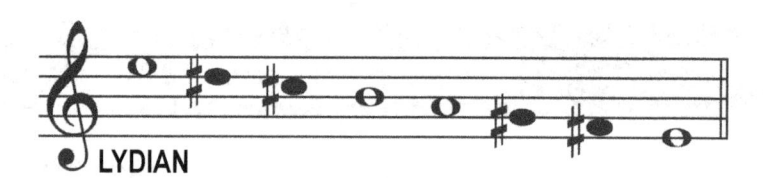

PHRYGIAN

"INSPIRES ENTHUSIASM... BACCHIC FRENZY AND ALL SIMILAR EMOTIONS... ARE BETTER SET TO THE PHRYGIAN THAN TO ANY OTHER MODE."

"SOFT OR DRINKING HARMONIES"; "DRUKENNESS AND SOFTNESS AND INDOLENCE ARE UTTERLY UNBECOMING THE CHARACTER OF OUR GUARDIANS"

LYDIAN

"ENFEEBLE[S] THE MIND"

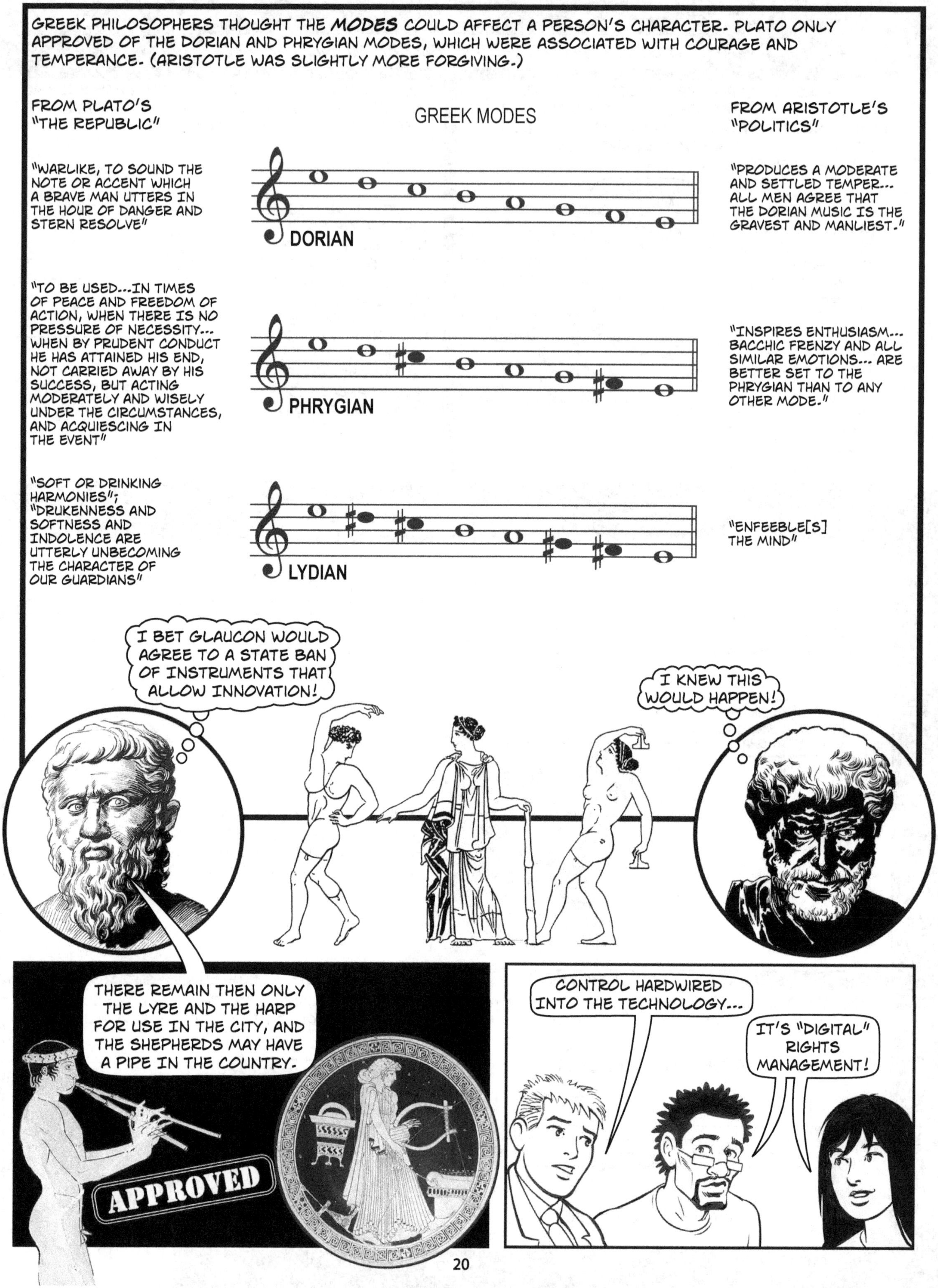

Plato: I BET GLAUCON WOULD AGREE TO A STATE BAN OF INSTRUMENTS THAT ALLOW INNOVATION!

Aristotle: I KNEW THIS WOULD HAPPEN!

Plato: THERE REMAIN THEN ONLY THE LYRE AND THE HARP FOR USE IN THE CITY, AND THE SHEPHERDS MAY HAVE A PIPE IN THE COUNTRY.

APPROVED

CONTROL HARDWIRED INTO THE TECHNOLOGY...

IT'S "DIGITAL" RIGHTS MANAGEMENT!

MIXING MUSICAL FORMS WAS ACTUALLY MEDDLING WITH THE ETHOS, AND THE ORDER OF THE COSMOS. IT THREATENED ANARCHY. SO PLATO DID WANT SOME KINDS OF "SAMPLING" FORBIDDEN. BUT NOT BECAUSE OF "PROPERTY RIGHTS."

THAT THEME OF THE NEED TO CONTROL MUSIC COMES UP AGAIN AS WE'LL SEE...

WHERE'S THE CAR?

UM, GUYS? LOOK OVER THERE.

GASP

IT SEEMS WE HAVE A NEW RIDE!

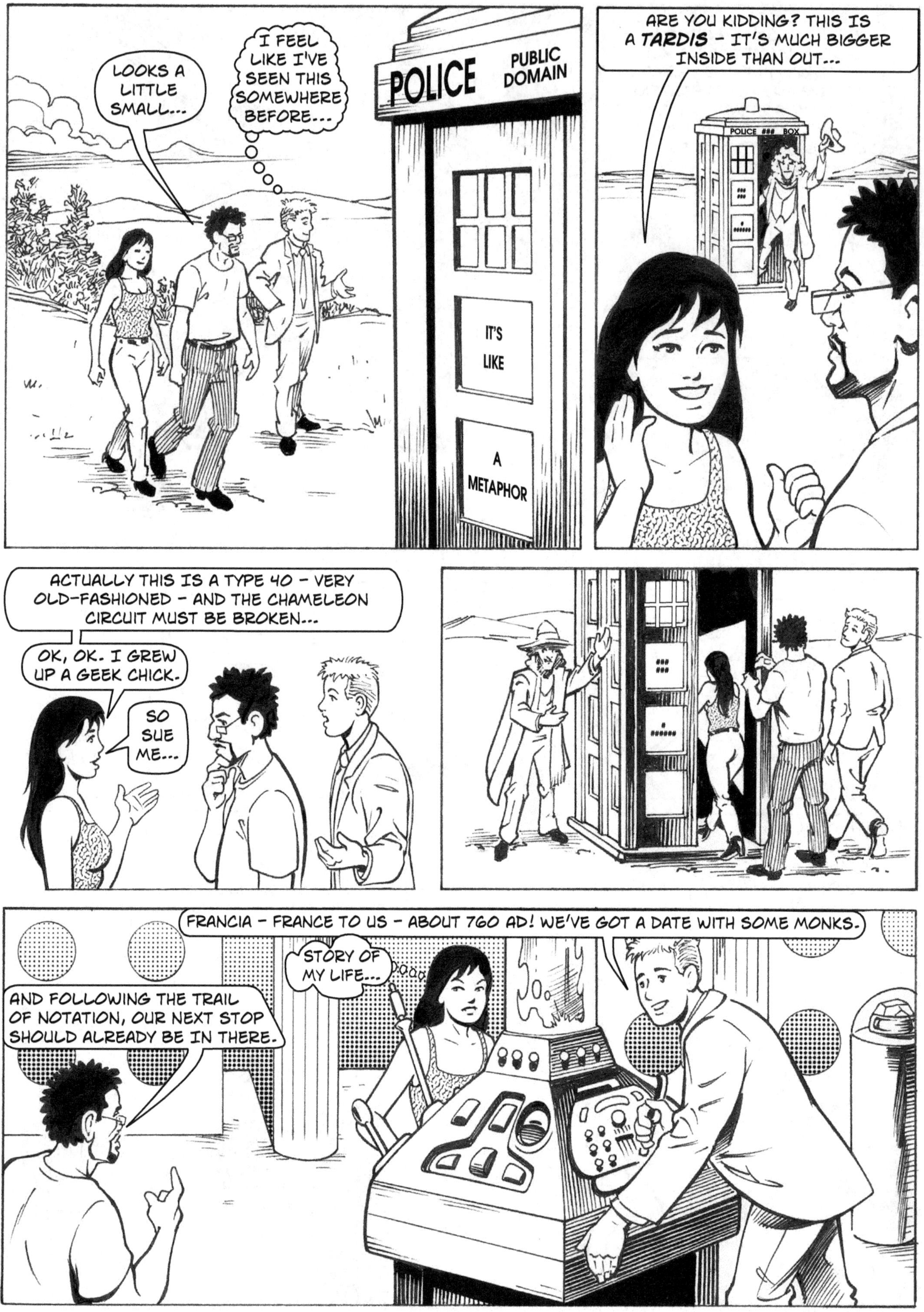

LOOKS A LITTLE SMALL...
I FEEL LIKE I'VE SEEN THIS SOMEWHERE BEFORE...
POLICE
PUBLIC DOMAIN
IT'S LIKE
A METAPHOR
ARE YOU KIDDING? THIS IS A *TARDIS* - IT'S MUCH BIGGER INSIDE THAN OUT...
POLICE ### BOX
ACTUALLY THIS IS A TYPE 40 - VERY OLD-FASHIONED - AND THE CHAMELEON CIRCUIT MUST BE BROKEN...
OK, OK. I GREW UP A GEEK CHICK.
SO SUE ME...
FRANCIA - FRANCE TO US - ABOUT 760 AD! WE'VE GOT A DATE WITH SOME MONKS.
STORY OF MY LIFE...
AND FOLLOWING THE TRAIL OF NOTATION, OUR NEXT STOP SHOULD ALREADY BE IN THERE.

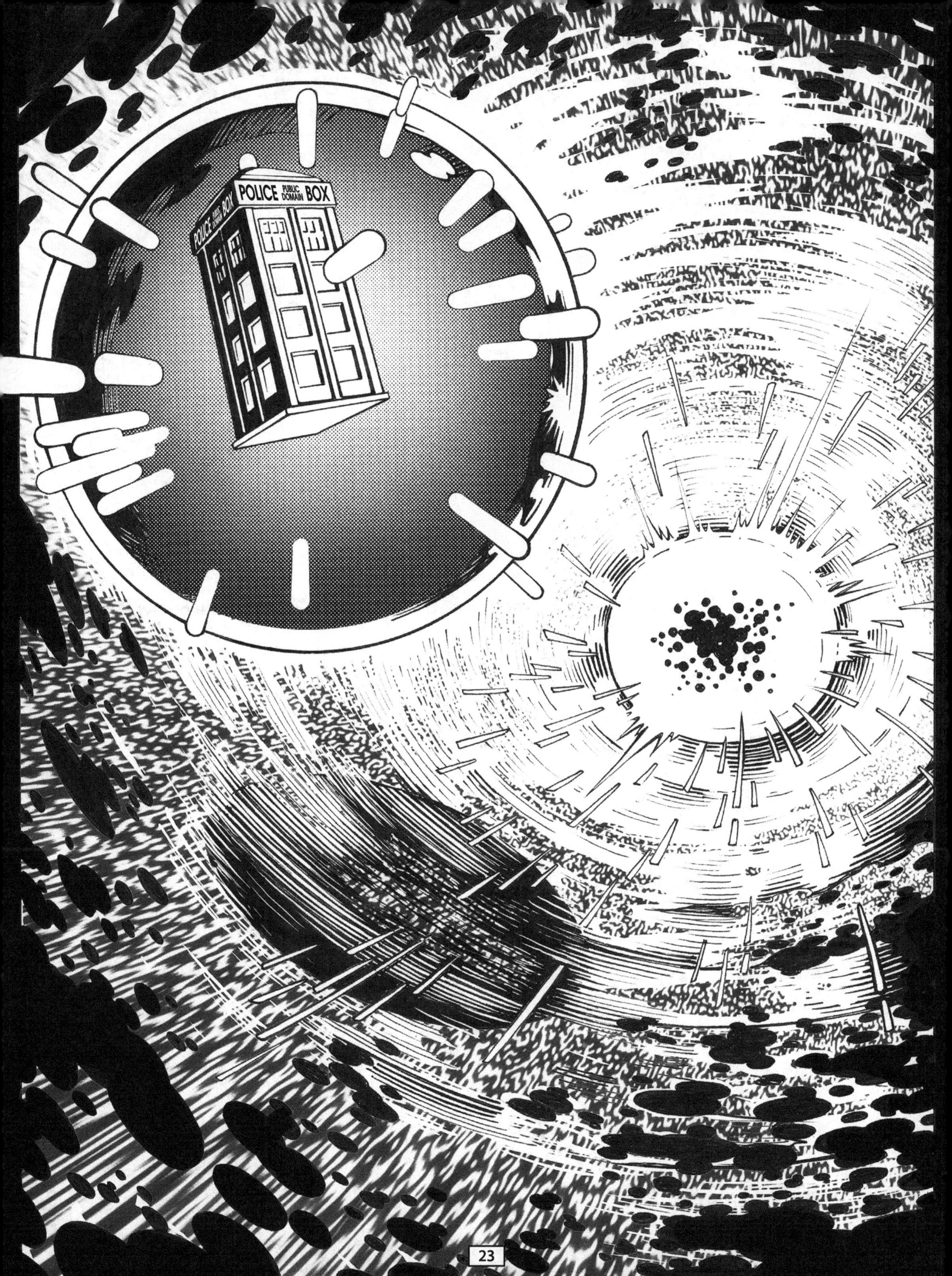
POLICE PUBLIC DOMAIN BOX

Panel 1:
?

Panel 2:
I CAN'T BELIEVE I HAVE TO WEAR THIS THING! WHY CAN'T I BE A NUN?

YOU THINK YOU HAVE PROBLEMS? WHAT ARE THEY GOING TO THINK IF THEY SEE ME?

Panel 3:
PAX VOBISCUM

QUOD ERAT DEMONSTRANDUM.

♪ MY FATHER BEAT YOUR FATHER AT DOMINOES... ♪

PAX VOBISCUM QUOQUE.

I STUDIED THIS PLACE! SO THIS IS THE COURT OF PIPPIN III, SOMETIMES KNOWN AS "PÉPIN LE BREF," OR "PIPPIN THE SHORT."

PIPPIN? WE'RE RESEARCHING HOBBITS, NOW?

C'MON! "MY FATHER BEAT YOUR FATHER AT DOMINOES"!?

I WAS BROUGHT UP SOUTHERN BAPTIST, OK? WE DIDN'T DO LATIN.

DUDE WASN'T TALL. BUT HE WAS THE DADDY OF CHARLEMAGNE.

THAT IS THE POPE'S "SCHOOL OF SINGERS."

THE "SCHOLA CANTORUM." POPE STEPHEN II BROUGHT THEM WITH HIM TO VISIT PIPPIN.

I'M TRAPPED IN THE 8TH CENTURY WITH TWO LUNATICS.

Salve Regina, mater misericordiae: Vita, dulcedo...

THE CHURCH SCORNED INSTRUMENTAL MUSIC, A DISTRACTION FROM THE GOSPEL MESSAGE. BUT THAT WASN'T THEIR ONLY STYLISTIC RULE...

MORE "FEAR AND LONGING," ALMOST LIKE THE GREEKS.

THE SCHOOL OF SINGERS WAS USED TO SHOW CONGREGATIONS HOW THINGS SHOULD SOUND – PART OF AN ATTEMPT TO IMPOSE A STANDARD LITURGY AND STANDARD MUSIC.

THE CHURCH WAS STRUGGLING TO IMPOSE UNIFORMITY, CENTRAL CONTROL. EVERYWHERE YOU WOULD HEAR THE SAME MUSIC, THE SAME LITURGY...
...ONE POPE, ONE CHURCH, ONE SONG.
SO INNOVATION IS BEING FORBIDDEN AGAIN? DON'T REMIX MY MASS?
SHHHHHH....
Ad te suspiramus, gementes et fluentes in hac lacrimarum valle...
SO BEAUTIFUL, IT REALLY DOES BRING PEACE...
...ergo, advocata nostra, illos tuos misericordes oculos...
THEY TRIED TO CRAM THIS MUSIC INTO THE GREEK MODES, BUT IT REALLY DOESN'T FIT. BOETHIUS SAID...
THIS ROBE HAS FLEAS!

IT WASN'T JUST A MATTER OF RELIGIOUS ORTHODOXY. PIPPIN GOT LEGITIMACY FROM THE CHURCH.	HE ACTUALLY CREATED THE POSITION OF "KING OF THE FRANKS" BY GETTING THE POPE TO BLESS HIS ELECTION.	AFTER THIS VISIT, HE DECLARED THE ROMAN LITURGY AND MUSIC TO BE THE ONLY OFFICIAL VERSION IN HIS KINGDOM.
		HE EVEN TRIED TO STAMP OUT LOCAL RITES AND MUSIC.
...A PROCESS THAT CHARLEMAGNE CONTINUED. INTERESTING. SO CHARLEMAGNE'S HOLY ROMAN EMPIRE IS PARTLY BUILT ON MUSICAL ORTHODOXY?		WELL, IT IS EASY TO OVERCLAIM. NOTHING IN HISTORY IS SIMPLE. BUT, YES, THAT WAS A SMALL PART OF BUILDING A RELIGIOUS EMPIRE.

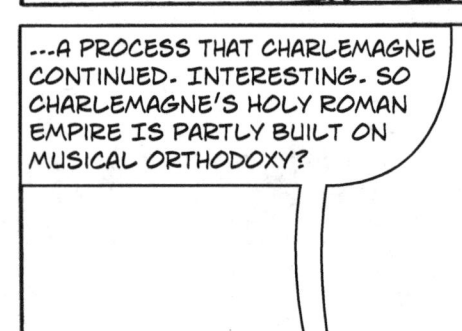

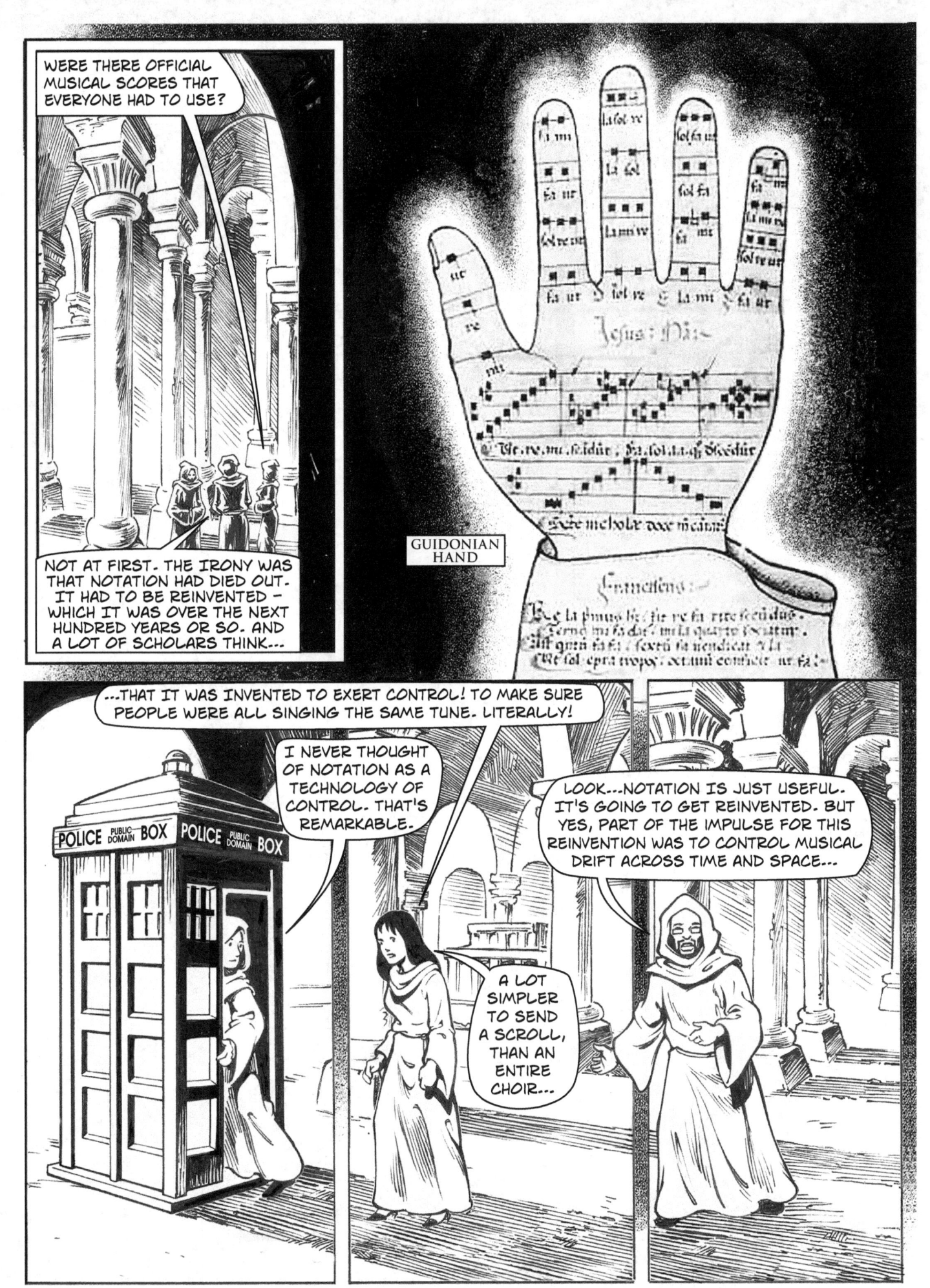

WERE THERE OFFICIAL MUSICAL SCORES THAT EVERYONE HAD TO USE?

NOT AT FIRST. THE IRONY WAS THAT NOTATION HAD DIED OUT. IT HAD TO BE REINVENTED — WHICH IT WAS OVER THE NEXT HUNDRED YEARS OR SO. AND A LOT OF SCHOLARS THINK...

GUIDONIAN HAND

...THAT IT WAS INVENTED TO EXERT CONTROL! TO MAKE SURE PEOPLE WERE ALL SINGING THE SAME TUNE. LITERALLY!

I NEVER THOUGHT OF NOTATION AS A TECHNOLOGY OF CONTROL. THAT'S REMARKABLE.

LOOK...NOTATION IS JUST USEFUL. IT'S GOING TO GET REINVENTED. BUT YES, PART OF THE IMPULSE FOR THIS REINVENTION WAS TO CONTROL MUSICAL DRIFT ACROSS TIME AND SPACE...

A LOT SIMPLER TO SEND A SCROLL, THAN AN ENTIRE CHOIR...

POLICE PUBLIC DOMAIN BOX

THOUGH IT'S NOT CLEAR HOW PRECISE THE NOTATION WAS...

...AT FIRST, IT WAS SIMPLE SIGNS LIKE THIS ABOVE THE WORDS TO INDICATE WHETHER THE TUNE WENT UP OR DOWN.

BUT NOTATION HELPED PEOPLE EXPERIMENT, INNOVATE...

...AND THEN PRESERVE AND TRANSMIT TUNES THEY'D CREATED.

ANOTHER UNRULY TECHNOLOGY, EH?

UNRULY?

WELL, IT SEEMS LIKE A HISTORY OF UNINTENDED CONSEQUENCES. METHODS OF CONTROL...

...THAT UNDERMINE THEMSELVES. THAT'S THE HISTORY OF MUSIC TOO, MAYBE.

COURTLY LOVE!!

THE ERA OF COURTLY LOVE! THAT'S WHERE WE ARE ARRIVING NOW.

TROUBADOURS AND JONGLEURS! ODES TO UNFULFILLED DESIRE!

YES... COURTLY LOVE...		"A TRUE LOVER CONSIDERS NOTHING GOOD EXCEPT WHAT HE THINKS WILL PLEASE HIS BELOVED. LOVE CAN DENY NOTHING TO LOVE." THAT'S SO SWEET! / THAT'S CAPELLANUS' DE AMORE.
	OF COURSE, HE ALSO CLAIMED ALL WOMEN WERE SHALLOW, ENVIOUS, AND SLANDEROUS, AND ADVISED TAKING PEASANT WOMEN BY FORCE, IF THE URGE CAME UPON YOU.	
I AM SERIOUS. PEOPLE WHO ROMANTICIZE THIS STUFF SHOULD READ IT FIRST.	SOUNDS LIKE A REAL PRINCE.	THERE ARE TIMES WHEN I THINK FEMINISM GOES TOO FAR. AND TIMES WHEN I THINK IT DOESN'T GO NEARLY FAR ENOUGH...

HOW COME IT WAS ALL MEN SINGING ABOUT WOMEN? DIDN'T THEY LET WOMEN BE TROUBADOURS?
ACTUALLY, THERE WERE FEMALE TROUBADOURS, THEY CALLED THEM "TROBAIRISES." IN THE LATE 1100s AND 1200s THEY WERE WRITING AND PERFORMING MUSIC FOR THE ARISTOCRACY OF WHAT'S NOW FRANCE.
WHAT, LIKE A BUNCH OF 12TH CENTURY JONI MITCHELLS?
THEY PAVED OCCITAN, AND PUT UP A PARKING LOT...
A CHANTAR M'ER DE SO QU'IEU NON VOLRIA...
CONTESSA DE DIA
WELL, YOU CAN LAUGH, BUT THEY WERE ACTUALLY PRETTY IMPORTANT IN TERMS OF WESTERN SECULAR MUSIC; THEY'RE THE FIRST FEMALE COMPOSERS THAT WE KNOW OF.
WE ARE FAMILY - I GOT TRO-BAI-RISES WITH ME...
YOU GO GIRLS!
SOME THINGS ARE JUST HERESY.

NICE...
MUCH NICER...
DO I ALWAYS HAVE TO DRESS LIKE THIS?
I'D SAY IT WAS GETTING TO BE A HABIT.
TEE HEE!
AHEM. WHERE ARE WE, AND WHEN?
1467. FRANCE.
Totz jois li deu humeliar e tota ricors obezir, Midons, per son bel acuillir e per son dous plazent esgar...
THOUGH THE IDEAS OF COURTLY LOVE HAVE BEEN AROUND FOR OVER 300 YEARS...

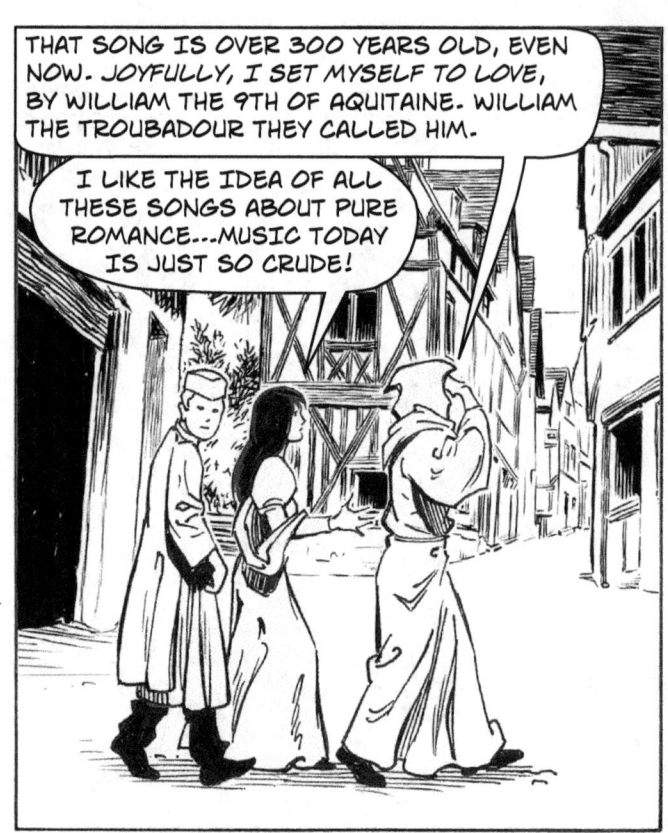

THAT SONG IS OVER 300 YEARS OLD, EVEN NOW. JOYFULLY, I SET MYSELF TO LOVE, BY WILLIAM THE 9TH OF AQUITAINE. WILLIAM THE TROUBADOUR THEY CALLED HIM.

I LIKE THE IDEA OF ALL THESE SONGS ABOUT PURE ROMANCE...MUSIC TODAY IS JUST SO CRUDE!

ACTUALLY, A LOT OF WILLIAM'S SONGS WOULD HAVE THE "EXPLICIT LYRICS" LABEL EVEN TODAY. HE WAS FOND OF...

...BOASTING ABOUT HIS EXPLOITS...IN ONE SONG HE PRETENDED TO BE MUTE, SO TWO LADIES WOULD THINK HE COULDN'T REVEAL THEIR SECRETS. THEN...

MADE SNOOP DOGG LOOK LIKE A CHOIRBOY.

ENOUGH!!! OK, SO OUR GENERATION DIDN'T INVENT DIRTY LYRICS. IS THAT THE POINT OF THIS TRIP?

I'D SAY THAT WE'RE LOOKING AT A CULTURE WAR...

HMM...

...AND MUSIC IS ONE OF THE BATTLEGROUNDS.

THE EARLY CHURCH DIDN'T AGREE WITH THE IDEAS OF COURTLY LOVE. YET THE TROUBADOUR THOUGHT LOVE FOR HIS LADY MADE HIM NOBLER. IT WASN'T JUST TEMPTATION TO SIN...

Allegiez moy, doulce plaisant brunette, ou Jesus Crist volt prendre char humaine...

THESE GUYS TAKE THEIR DATES TO CHURCH!

THAT'S MOLINET'S OROISON A NOSTRE DAME — THE PRAYER TO OUR LADY. THIS MUST BE THE FIRST PERFORMANCE.

IT IS BEAUTIFUL!

HAUNTING...

THE FUNNY THING IS, THE FIRST AND LAST LINES OF EACH VERSE ARE ACTUALLY TAKEN FROM POPULAR SONGS...SECULAR SONGS.

STRANGE TO DESCRIBE THE VIRGIN MARY AS A "SWEET, PLEASING BRUNETTE."

WELL, THAT LINE IS STRIKING — THE POPULAR SONG IT IS TAKEN FROM GOES LIKE THIS...

Allegiez moy, doulce plaisant brunette, desous la boudinette- SOOTHE ME, SWEET PLEASANT BRUNETTE, JUST BELOW THE....

STOP! WE'LL END THIS TRANSLATION RIGHT THERE, THANK YOU. OR THIS PARTICULAR BRUNETTE WILL BE NEITHER SWEET NOR PLEASANT FOR THE REST OF THE TRIP.

SHHH!!

SORRY...

Pax vobiscum quoque.

SORRY...

35

"THE POINT IS, THAT OUR IDEAS ABOUT BOTH LOVE AND RELIGIOUS ADORATION WERE PROFOUNDLY SHAPED BY THIS MOMENT IN HISTORY..."

"...AND THE TWO-WAY BORROWING IN MUSIC WAS PART OF THE CONVERSATION."

♪ A COMPLETE UNKNOWN... ♪

WHAT DO YOU MEAN, PART OF THE CONVERSATION?
THE TROUBADOURS ROMANTICIZED THEIR LADY LOVES. SOME OF THAT ROMANCE SEEPED INTO THE IDEALIZATION OF THE VIRGIN MARY.
THE SENSUALITY WAS REMOVED. BUT THAT LEFT TRANSCENDENT LOVE, PASSING ALL UNDERSTANDING.
HM...THIS SWIVELS!
OOPS!
WHOOSH
WHACK!!
RATS IN THE DONJON, PLAGUE FLEAS DOWNTOWN...
SO THE RELIGIOUS COMPOSERS COULD BORROW TUNES AND LYRICS FROM THOSE BAWDY SONGS AND NOT FEEL THEY WERE COMMITTING HERESY.
INTERESTING...
History of Music Copyright CARROLL

I WAS JUST GETTING USED TO THE LAST ONE... POSTMODERNISM IS FUN TO READ, BUT IT'S REALLY DISORIENTING TO TRAVEL BY.
ANOTHER NEW RIDE!
Scaramouche, Scaramouche...
I THINK I GET THE POINT. BUT IS ALL THIS BORROWING HAPPENING AS PART OF AN ORAL TRADITION? HANDWRITTEN MANUSCRIPTS? WHAT?
FUNNY YOU SHOULD ASK...
Germany 1467
IS THAT GUTENBERG?!
THAT'S HIM. IT'S 1467. POOR GUY IS GOING TO DIE NEXT YEAR, BUT THAT THING IN FRONT OF HIM HAS ALREADY BEGUN TO CHANGE THE WORLD FOREVER.

MUSICAL PRINTING WAS FIRST USED IN THE 1470s, AND REALLY CAUGHT ON DURING THE 1500s. LET'S TAKE A LITTLE HOP TO VENICE IN 1498...

Venice 1498

...WHERE PRINTER OTTAVIANO PETRUCCI IS ABOUT TO GET A "PATENT."

HOPE THIS JALOPY HAS PONTOONS.

Spinacino
THIS ISN'T VENICE!!
NO. IT'S ONE OF PETRUCCI'S SCORES.
THIS REALLY IS POSTMODERNISM!
IL N'Y A PAS DE HORS-TEXTE.

WAIT. THIS MUSIC WE'RE IN IS PATENTED?

NOT THE MUSIC. PRINTING MUSICAL SCORES WAS **HARD** IN THE 15TH & 16TH CENTURIES. PETRUCCI HAD AN INTRICATE BUT ACCURATE WAY TO DO IT. HE ASKED FOR A 20 YEAR MONOPOLY OVER **ALL MUSICAL PRINTING** IN VENICE AS A REWARD.

Ottaviano dei Petrucci of Fossombrone...a very ingenious man, has, at great expense and with most watchful care, invented what many, not only in Italy but also outside of Italy, have attempted in vain, which is to print, most conveniently, figured music: and in consequence even more easily plainchant: a thing very important to the Christian religion...

[Petrucci pleads that the Signory] Accord him, as first inventor, a special grace, that, for twenty years no other be empowered to print figured music in the land subject to your signory... nor to import said things, printed outside in any other place whatsoever.

WAIT — HE WAS THE **ONLY** PERSON WHO COULD LEGALLY PRINT MUSIC IN VENICE?

A MUSICAL MONOPOLIST! THE MICROSOFT OF MADRIGALS.

PETRUCCI WAS A SAVVY INNOVATOR — BUT WHAT HE AND THE OTHER PRINTERS DID CHANGED THE FACE OF MUSICAL STYLE.

WAIT. HOW DOES PRINTING CHANGE MUSICAL STYLE?

UNTIL THIS, MOST MUSIC WAS PLAYED FROM MEMORY. THAT WORKS IF YOU ARE PLAYING A SIMPLE SINGLE TUNE — BUT HOW TO COORDINATE LOTS OF DIFFERENT MUSICIANS PLAYING DIFFERENT PARTS?

BUT WERE THE COMPOSERS GETTING THEIR CUT OF THE ACTION?

SO CHEAP PRINTED MUSIC MAKES POLYPHONIC MUSIC SPREAD AND ENCOURAGES EXPERIMENTATION — THE TECHNOLOGY ALLOWS A NEW KIND OF COMPLEXITY!

COMPOSERS?

WELL, MOST OF THEM DIDN'T HAVE PRINTING RIGHTS. THOSE BELONGED TO THE PUBLISHER.
THANKS!
PEOPLE WERE STARTING TO THINK OF COMPOSERS AS ARTISTS, NOT ARTISANS, BUT THEIR PAYMENT CAME FROM WAGES OR PATRONAGE. THEY JUST DIDN'T HAVE OUR CONCEPT OF COPYRIGHT.
SO COMPOSERS DIDN'T GET LEGAL CONTROL OF THE WORKS THEY CREATED?
ONLY A FEW. GENERALLY BECAUSE THEY WERE COURT FAVORITES OR BECAUSE THEY "WORKED HARD" AND LOBBIED. NOT BECAUSE THEY WERE AUTHORS OF SOMETHING "ORIGINAL."
SO...WHO IS THAT GUY?
THAT'S THE EXCEPTION. ***ORLANDO DI LASSO.***

Panel 1: I'M SURE HE'S IN A LOT OF PEOPLE'S COLLECTIONS. WELL, NOT QUITE, BUT IF YOU'VE EVER SEEN SHAKESPEARE'S HENRY IV, PART II, YOU'VE HEARD A DI LASSO SONG.

Panel 2: THE DRUNKEN JUSTICE SILENCE! I *LOVE* SONGS BY INEBRIATED JUDGES!

Panel 3: NOW *THAT'S* A SPECIALIZED PLAYLIST...

Panel 4: ♪ For women are shrews, both short and tall: 'Tis merry in hall when beards wag all; And welcome merry Shrovetide. Be merry, be merry. ♪

OH FOR A SONG WHERE WOMEN ARE NEITHER SHREWS NOR SEXPOTS.

Panel 5: SO I CAN ADD DI LASSO TO MY LIST? NO, THE WORDS ARE SHAKESPEARE'S. TO BE FAIR, THE CHARACTER SINGING THEM IS AN IDIOT.

Panel 6: I AM DETECTING A THEME IN THIS HISTORY.

THOUGH DI LASSO DID TURN A SONG CALLED YOU 15 YEAR OLD GIRLS INTO A MASS CALLED ENTRE VOUS FILLES. THE ORIGINAL WAS PRETTY RACY...

"YOU GIRLS, FIFTEEN YEARS OLD, DON'T COME TO GET WATER AT THE FOUNTAIN, BECAUSE YOU HAVE DARLING EYES, PERT BREASTS, LAUGHING MOUTHS..."

TAKING BAWDY PROFANE SONGS AND MAKING THEM HOLY. NICE THAT HE FOUND THE ORIGINAL SO "INSPIRING."

SO NOW COMPOSERS WERE BEGINNING TO CLAIM THE ECONOMIC BENEFITS OF COPYRIGHT?

WELL, DI LASSO'S MOTIVES WERE MIXED. HE HAD FOUND INACCURATE VERSIONS OF HIS WORKS AND WANTED THE RIGHT TO CONTROL QUALITY — TO PROTECT THE WORK "IN WHICH HE HAS INVESTED HIS LIFE'S BLOOD."

AND THAT IDEA OF "THE AUTHORIZED VERSION" RESONATED WITH MONARCHS WHO WANTED TO AVOID COMPETING VERSIONS OF THE MASS OR THE SCRIPTURE.

RIGHT. SO DI LASSO GOT THE EXCLUSIVE RIGHT TO SAY WHO PRINTED HIS WORK, OR IF HIS WORK GOT PRINTED AT ALL. BUT HE WAS THE EXCEPTION. HARDLY ANY COMPOSERS HAD ANYTHING COMPARABLE. DI LASSO GOT HIS PRIVILEGES IN THE 1570s.

AND IT WASN'T UNTIL 1710 THAT THE FIRST COPYRIGHT STATUTE WAS PASSED — THE "STATUTE OF ANNE" GAVE **AUTHORS** A LEGAL RIGHT OVER THEIR CREATIONS.

TOOK YOU LAWYERS LONG ENOUGH TO DECIDE TO PROTECT CREATORS!

ACTUALLY, IT WAS A LITTLE MORE COMPLEX...

ALL KINDS OF THINGS WENT INTO THE MIX. RESENTMENT AGAINST THE CONTROL THE PUBLISHING GUILDS HAD OVER WHAT WAS PRINTED...

...CHANGING IDEAS OF AESTHETICS...

THE LAPSE OF THE PRESS LICENSING ACT...

YES, THE PUBLISHERS WANTED NEW RIGHTS, PERPETUAL ONES...

EVEN A CONTINUING SUSPICION OF STATE GRANTED MONOPOLIES...

...THAT WENT ALL THE WAY BACK TO THE STATUTE OF MONOPOLIES OF 1624.

BUT I AM SURE **YOU** ARE AWARE OF ALL THAT.

NOW WE ARE TALKING ABOUT SOMETHING I KNOW A LOT ABOUT.
OF COURSE, THE RIGHTS LOOKED VERY DIFFERENT THAN THEY DO TODAY.
THE COPYRIGHT TERM WAS 14 YEARS, WITH A MAXIMUM OF 28 YEARS. IMAGINE IF WE HAD THAT TODAY. MUCH OF THE CULTURE OF THE 20TH CENTURY WOULD ALREADY BE FREE FOR US TO USE.
AND AT FIRST, IT WASN'T CLEAR THAT COMPOSERS GOT ANY RIGHTS UNDER THE STATUTE...
UNTIL J.C. BACH SUED A PUBLISHER IN 1777...
WHICH BACH IS THAT? I GET CONFUSED.
THAT ONE I CAN ANSWER...
JOHANN CHRISTIAN BACH WAS THE 18TH CHILD OF JOHANN SEBASTIAN BACH. THEY CALLED HIM THE "ENGLISH BACH."
J.C. BACH
BACH IN THE UK, UR!

SORRY...ANYWAY, HE SUED A PUBLISHING FIRM CALLED LONGMAN AND THE COURT HAD TO DECIDE WHETHER MUSICAL COMPOSITIONS WERE "WRITINGS" COVERED BY THE STATUTE.

IT HELD THEY WERE.

"MUSIC IS A SCIENCE; IT MAY BE WRITTEN; AND THE MODE OF CONVEYING THE IDEAS, IS BY SIGNS AND MARKS. A PERSON MAY USE THE COPY BY PLAYING IT, BUT HE HAS NO RIGHT TO ROB THE AUTHOR OF THE PROFIT, BY MULTIPLYING COPIES AND DISPOSING OF THEM FOR HIS OWN USE.... THERE IS NO COLOUR FOR SAYING THAT MUSIC IS NOT WITHIN THE ACT."

...DIDN'T DO HIM MUCH GOOD. HE DIED PENNILESS A FEW YEARS LATER. HIS CREDITORS TRIED TO SELL HIS BODY TO MEDICAL SCHOOLS TO COVER HIS DEBTS.

WOW. I THOUGHT THE **RIAA** WAS HARD CORE.

RIP
UNDER NEW MANAGEMENT
J.C. BACH

SO WHAT DID THESE COPYRIGHTS COVER?

BASICALLY JUST REPRINTING. YOU COULD PERFORM THE MUSIC WITHOUT PERMISSION, YOU COULD **BORROW** FRAGMENTS FROM THE MUSIC, YOU JUST COULDN'T REPRINT THE ENTIRE WORK.

BORROW? THESE ARE CLASSICAL COMPOSERS, NOT SAMPLERS LIKE P DUDDY OR THAT GIRLSPEAK FELLOW.
THAT'D BE PUFF DADDY AND GIRL TALK.
I DON'T THINK THEY'D BE GOING AROUND BORROWING FROM EACH OTHER'S MUSIC!!
HA HA
?
HA HA Ha HA
?
ARE YOU KIDDING?!!! CLASSICAL MUSICIANS BORROWED FROM EACH OTHER ALL THE TIME! KEEPING TRACK OF THE BORROWING CAN DRIVE YOU CRAZY. IT'S LIKE AN INSANE GAME OF MUSICAL CHUTES AND LADDERS.

ACTUALLY, THAT'S A GAME I'D LIKE TO PLAY!

51

GEORG FRIEDRICH HANDEL (1685–1759)

Borrowed from Astorga, Bononcini, Carissimi, Cavalli…
…Kerll, Kuhnau, Legrenzi,
…Stradella, Telemann, Urio

"AND HE SHALL REIGN FOR EVER AND EVER…"

"I LOVE THAT PASSAGE, HANDEL'S MESSIAH!"

LUDWIG VAN BEETHOVEN (1770–1827)

"YES, WHICH BEETHOVEN QUOTED IN MISSA SOLEMNIS."

"HANDEL ONLY MANAGED TO COMPOSE MESSIAH SO FAST BECAUSE HE BORROWED FROM HIS OWN PRIOR SECULAR WORK."

"YOU WANT THE TRUTH? YOU CAN'T **HANDEL** THE TRUTH!"

"…AND A VERY SIMILAR PHRASE REAPPEARS IN MAHLER'S FIRST SYMPHONY…"

"STRAVINSKY'S OPERA OEDIPUS REX PARODIED HANDEL."

"PARODEIA IS GREEK FOR 'A SONG SUNG ALONGSIDE ANOTHER.'"

"WHEE!"

"THE OWNERS OF HAPPY BIRTHDAY AGREED! THEY COMPLAINED THAT STRAVINSKY USED IT IN A FANFARE. THEN IT TURNED OUT THAT THEY DIDN'T EVEN OWN HAPPY BIRTHDAY!"

"A GOOD COMPOSER DOES NOT IMITATE; HE STEALS."

"STRAVINSKY'S THE RITE OF SPRING WAS USED BY BERIO."

"GOOD THING IT WASN'T THE COPYRIGHT OF SPRING!"

IGOR STRAVINSKY (1882–1971)

BRAHMS'S FIRST SYMPHONY WAS SO SIMILAR TO BEETHOVEN'S MUSIC...
...THAT ONE CONDUCTOR CALLED IT "BEETHOVEN'S TENTH."
!
OUCH!
?
YES INDEED, AND WHAT IS REMARKABLE IS THAT EVERY JACKASS HEARS AS MUCH!
JOHANNES BRAHMS (1833–1897)
THRIFTY!
BERIO... IS... TOO... STRONG! MUST... HANG... ON!
AND THEN MAHLER'S THIRD SYMPHONY QUOTED FROM BRAHMS'S FIRST...
...WHICH HAD BORROWED FROM BEETHOVEN!
AND THEN THE POSTMODERN COMPOSER BERIO BORROWED DIRECTLY FROM THE SCHERZO MOVEMENT OF MAHLER'S SECOND...
...AND FROM EVERYONE ELSE TOO! THAT WAS HIS POINT!
GUSTAV MAHLER (1860–1911)
LUCIANO BERIO (1925–2003)

WOW. I HAVEN'T HAD AS MUCH FUN AS THAT SINCE SPACE MOUNTAIN...

SHE WENT TO DISNEY WORLD!? I HAD HER DOWN AS THE VIOLIN/MATH CAMP TYPE.

"BORROWING IS PERMISSIBLE; BUT ONE MUST RETURN THE OBJECT BORROWED WITH 'INTEREST,'" MEANING YOU HAVE TO IMPROVE ON THE ORIGINAL...

YEAH, SOMEONE'S SUBCONSCIOUS WAS WORKING OVERTIME.

THAT'S FROM 1739 – MATTHESON'S THE PERFECT CHAPEL MASTER.

BUT WHAT THAT DOESN'T SHOW YOU IS HOW **NORMAL** BORROWING WAS – HOW IT WAS JUST PART OF WHAT COMPOSERS DID. LOOK AT THIS BOOK OVER HERE...

SO SLAVISH IMITATION WASN'T GOOD, BUT OTHER KINDS WERE OK?

ABSOLUTELY. THE 18TH CENTURY COMPOSERS REWORKED MATERIAL ALL THE TIME, THEIR OWN AND OTHERS...BUT WHAT WAS ACCEPTABLE CHANGED OVER TIME.

"BY THE EARLY 19TH CENTURY HANDEL STOOD ACCUSED OF PLAGIARISM FOR PRACTICES THAT SEEM TODAY LIKE PARTICULARLY EXCELLENT EXAMPLES OF WHAT HAD BEEN A LONG AND DISTINGUISHED TRADITION OF CREATIVELY RESHAPING BORROWED MATERIAL."

DID THEY DISTINGUISH BETWEEN DIFFERENT KINDS OF BORROWING?

THEY DID... HMM...

BURKHOLDER

YOU SAID YOU LIKED THE CHUTES AND LADDERS. DID YOU PLAY MANY VIDEO GAMES WHEN YOU WERE A KID?
SURE... WHY...?
Pull
YANK!

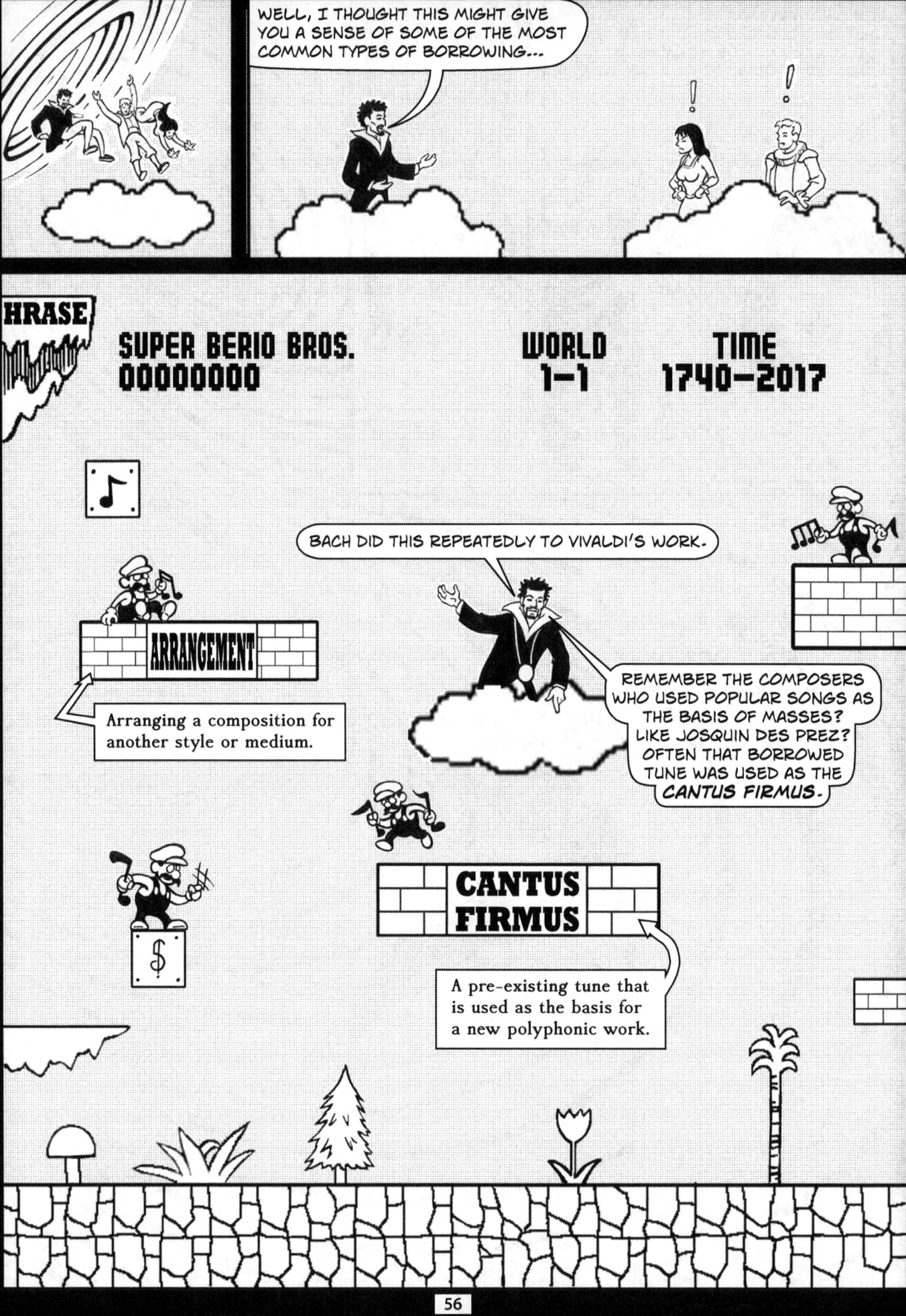

WELL, I THOUGHT THIS MIGHT GIVE YOU A SENSE OF SOME OF THE MOST COMMON TYPES OF BORROWING...

SUPER BERIO BROS.
00000000

WORLD
1-1

TIME
1740-2017

ARRANGEMENT

Arranging a composition for another style or medium.

BACH DID THIS REPEATEDLY TO VIVALDI'S WORK.

REMEMBER THE COMPOSERS WHO USED POPULAR SONGS AS THE BASIS OF MASSES? LIKE JOSQUIN DES PREZ? OFTEN THAT BORROWED TUNE WAS USED AS THE *CANTUS FIRMUS*.

CANTUS FIRMUS

A pre-existing tune that is used as the basis for a new polyphonic work.

PARODY
Mozart parodied his contemporaries, but then his own Magic Flute was parodied.

"What's 'source for the Amadeuce is source for the slander.'" "Zoloft."

QUOTATION
Tchaikovsky's *1812 Overture* conjures up the Russian and French armies by quoting their national anthems...

...and then that cool cannon goes off!

MODELING
John Williams' Empire theme for *Star Wars* was modeled on Holst's *The Planets*.

"Princess Leia!"

SUPER BERIO BROS.
00001000

WORLD
1-1

TIME
1740-2017

PARODY — Evoking another musical work in a humorous or satirical way.

QUOTATION — Using a brief quote of another tune in order to conjure up the original, humorously, as homage, or to evoke an emotion.

MODELING — Taking a prior work as the structure or pattern for a new one.

THEME & VARIATIONS

ALLUSION

57

LOOK "SUPER BERIO BROS" IS ALL VERY CUTE AND SO WAS "SIX DEGREES OF INSPIRATION."

I GET IT.

BAROQUE AND CLASSICAL COMPOSERS BORROWED A LOT, FOR LOTS OF DIFFERENT REASONS. THEIR BORROWING WAS PART OF THE MUSICAL TRADITION, NOT A CAUSE FOR A LAWSUIT.

YES, THE VITAL DIFFERENCE BETWEEN OBSERVED BEHAVIOR AND EXPERIENCED MEANING!

GREAT. BUT THAT'S NOT ENOUGH. IT TELLS ME WHAT THEY DID. NOT WHAT THEY FELT...

HMMM... CUTE AND SMART?

IF I WANT TO KNOW HOW MUSIC TODAY IS DIFFERENT FROM MUSIC MADE 200 OR 2000 YEARS AGO, IT ISN'T ENOUGH TO KNOW WHAT WAS IN THEIR COMPOSITIONS...

...I NEED TO KNOW WHAT WAS IN THEIR HEADS.

Panel 1:

Panel 2: AHEM... AHEM... AHEM...

Panel 3: THAT IS THE QUESTION. BUT TO ANSWER IT WE NEED PERISCOPIC VISION.
TELESCOPIC?
PERIPATETIC?

Panel 4: MARE MUSICUM
NO... PERISCOPIC. WE NEED TO GET BELOW THE SURFACE OF MUSIC, SEE HOW MUSICIANS WERE PAID, WHAT THEIR MUSIC WAS MADE FOR, HOW IT WAS DISTRIBUTED AND EXPERIENCED.

Panel 5: ...BUT AT THE SAME TIME, WE NEED TO LOOK ABOVE THE SURFACE, SEE WHAT COMPOSERS AND MUSICIANS WERE SAYING AND THINKING ABOUT THEIR ART AND WHO OWNED IT.

Panel 6:

Panel 7:

Panel 8: *THAT'S DE-E-E-P....*

ATTITUDES & NORMS

RENAISSANCE TIMELINE

← 1400–1500 — 1500–1600 →

ISLE OF MAD COMPOSERS

BY 1500 PRINTING PRESSES COULD RENDER COMPLEX MUSICAL SCORES.

"OUR BUDDY PETRUCCI!"

SOME PRINTERS WERE GIVEN EXCLUSIVE RIGHTS TO PRINT PARTICULAR BOOKS THROUGH PRINTING PRIVILEGES.

PAYMENT & TECHNOLOGIES

Patent for Method of Printing Music

LAW

ATTITUDES & NORMS
RENAISSANCE
1500-1600
TIMELINE
BAROQUE
1600-1750
*@÷>[?ε
!÷¿*%+
COMPOSERS DID COMPLAIN ABOUT POORLY PRINTED VERSIONS OF THEIR WORK.
BUT DIDN'T COMPLAIN WHEN OTHERS REWORKED IT. CREDIT, NOT OWNERSHIP!
ISLE OF MAD COMPOSERS
MOST COMPOSERS DEPENDED ON PATRONAGE. MUSIC WAS CREATED FOR A PARTICULAR PERSON AND OFTEN A PARTICULAR EVENT.
PAYMENT & TECHNOLOGIES
1575:
Composer's Printing Privilege
DI LASSO WAS ONE OF THE FIRST COMPOSERS TO GET A PRINTING PRIVILEGE.
LAW

ATTITUDES & NORMS

BAROQUE TIMELINE

1600–1700 ←————————————————→ 1700–1750

"The type of borrowing practiced in the Baroque era that has seemed most foreign to later centuries was the re-use or reworking of entire pieces...."

—J. Peter Burkholder

BURKHOLDER LITERALLY WROTE THE BOOK ON MUSICAL BORROWING.

REVERSIONED VIVALDI!

RE-HASHED HANDEL!

ISLE OF PUBLISHING COMPOSERS

SO UNDER PATRONAGE, IF MUSIC WAS COMPOSED FOR PARTICULAR EVENTS OR PEOPLE, YOU WOULD PROBABLY HAVE TO REVISE IT.

PAYMENT & TECHNOLOGIES

1624: STATUTE OF MONOPOLIES LIMITS GRANTING OF MONOPOLIES AND CHARTERS "EXCEPT" LETTERS PATENTS FOR INVENTORS.

1710: STATUTE OF ANNE WAS THE FIRST TRUE COPYRIGHT STATUTE...IT COVERED THE RIGHT TO REPRINT THE ENTIRE WORK – NEITHER BORROWING NOR PERFORMING WERE AFFECTED.

Anno Octavo
Annæ Reginæ.

LAW

62

ATTITUDES & NORMS

BAROQUE TIMELINE 1710 — 1750

"COME ON NOW... WHERE'S THE PARTY AT??!?"

BACH WOULD ARRANGE OTHER PEOPLE'S WORKS FOR DIFFERENT INSTRUMENTS APPROPRIATE FOR A NEW SETTING.

"BRICOLAGE BACH?"

SO THE COMPOSER WAS ALMOST LIKE THE DJ — PROVIDING THE RIGHT MUSIC FOR THE RIGHT OCCASION — CUSTOMIZING AS HE WENT ALONG — HIS OWN STUFF AND OTHERS'.

WELL... I SEE WHAT YOU MEAN, BUT, NO DISRESPECT TO DJ KOOL HERC, THIS WAS **BACH**!

AS THE MARKET FOR PRINTED MUSIC EXPANDED, COMPOSERS STARTED TO CLAIM A SHARE OF THE MONEY FROM PUBLISHING THEIR WORKS.

HANDEL DID THAT, RIGHT? HE EVEN "FREELANCED" AS A COMPOSER.

"MESSIAH FOR HY-AH! WATER MUSIC ON TAP!"

PAYMENT & TECHNOLOGIES

LAW

63

SO HOW DID THAT CHANGE IN CLASSICAL MUSIC?

ATTITUDES & NORMS

CLASSICAL TIMELINE

← 1750

1820 →

BY THE MIDDLE OF THE 18TH CENTURY, THE IDEAS BEGAN TO CHANGE IN LITERATURE AND THEN IN MUSIC. ART CAME TO BE DEFINED IN TERMS OF ORIGINAL GENIUS —

MY PRINCIPAL SOURCE OF INSPIRATION IS ME!!

COMPOSERS DISTINGUISHED THEMSELVES THROUGH NOVELTY, NOT BRILLIANTLY REWORKING TRADITIONAL MATERIALS.

AND THAT IDEA OF THE ORIGINAL AUTHOR ENDS UP BEING THE ORGANIZING PRINCIPLE OF COPYRIGHT! IT ALL CONNECTS.

THE INVENTION OF LITHOGRAPHY IN 1796 MEANT PRINTING MUSIC, WITH ATTRACTIVE PICTURES, WAS SUDDENLY CHEAPER AND EASIER.

LA LUTTE ARTISTIQUE
POUR LE PIANO PAR E. MARIE

SO IS THIS WHEN COMPOSERS SHIFT TO SELLING THEIR MUSIC TO THE PUBLIC, NOT TO SOME PATRON?

PARTLY. BUT PATRONAGE DOESN'T DISAPPEAR. EVEN THOUGH HE FREELANCED, LISZT WAS STILL RELYING ON A DUKE'S PATRONAGE IN THE 1880s.

AT ONE POINT, HE AND HANS CHRISTIAN ANDERSON WERE BOTH BEING SUPPORTED BY THE DUKE OF WEIMAR. NOW *THAT'S* WHAT I CALL TALENT SPOTTING.

PAYMENT & TECHNOLOGIES

1793: FIRST FRENCH COPYRIGHT LAW COVERING ALL THE "BEAUX ARTS"

1777: BACH v. LONGMAN (UK) MUSIC IS COVERED BY COPYRIGHT. DOESN'T AFFECT BORROWING OR PERFORMING — JUST REPRINTING.

LAW

64

ATTITUDES & NORMS

ROMANTIC TIMELINE 1780 — 1910

CLASSICAL | ROMANTIC

"THERE ARE AND THERE WILL BE THOUSANDS OF PRINCES. THERE IS ONLY ONE BEETHOVEN."

"MODEST..."

"IT AIN'T BRAGGIN' IF YOU CAN BACK IT UP. BEETHOVEN WAS SEEN AS THE PERSONIFICATION OF THE NEW STYLE OF COMPOSER. HE'S A TRANSITIONAL FIGURE."

"THE TECHNOLOGY WASN'T JUST CHANGING PUBLISHING. IN THE LATE 18TH CENTURY PIANOS WERE LABORIOUSLY MADE BY HAND. BY 1850 THE INDUSTRIAL REVOLUTION MEANT THAT PIANOS COULD BE MASS PRODUCED IN STEAM-DRIVEN FACTORIES."

"THAT IS SO STEAM PUNK!"

PAYMENT & TECHNOLOGIES

1833: DRAMATIC LITERARY PROPERTY ACT (UK) PROTECTS PERFORMANCES OF DRAMATIC WORKS – SUCH AS OPERAS.

LAW

65

ATTITUDES & NORMS

ROMANTIC TIMELINE 1810 ←——————————→ 1910

"SO THIS IS WHERE WE START SEEING COMPLAINTS THAT IMITATION IS PLAGIARISM, NOT JUST SINCERE FLATTERY?"

"EXACTLY. BUT BORROWING DIDN'T STOP, IT JUST CHANGED SHAPE. YOU COULD COPY FOLK SONGS TO SET A SCENE..."

"CHOPIN, TCHAIKOVSKY, DVORAK..."

"...OR YOU COULD TIP THE HAT TO AN EARLIER COMPOSER, OR EVEN MAKE FUN..."

"I'D LIKE TWENTY ASSORTED SLAVIC FOLK SONGS AND A BUSHEL OF NAIVE MELODIES, PLEASE."

"...AND A BIG SHOUTOUT GOES OUT TO MY MAN, MOZART."

"ALL THOSE PIANOS IN MIDDLE CLASS DRAWING ROOMS NEEDED MUSIC..."

"AND THE ROMANTIC COMPOSERS WERE READY TO PROVIDE IT."

"ORIGINALITY WASN'T JUST AN AESTHETIC, IT WAS A WAY TO DISTINGUISH YOURSELF FROM YOUR COMPETITORS..."

PAYMENT & TECHNOLOGIES

1851: SACEM COLLECTING SOCIETY ESTABLISHED IN FRANCE TO COLLECT COMPOSERS' AND PUBLISHERS' PERFORMANCE ROYALTIES FROM PUBLIC VENUES.

1886: BERNE CONVENTION – THE FIRST MAJOR INTERNATIONAL COPYRIGHT AGREEMENT.

LAW

YOU KNOW, THIS IS FASCINATING, I MUST ADMIT.

CHANGING NOTIONS OF COMPOSITION, OF GENIUS, NEW TECHNOLOGIES, NEW WAYS OF GETTING PAID, THE BEGINNINGS OF OUR IDEAS OF ORIGINALITY, THE DEVELOPMENT OF COPYRIGHT...

YOU WERE RIGHT. AT FIRST I THOUGHT THAT LOOKING AT THESE THINGS WOULD DISTRACT FROM THE BEAUTY OF MUSIC.

IT DOESN'T. ANY MORE THAN UNDERSTANDING ANATOMY DISTRACTS FROM THE BEAUTY OF THE STATUE...

AND WE *DO* NEED TO UNDERSTAND IT ALL TOGETHER. MUSICAL NORMS, TECHNOLOGY, LAW, AESTHETICS...EACH INFLUENCES THE OTHERS. WE CAN'T UNDERSTAND CREATIVITY OR BORROWING WITHOUT SEEING THEM ALL...

AUDIENCES MATTER... TECHNOLOGIES MATTER... LAW IS STARTING TO MATTER...

PATRONAGE PRODUCED ONE KIND OF MUSIC...

AIMED AT THE EARS, AND PRIDE, OF ARISTOCRATIC LISTENERS.

TECHNOLOGY ALLOWED MUSIC TO REACH REMOTE EARS...

PRINTERS WERE THE FIRST TECHNOLOGICAL INTERMEDIARIES...

SOME RECEIVED LEGAL RIGHTS TO PRINT MUSIC...OR THE RIGHTS TO PARTICULAR SONGS...

WITH THE DEVELOPMENT OF COPYRIGHT, THE RIGHT SHIFTS TO THE AUTHOR...

COMPOSERS DON'T USE THE SYSTEM MUCH AT FIRST...

LISZT	UP 1...
BEETHOVEN	DOWN 7...
MOZART	UP 13...
TCHAIKOVSKY	DOWN 2...
BRAHMS	UP 7...
MAHLER	DOWN 3...

EVEN SO, MUSIC IS NOW DRIVEN BY A MUCH LARGER MARKET...

MUSIC FOR DRAWING ROOMS AND MUSIC HALLS AS WELL AS PALACES AND CHURCHES...

AND THERE'S AN AESTHETIC CHANGE, A NEW FOCUS ON ORIGINALITY...

GRADUALLY COMPOSERS MAKE MORE USE OF COPYRIGHT...

THERE ARE STILL POWER IMBALANCES...BUT COPYRIGHT IS A WONDERFUL TOOL!

CREATORS CAN DREAM OF GIVING UP WAITING TABLES...CONCENTRATE ON THEIR ART...

AND REACH AN AUDIENCE OF THOUSANDS, MAYBE MILLIONS...

70

IT'S 1814...

...AND THAT'S FRANCIS SCOTT KEY WATCHING FORT McHENRY BEING BOMBARDED BY THE BRITISH...

HE WROTE A POEM ABOUT IT CALLED THE DEFENCE OF FORT McHENRY...

BUT IT DIDN'T ACHIEVE TRUE FAME UNTIL HE SET IT TO THE TUNE OF...

THE ANACREONTIC SONG — A BRITISH DRINKING SONG FROM 1778 — AND IT BECAME...

THE STAR-SPANGLED BANNER...

WHICH BECAME THE MUSICAL EMBLEM OF THE NATION.

...SO IN 1904 WHEN PUCCINI WROTE MADAME BUTTERFLY, HE MADE IT THE THEME OF PINKERTON, THE AMERICAN NAVAL OFFICER...

...BUT EVEN A PINKERTON DETECTIVE COULDN'T HAVE IMAGINED WHAT THE SONG WOULD SOUND LIKE, 71 YEARS LATER, PLAYED BY A YOUNG MAN NAMED...

JIMI HENDRIX!!

WAIT, WE BORROWED OUR NATIONAL ANTHEM FROM THE COUNTRY **WE REVOLTED AGAINST**? THAT'S CHEEKY. AT LEAST WE STILL HAVE *MY COUNTRY, 'TIS OF THEE*.
ACTUALLY, THAT'S THE **BRITISH** NATIONAL ANTHEM – WORDS BY SAMUEL FRANCIS SMITH SET TO THE TUNE FROM *GOD SAVE THE QUEEN*.
SWEET LAND OF LIBERTY...
...TO STEAL YOUR TUNES.
THE BATTLE HYMN OF THE REPUBLIC?
THE MUSIC IS BORROWED FROM WILLIAM STEFFE'S *CANAAN'S HAPPY SHORE*, THE SONG THAT BECAME *JOHN BROWN'S BODY*.
THE BORROWING DIDN'T STOP THERE. *THE BATTLE HYMN OF THE REPUBLIC'S* LYRICS WERE WRITTEN BY THE ABOLITIONIST JULIA WARD HOWE...
...BUT A BRITISH FOLK SONG COLLECTOR NAMED CECIL SHARP PUT HIS NAME ON THE COPYRIGHT.
MINE EYES HAVE SEEN THE GLORY OF THE STEALING OF MY WORDS...
THE MARINE HYMN?
NOPE. FIRST SET TO AN OLD SPANISH FOLK SONG, THEN TO A MELODY FROM THE OPERA *GENEVIEVE DE BRABANT* BY JACQUES OFFENBACH.
REMIX ISN'T OUR FUTURE... IT'S OUR **PAST**.

"ISN'T ONE DIFFERENCE BETWEEN MUSIC IN THE OLD WORLD AND THE NEW THAT THE CONSTITUTION *REQUIRES* THE PROTECTION OF CREATORS' RIGHTS? SPEAKING AS A COMPOSER, I LIKE THAT!"

"WELL, NOT EXACTLY..."

"THIS IS NOT THE EXCELLENT ADVENTURE I HAD IN MIND..."

73

Panel 1:
?
DON'T MIND US...
...GOOD JOB CROSSING THE DELAWARE, BY THE WAY.

Panel 2:
?
DON'T COMPROMISE THOSE PRINCIPLES IN THE DECLARATION OF INDEPENDENCE. IT SAYS "ALL MEN..."
LISTEN TO MARTHA MORE...!

Panel 3:
THAT WAS *NOT* THE WAY I HAD PLANNED TO ARRIVE!

Panel 4:
JUST ADDING SOME UNDERREPRESENTED OPINIONS...

Section. 8. The Congress shall have Power To promote the Progress of Science and useful Arts, by securing for limited Times to Authors and Inventors the exclusive Right to their respective Writings and Discoveries;

SOME OF THE FRAMERS OF THE CONSTITUTION HAD CORRESPONDED ABOUT DIFFERENT WAYS TO ENCOURAGE INNOVATION AND THE SPREAD OF LEARNING...

LAND GRANTS... PRIZES...

THEY SETTLED ON COPYRIGHTS AND PATENTS. CONGRESS IS GIVEN THE POWER TO "PROMOTE THE PROGRESS OF SCIENCE AND USEFUL ARTS" BY GIVING EXCLUSIVE RIGHTS FOR LIMITED TIMES TO AUTHORS AND INVENTORS.

HOW LONG IS THE "LIMITED TIME"?

IN THE FIRST COPYRIGHT ACT IT WAS 14 YEARS... RENEWABLE FOR ANOTHER 14...

SO IF THE ANACREONTIC SONG HAD BEEN COPYRIGHTED BACK THEN IT WOULD HAVE BEEN IN THE PUBLIC DOMAIN BY THE TIME FRANCIS SCOTT KEY USED IT FOR THE NATIONAL ANTHEM!

HOW LONG DOES COPYRIGHT LAST NOW?

BUT THAT ACT DIDN'T MENTION MUSIC. CONGRESS WAS MORE CONCERNED ABOUT MAPS AND BOOKS. IT WASN'T UNTIL 1831 THAT MUSIC WAS EXPLICITLY INCLUDED. THE COPYRIGHT LASTED 28 YEARS, RENEWABLE FOR ANOTHER 14.

NOW IT IS THE LIFE OF THE AUTHOR...

...PLUS 70 YEARS.

!!!

SO A SONG WRITTEN BY A 25 YEAR OLD TODAY WILL BE ENTERING THE PUBLIC DOMAIN...

...FOR THE FRANCIS SCOTT KEYS OF THE MODERN WORLD TO REMIX...

IN ABOUT 120 YEARS.

IF YOU WANT A SYMBOL OF WHY EARLY AMERICAN COMPOSERS WANTED COPYRIGHT PROTECTION, LOOK AT STEPHEN FOSTER.

I GUESS IT'S ASKING A LITTLE MUCH THAT I WOULD KNOW ANY OF HIS TUNES?

OH, YOU DO... OH! SUSANNA, CAMPTOWN RACES, WAY DOWN UPON THE SWANEE RIVER, JEANIE WITH THE LIGHT BROWN HAIR, MY OLD KENTUCKY HOME...

FOSTER WAS TRYING TO MAKE A LIVING AS A PROFESSIONAL SONGWRITER — NOT DEPENDING ON PATRONAGE OR PERFORMANCE.

ONE MAN WROTE ALL THOSE!

YES, AND A LOT MORE.

EVEN THOUGH MUSIC WAS FORMALLY PROTECTED BY COPYRIGHT BY THE TIME HE WAS WRITING, THE BUSINESS MODEL WE KNOW NOW DIDN'T EXIST.

STEPHEN FOSTER
(1826–1864)

HIS SONGS WERE INCREDIBLY POPULAR BUT NOT MUCH OF THAT MONEY CAME TO HIM. HE DIED AT AGE 37 AND LEGEND HAS IT HE HAD ONLY 37 CENTS TO HIS NAME.

MUSICALLY, THOUGH, FOSTER EMBODIES A DIFFERENT STORY. IT'S A VERY AMERICAN STORY. A STORY OF REMIX...

...SOMETIMES FORCIBLE REMIX.

THE PEOPLE WHO CAME TO THE U.S. ALL BROUGHT THEIR OWN MUSIC...FOR SOME OF THEM THE JOURNEY WAS A GREAT ADVENTURE INTO FREEDOM...AND THEIR MUSIC CARRIED MEMORIES OF THEIR HOME.

FOR OTHERS...

...THE JOURNEY WASN'T...

...A VOLUNTARY ONE!

SLAVES DIDN'T JUST BRING THEIR MUSICAL TRADITIONS, THEY BROUGHT MEMORIES OF HOW TO MAKE THEIR INSTRUMENTS... STRINGED INSTRUMENTS THAT USED A GOURD AS A SOUND BOX... THE AKONTING SPIKE LUTES FROM SENEGAL...COMBINED...THEY BECAME A CLASSICALLY AMERICAN INSTRUMENT, THE BANJO.

WASN'T BANJO MUSIC A KEY TO FOSTER'S SUCCESS?

YES. THERE'S EVIDENCE THAT FOSTER HAD SOME CLASSICAL MUSICAL TRAINING FROM A GERMAN IMMIGRANT CALLED HENRY KLEBER, BUT WE KNOW HE WAS FASCINATED BY MINSTRELSY... THE SONGS THAT WERE CALLED "*ETHIOPIAN*" AT THE TIME.

ARE YOU TALKING ABOUT THOSE AWFUL, DEMEANING MINSTREL SHOWS?

YES. THE MINSTREL SONGS WERE SUNG BY WHITE PERFORMERS WHO DRESSED UP IN "BLACKFACE" AND THE LYRICS WERE FULL OF RACIST STEREOTYPES...

...IT'S EASIER TO LIVE WITH A SYSTEM LIKE SLAVERY IF YOU CAN CARICATURE THE PEOPLE YOU ARE ENSLAVING...SLAVERY APPROPRIATED PEOPLE. MINSTRELSY APPROPRIATED STEREOTYPES.*

*MINSTRELSY PERSISTED. THE LAST BLACK AND WHITE MINSTREL SHOW ON BBC WAS IN 1978! —EDS.

78

FOSTER'S SONGS HAVE THOSE SAME CARICATURES. BUT HE WAS COMPLICATED.

HE USED THE MINSTREL TRADITION, BUT HE ALSO TRIED TO GET HIS AUDIENCE TO EMPATHIZE WITH THE PEOPLE HE WROTE ABOUT...

A SONG LIKE NELLY WAS A LADY SOUNDS CONDESCENDING TO US...

...BUT, IN 1849, DESCRIBING AN AFRICAN-AMERICAN WOMAN AS A "LADY" MOURNED BY HER WIDOWER HUSBAND WAS PROBABLY SHOCKING IN A WORLD WHERE "NELLY" COULD ALSO BE BOUGHT AND SOLD.

NELLY WAS A LADY, LAST NIGHT SHE DIED...

AND PEOPLE RESPONDED.

FOSTER'S SONGS WERE WILDLY POPULAR.

THEY STILL ARE! SO WHY WASN'T HE A COMMERCIAL SUCCESS?

HE GOT CHEATED! ABOUT 20 PUBLISHERS PRINTED OH! SUSANNA AND ONLY ONE OF THEM PAID HIM — A MEASLY $100.

79

THAT WAS PART OF IT. BUT YOU ALSO HAVE TO REMEMBER THIS WAS A DIFFERENT WORLD. AT FIRST COPYRIGHT ONLY COVERED THE RIGHT TO PRINT. NO ONE THOUGHT THERE WAS A RIGHT TO KEEP PEOPLE FROM PERFORMING THE SONG.

NO PEOPLE MONITORING THE MUSIC HALLS AND DEMANDING PAYMENT FOR EACH PERFORMANCE?

EXACTLY! AND FRANKLY, THE PUBLISHERS HAD THE POWER.

MMM...

2314
OUR DIGITAL DETECTORS REVEAL OVER 150 PERFORMANCES OF CAMPTOWN RACES THIS MONTH ALONE!

GRUMBLE...

RECORDING CONTRACTS...

AND *THAT* HASN'T CHANGED! I COULD SHOW YOU RECORDING CONTRACTS...!

FOSTER DID MAKE A LIVING FROM HIS MUSIC — HE AVERAGED ABOUT $1300 A YEAR — ABOUT $38,000 TODAY. HE JUST DIDN'T EARN WHAT HE COULD NOW. AND SOME OF THAT HAD TO DO WITH THE RELATIVE POWER OF THE ARTISTS AS OPPOSED TO THE INTERMEDIARIES — THE PRINTERS.

RECORDING CONTRACTS...

RECORDING CONTRACTS!!!

Label shall be the exclusive, perpetual owner of all copyrights throughout the universe ... "Work for hire" ... "Controlled composition" ... No royalties shall be payable to you for the following ... Label may recoup "advances" from your royalties ...

PLEASE! YOUNG KIDS MIGHT READ THIS COMIC.

80

SO WHEN THEY CALL FOSTER "THE FATHER OF AMERICAN POPULAR MUSIC" IT'S TRUE IN MORE THAN ONE WAY.

HE'S AN EARLY EXAMPLE OF A PROFESSIONAL POPULAR SONGWRITER – NOT A PERFORMER – WHOSE ROYALTIES COME FROM A LARGE MARKET REACHED THROUGH MECHANICAL DISTRIBUTION, A MARKET BUILT AROUND COPYRIGHTED MUSIC.

AND TO ATTRACT THAT MARKET FOSTER TOOK FRAGMENTS OF THE MUSICAL TRADITIONS THAT AMERICA HAD MINGLED TOGETHER – PLANTATION CHANTS, BANJO MUSIC AND MINSTRELSY, BUT ALSO CELTIC AND GERMAN FOLK TUNES, EVEN SNIPPETS OF OPERA.

I CAN SEE A HINT OF CONFLICT BETWEEN THE WAY COMPOSERS ARE BEGINNING TO GET PAID AND THE WAY MUSIC GETS MADE.

...THE MARKET IS BUILT AROUND PROPERTY RIGHTS OVER MUSIC. BUT IN THE PROCESS OF MUSICAL CREATION, COMPOSERS HAD TREATED THEIR MUSICAL HERITAGE AS A COMMONS – BORROWING AND REMIXING TO MAKE NEW STYLES AND SONGS.

WHAT'S GOING TO HAPPEN WHEN THE TWO...

COLLIDE?

IS THIS WHEN WE GET THE FIRST LAW SUIT CLAIMING ONE TUNE WAS COPIED FROM ANOTHER?

YES. REED v. CARUSI IN 1845.

IN *REED v. CARUSI*, SAMUEL CARUSI WAS ORDERED TO PAY $200 FOR PRODUCING A MUSICAL VERSION OF A POEM CALLED *THE OLD ARM CHAIR*. THE JURY THOUGHT CARUSI'S VERSION WAS TOO SIMILAR TO HENRY RUSSELL'S VERSION OF THE SONG. CARUSI CLAIMED THAT RUSSELL'S SONG ITSELF WAS BUILT ON TWO EARLIER SONGS, *THE BLUE BELLS OF SCOTLAND* AND *THE SOLDIER'S TEAR*, WHILE HIS OWN WAS BUILT ON A SONG CALLED *NEW ENGLAND*. THE COURT DISAGREED!

BORROWING FOR ME BUT NOT FOR THEE!

WE'VE COME QUITE SOME WAY FROM THE GREEKS, WHEN THE CUTTING EDGE TECHNOLOGY WAS "NOTATION" AND THE REASON TO RESIST REMIX WAS BECAUSE PLATO THOUGHT IT WOULD UNDERMINE PHILOSOPHY AND THE STATE!

AND THE PACE OF CHANGE WAS ONLY...

...INCREASING...

IF I GET NOTHING OUT OF THIS TRIP BUT THIS HAT, IT WILL HAVE BEEN WORTH IT!

THE MASS PRODUCTION OF PIANOS WAS ONLY THE BEGINNING. BY THE 1890s THE MARKET FOR PRINTED MUSIC WAS GROWING FAST. SHEET MUSIC SALES BOOMED.

WHAT KIND OF MUSIC WERE PEOPLE LISTENING TO?

AS THE 19TH CENTURY CAME TO A CLOSE, THE SOUND OF THE MOMENT WAS RAGTIME.

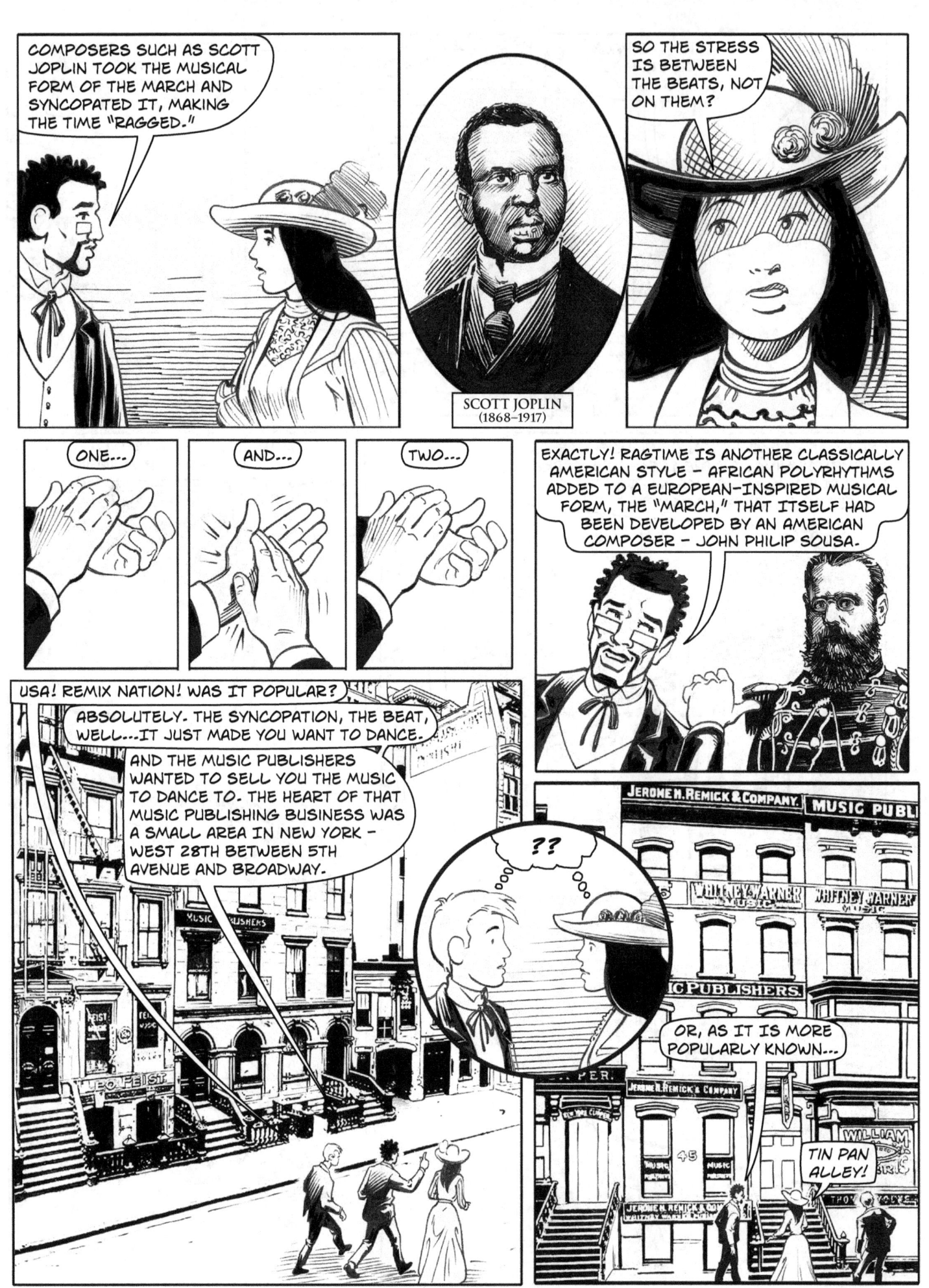

COMPOSERS SUCH AS SCOTT JOPLIN TOOK THE MUSICAL FORM OF THE MARCH AND SYNCOPATED IT, MAKING THE TIME "RAGGED."

SO THE STRESS IS BETWEEN THE BEATS, NOT ON THEM?

SCOTT JOPLIN
(1868–1917)

ONE...

AND...

TWO...

EXACTLY! RAGTIME IS ANOTHER CLASSICALLY AMERICAN STYLE — AFRICAN POLYRHYTHMS ADDED TO A EUROPEAN-INSPIRED MUSICAL FORM, THE "MARCH," THAT ITSELF HAD BEEN DEVELOPED BY AN AMERICAN COMPOSER — JOHN PHILIP SOUSA.

USA! REMIX NATION! WAS IT POPULAR?

ABSOLUTELY. THE SYNCOPATION, THE BEAT, WELL...IT JUST MADE YOU WANT TO DANCE.

AND THE MUSIC PUBLISHERS WANTED TO SELL YOU THE MUSIC TO DANCE TO. THE HEART OF THAT MUSIC PUBLISHING BUSINESS WAS A SMALL AREA IN NEW YORK — WEST 28TH BETWEEN 5TH AVENUE AND BROADWAY.

??

OR, AS IT IS MORE POPULARLY KNOWN...

TIN PAN ALLEY!

DIDN'T THE MUSIC PUBLISHERS HIRE MUSICIANS WHO WENT AROUND TO PROMOTE THEIR MUSIC TO STORES AND TO THE PUBLIC?

YES, THEY WERE CALLED "SONG PLUGGERS." SOME PEOPLE SAY THE TINNY PIANOS THEY USED GAVE TIN PAN ALLEY ITS NAME.

THE AMAZING THING IS THAT THIS IS A MUSIC INDUSTRY BUILT ON PERFORMANCE BY ITS CUSTOMERS. YOU NEED A PLAYER — A HUMAN INTERMEDIARY BETWEEN THE NOTATION AND THE LISTENER'S EAR.

THAT WAS CHANGING, RIGHT?

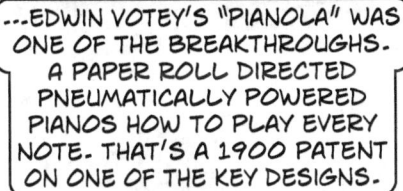

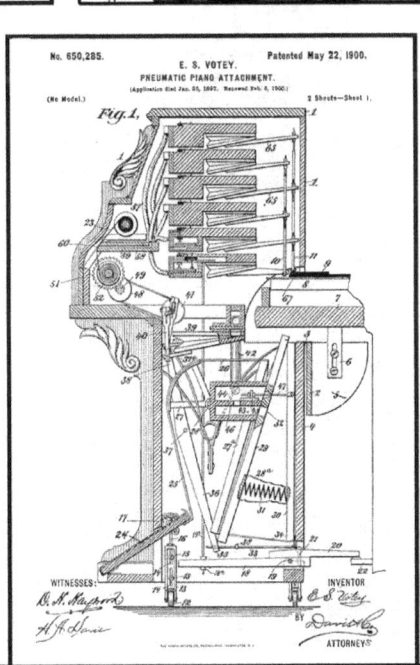

OH, YES. INVENTORS WERE HARD AT WORK ON TURNING THE "SCORE" DIRECTLY INTO MUSIC...

OH GO WAY MAN I CAN HYPNOTIZE DIS NATION, I CAN SHAKE DE EARTH'S FOUNDATION WID DE MAPLE LEAF RAG.

...EDWIN VOTEY'S "PIANOLA" WAS ONE OF THE BREAKTHROUGHS. A PAPER ROLL DIRECTED PNEUMATICALLY POWERED PIANOS HOW TO PLAY EVERY NOTE. THAT'S A 1900 PATENT ON ONE OF THE KEY DESIGNS.

SO "NOTATION" BECOMES "PROGRAMMING" — INSTRUCTING THE INSTRUMENT WITHOUT A HUMAN IN BETWEEN. THAT'S BRILLIANT.

AT FIRST THE COSTS WERE HIGH.

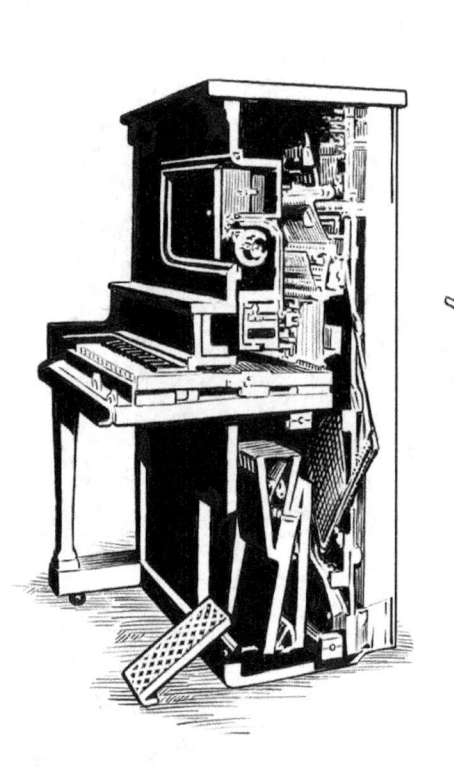

AND THERE WERE "FORMAT WARS," RIGHT? DIFFERENT NUMBERS OF KEYS AND SIZES OF PIANO ROLLS?

I THOUGHT THAT WAS ONLY A PROBLEM OF OUR GENERATION. I BOUGHT HD DVD INSTEAD OF BLU-RAY!

BUT THEY STANDARDIZED AND PRICES KEPT DROPPING.

BY THE 1920s MOST PIANOS MANUFACTURED IN THE U.S. HAD A "PLAYER PIANO" INSIDE...MIMICKING EXACTLY THE STYLE OF THE PIANIST WHO HAD "RECORDED" THE TRACK.

BUT THERE WAS A COMPETITIVE TECHNOLOGY...

WHEN *DID* EDISON INVENT THE PHONOGRAPH?

EDISON'S PHONOGRAPH WAS INVENTED IN 1877. EMILE BERLINER'S GRAMOPHONE, WHICH LOOKED MORE LIKE A RECORD PLAYER, CAME ALONG TEN YEARS LATER.

WITHIN TWO YEARS, THE FIRST PHONOGRAPH PARLOR OPENED. YOU YELLED YOUR SELECTION INTO A SPEAKING TUBE AND THEN LISTENED THROUGH A HORN TO THE MUSIC PLAYING FROM A GRAMOPHONE DOWNSTAIRS.

IN 1901 BERLINER JOINED FORCES WITH E.R. JOHNSON, WHO HAD SOLVED THE PROBLEM OF THE GRAMOPHONE'S MOTOR, DOING BUSINESS AS THE VICTOR TALKING MACHINE COMPANY. YOU MAY RECOGNIZE THE TRADEMARK...
GADZOOKS! THIS DEVICE WILL UNSETTLE THE POLITICAL ECONOMY OF MUSIC MAKING...! ALSO, I THINK THE TECHNICIAN DROPPED SOME BACON DOWN THAT HORN...
THE RECORDING INDUSTRY EXPANDED FAST. CARUSO MADE HIS FIRST RECORDING IN 1902...
THAT EARLY! THE COMPOSERS AND PUBLISHERS MUST HAVE WELCOMED THIS NEW MARKET FOR THEIR WORK.
NOT EXACTLY.
(No Model.)
E. BERLINER.
GRAMOPHONE.
No. 372,786.
Patented Nov. 8, 1887.
WITNESSES
INVENTOR

Panel 1:

"REMEMBER COPYRIGHT LAW IS A STATUTORY MONOPOLY — YOU ONLY HAVE THE RIGHTS THE STATUTE GIVES YOU. AND THE STATUTE SAID NOTHING ABOUT PIANO ROLLS OR RECORDINGS."

"WHAT DO YOU MEAN?"

"COPYRIGHT ISN'T A RIGHT TO CONTROL EVERY ASPECT OF THE WORK... JUST SELECTED ONES SUCH AS REPRODUCTION OR PUBLIC PERFORMANCE."

"IF YOU ARE IN A BOOKSTORE AND YOU READ A BOOK JUST STANDING THERE, THAT DOESN'T VIOLATE COPYRIGHT. IF YOU SING IN THE SHOWER, THAT DOESN'T VIOLATE COPYRIGHT."

"GOOD TASTE BUT NOT COPYRIGHT?"

Panel 2:

"BACK THEN THE RIGHTS WERE MUCH 'THINNER.' THEY JUST COVERED PRINTING AND PUBLIC PERFORMANCE. THE PIANO ROLL MAKERS AND RECORD MAKERS WEREN'T DOING EITHER."

"THE RECORDING INDUSTRY IS SO CONCERNED ABOUT THE EFFECTS OF TECHNOLOGICAL 'PIRACY' ON ARTISTS TODAY. I'M SURE THEY FELT THE SAME WAY BACK THEN!"

Panel 3:

"SURELY THEY WANTED COMPOSERS TO GET PAID FOR USES OF THEIR WORKS IN NEW TECHNOLOGIES?"

Panel 4:

"YOU ARE A CYNICAL MAN. LET'S HAVE THEM SPEAK FOR THEMSELVES. HERE ARE THE REPRESENTATIVES OF THE RECORDING AND PIANO ROLL INDUSTRIES TESTIFYING IN CONGRESS IN 1906!"

"ALL TALK ABOUT 'DISHONESTY' AND 'THEFT' IN THIS CONNECTION, FROM HOWEVER HIGH A SOURCE, IS THE MEREST CLAPTRAP, FOR THERE EXISTS NO PROPERTY IN IDEAS, MUSICAL, LITERARY OR ARTISTIC, EXCEPT AS DEFINED BY STATUTE."

PHILIP MAURO
AMERICAN GRAPHOPHONE COMPANY

"IT IS THEREFORE PERFECTLY DEMONSTRABLE THAT THE INTRODUCTION OF AUTOMATIC MUSIC PLAYERS HAS NOT DEPRIVED ANY COMPOSER OF ANYTHING HE HAD BEFORE THEIR INTRODUCTION."

"WE HAVE A RIGHT UNDER THE LAW OF THE LAND AS IT STANDS TODAY TO REPRODUCE...MUSIC: PAST, PRESENT OR FUTURE. THIS BILL SAYS TO US THAT WE CANNOT REPRODUCE THAT IF SOME FELLOW TELLS US WE CANNOT."

"THE COMPOSERS AND THE PUBLIC ALIKE WERE DEPENDENT A FEW YEARS AGO FOR THE RENDITION OF THESE COMPOSITIONS... ENTIRELY UPON THE HUMAN VOICE OR UPON INSTRUMENTS MANIPULATED BY HUMAN FINGERS. HENCE THERE WAS A VERY NARROW LIMIT TO THE AUDIBLE RENDITION OF MUSICAL COMPOSITIONS, AND THE AVERAGE QUALITY THEREOF WAS VERY LOW, BEING DETERMINED BY THE SKILL OF THE HUMAN PERFORMER...IN A FEW YEARS THE GENIUS OF THE INVENTOR HAS BROUGHT ABOUT A MARVELOUS CHANGE...THE COMPOSERS AND PUBLISHERS HAVE NOT CONTRIBUTED IN THE SLIGHTEST DEGREE TO THIS CHANGE...YET THE PUBLISHER DOES NOT SCRUPLE TO DEMAND RADICAL CHANGE OF LEGISLATION IN ORDER TO GIVE HIM THE ENTIRE MONOPOLY OF THE BENEFITS...AND HAS THE EFFRONTERY TO APPLY VITUPERATIVE EPITHETS TO THOSE WHO VENTURE TO OPPOSE HIS SCHEME OF GREED."

ALBERT WALKER
AUTO-MUSIC PERFORATING COMPANY OF NEW YORK

GEORGE POUND
DE KLEIST MUSICAL INSTRUMENT MANUFACTURING COMPANY & RUDOLPH WURLITZER COMPANY

Panel 1: SO THE RECORDING INDUSTRY BACK THEN WANTED NEW TECHNOLOGIES TO HAVE THE FREEDOM TO COPY? IRONY! AND THEY WERE **INDIGNANT** ABOUT THE SUGGESTION THEY SHOULD HAVE TO PAY COMPOSERS FOR RECORDING THEIR SONGS?

Panel 2: ABSOLUTELY. THEY THOUGHT THAT THEIR TECHNOLOGY HAD CREATED A NEW MARKET AND CLAIMED IT WOULD BE BETTER FOR THE PUBLIC IF RECORDINGS WERE FREELY MADE. JOHN PHILIP SOUSA DIDN'T AGREE.

Panel 3: "THESE PERFORATED ROLL COMPANIES AND THESE PHONOGRAPH COMPANIES TAKE MY PROPERTY AND PUT IT ON THEIR RECORDS...WHEN THEY MAKE MONEY OUT OF MY PIECES, I WANT A SHARE OF IT...THEY HAVE TO BUY THE WOOD THAT THEY MAKE THE BOX OUT OF, AND THE MATERIAL FOR THE DISK, AND THAT DISK AS IT STANDS, WITHOUT THE COMPOSITION OF AN AMERICAN COMPOSER ON IT, IS NOT WORTH A PENNY. PUT THE COMPOSITION OF AN AMERICAN COMPOSER ON IT AND IT IS WORTH $1.50. WHAT MAKES THE DIFFERENCE? THE STUFF THAT WE WRITE."

Panel 4: YEAH! THAT'S WHAT I'M TALKING ABOUT! SOMEONE NEEDS TO STAND UP FOR THE COMPOSER. MAN, THAT GUY TALKED JUST LIKE HE COMPOSED. MAKES YOU WANT TO GET UP AND **MARCH**!

Panel 5: HMMPH. I THINK THE RECORDING INDUSTRY GUYS HAD A POINT. THEY WERE WORRIED THAT THE PUBLISHERS HAD FORMED A CARTEL TO MONOPOLIZE MUSIC.

Panel 6: MAYBE YOU DISAGREE WITH SOUSA BECAUSE NO ONE WOULD EVER WANT TO COPY ANYTHING YOU WROTE?

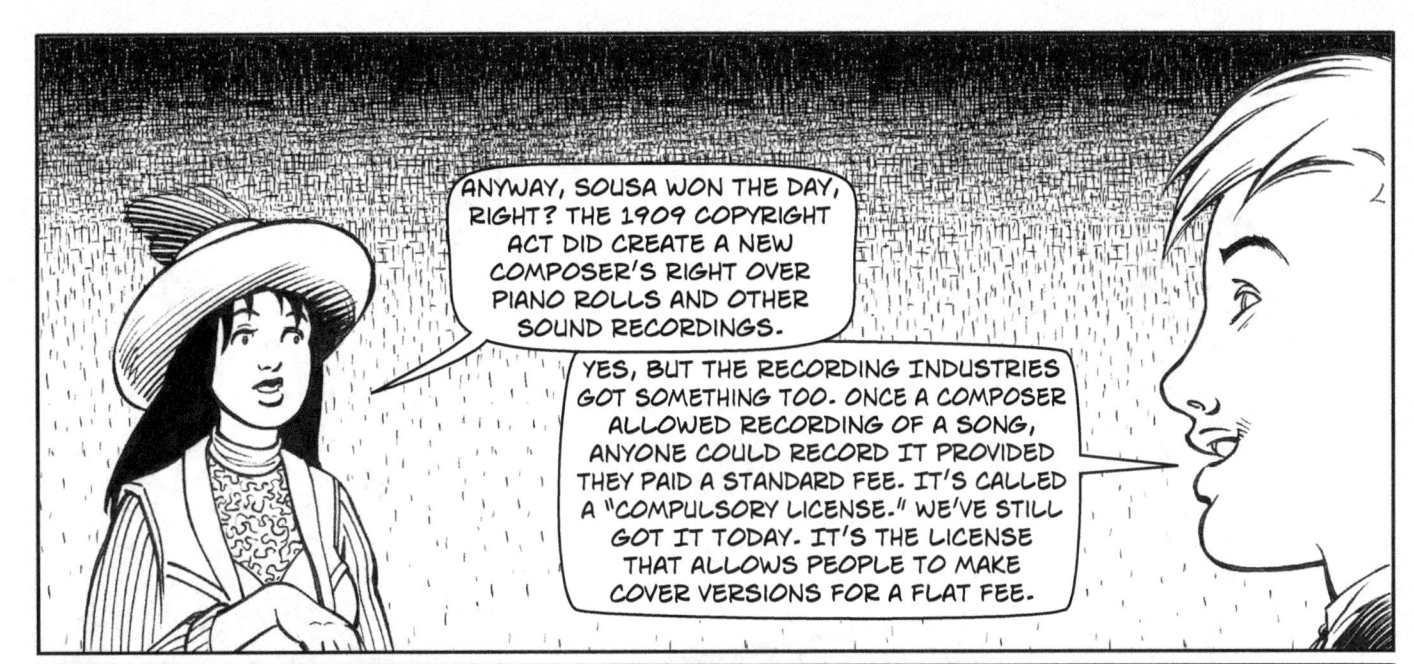

"ANYWAY, SOUSA WON THE DAY, RIGHT? THE 1909 COPYRIGHT ACT DID CREATE A NEW COMPOSER'S RIGHT OVER PIANO ROLLS AND OTHER SOUND RECORDINGS."

"YES, BUT THE RECORDING INDUSTRIES GOT SOMETHING TOO. ONCE A COMPOSER ALLOWED RECORDING OF A SONG, ANYONE COULD RECORD IT PROVIDED THEY PAID A STANDARD FEE. IT'S CALLED A "COMPULSORY LICENSE." WE'VE STILL GOT IT TODAY. IT'S THE LICENSE THAT ALLOWS PEOPLE TO MAKE COVER VERSIONS FOR A FLAT FEE."

"A PEACE TREATY FOR THE MUSIC WARS!! IT DESERVES ITS OWN SONG!"

"YOU SAY HYPOCRITICAL, I SAY PIRATICAL... YOU SAY PRO-TECHNICAL, I SAY HERETICAL... 'POCRITICAL, PIRATICAL, PRO-TECHNICAL, HERETICAL... LICENSE THE WHOLE THING OFF!"

Panel 1:
"FUNNY YOU SHOULD PICK THAT TUNE...LOOK. THAT'S THE SAME STORE. WAIT, WHAT'S CHANGED...?!!"

Panel 2:
"SOMEONE SHOT A COUCH AND SKINNED IT! MUST...NOT...LAUGH... AND DARN, I LOST THAT HAT."

Panel 3:
"LOOK!"

"REMICK'S BRINGS YOU THE BEST SONGS OF 1914!"

♪♪♪ "YOUR LIPS WERE SWEETER THAN JULEP WHEN YOU WORE THAT TULIP..." ♪

BETWEEN 1890 AND 1909 MUSIC SALES HAD TRIPLED. TIN PAN ALLEY'S BUSINESS WAS BOOMING, EVEN WITHOUT THE MONEY FOR PIANO ROLLS AND RECORDS.

Panel 4:
"COMPOSERS AND PUBLISHERS DID HAVE THE RIGHT TO GET PAYMENT FOR PUBLIC PERFORMANCE, RIGHT?"

"YES, THEY GOT THAT IN 1897, BUT IT WAS SPARINGLY USED AT FIRST. PERFORMANCE WAS SEEN AS FREE PUBLICITY. IN 1909 THE LAW ADDED A 2 CENT STATUTORY ROYALTY FOR EVERY PIANO ROLL OR RECORD. AND COPYRIGHT HAD BEEN EXTENDED AGAIN. NOW IT LASTED 28 YEARS, RENEWABLE FOR ANOTHER 28."

"WHICH MEANS THAT, IN 1914, THE YOUNG MAN PLAYING THAT PIANO MIGHT EXPECT ANY NEW SONG HE PLAYED TO BE COPYRIGHTED UNTIL 1942. 1970 IF THEY RENEWED."

A COPYRIGHT FROM 1914 THAT LASTS PAST 1969! FEELS LIKE A LONG WAY FROM WOODSTOCK. WHO'S THE YOUNG GUY?
THE NAME'S GERSHWIN, GEORGE GERSHWIN. HE'S NOT A SONGWRITER YET, JUST THE YOUNGEST SONG PLUGGER IN THE BUSINESS. AT 15 HE'S SELLING OTHER PEOPLE'S SONGS, EVEN SONGS LIKE THAT. BUT HE'S ABOUT TO BECOME ONE OF THE GREAT COMPOSERS OF THE CENTURY.
REMICK'S
MUSIC
COME JOSEPHINE IN MY FLYING MACHINE, GOING UP SHE GOES! UP SHE GOES!
1913
1917
1930
1945
1950
1961
1968
1969
MUSIC PUBLISHERS
LEO. FEIST
PLUGGING SONGS AT 15 IS PRETTY PRECOCIOUS!
AND HE WAS WRITING THEM BY 17. HE HAD HIS FIRST BIG HIT – SWANEE – IN 1919, JUST AROUND HIS 21ST BIRTHDAY. AL JOLSON WOULD MAKE IT FAMOUS – AND VICE VERSA.
SWANEE
WORDS BY I. CAESAR MUSIC BY GEORGE GERSHWIN
SWANEE! HOW I LOVE YOU, HOW I LOVE YOU, MY DEAR OLD SWANEE!!
Successfully Introduced by AL JOLSON in "SINBAD" at the Winter Garden New York
6
T. B HARMS AND FRANCIS, DAY & HUNTER NEW YORK

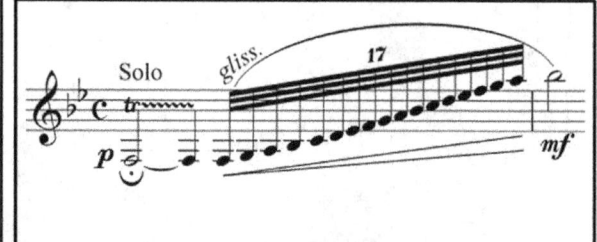

GERSHWIN HAD LOTS OF HITS AFTER THAT — EVER HEAR OF LADY BE GOOD OR FASCINATING RHYTHM?

BUT HIS FIRST MAJOR PIECE WAS RHAPSODY IN BLUE IN 1924.

IT DREW ON EVERYTHING — JAZZ, FOXTROT, "BLUE" NOTES, MODERNIST MUSIC, THE SYNCOPATION OF RAGTIME — MANY HAVE CALLED IT "A MELTING POT."

...AND I WROTE IT IN THREE WEEKS!

WHOOSH!

I LOVE THAT PIECE. EVEN THOUGH I HAD TO PLAY IT A MILLION TIMES AT PIANO RECITALS AS A KID.

???

YEAH — THE CHILD PIANO PRODIGY, WITH BIG HAIR, BRACES AND TWO VERY PROUD PARENTS. IT'S A PERIOD OF MY LIFE I'D RATHER FORGET.

THAT'S MY DAUGHTER!

SHH!! SHH!! SHH!!

THE PUBLIC DOMAIN
IT'S FUNNY THAT YOU SHOULD MENTION RHAPSODY IN BLUE AND 1924. SONGS PUBLISHED BEFORE 1923 – INCLUDING SWANEE – ARE ALL IN THE PUBLIC DOMAIN. YOU CAN SING THEM, REPRINT THEM, ADAPT THEM, INCORPORATE THEM INTO NEW PLAYS AND MOVIES.
WHEN GERSHWIN WROTE RHAPSODY IN BLUE THE "DEAL" COPYRIGHT GAVE HIM WAS SIMPLE. THE COPYRIGHT TERM LASTED 28 YEARS...UNTIL 1952.
?
1952
CRANK
CREAK
CRANK
FEELS PRETTY GOOD!
CRANK
RHAPSODY IN BLUE
28 Years
MIGHT BE NICE TO RENEW...
1924
...UNLESS HE RENEWED THE COPYRIGHT.
IN WHICH CASE IT WOULD LAST FOR ANOTHER 28 YEARS, UNTIL 1980...
THE PUBLIC DOMAIN
1980
CRANK
CRANK
C-C-CRANK
UGH...THIS PROBABLY... UGH...HAS ALL KINDS OF LUMBAR BENEFITS.
CRANK
CREAK
28 Years
56 Years
RHAPSODY IN BLUE
28 Years
CRANK
CRANK
C-C-C-R-A-N-K
1924

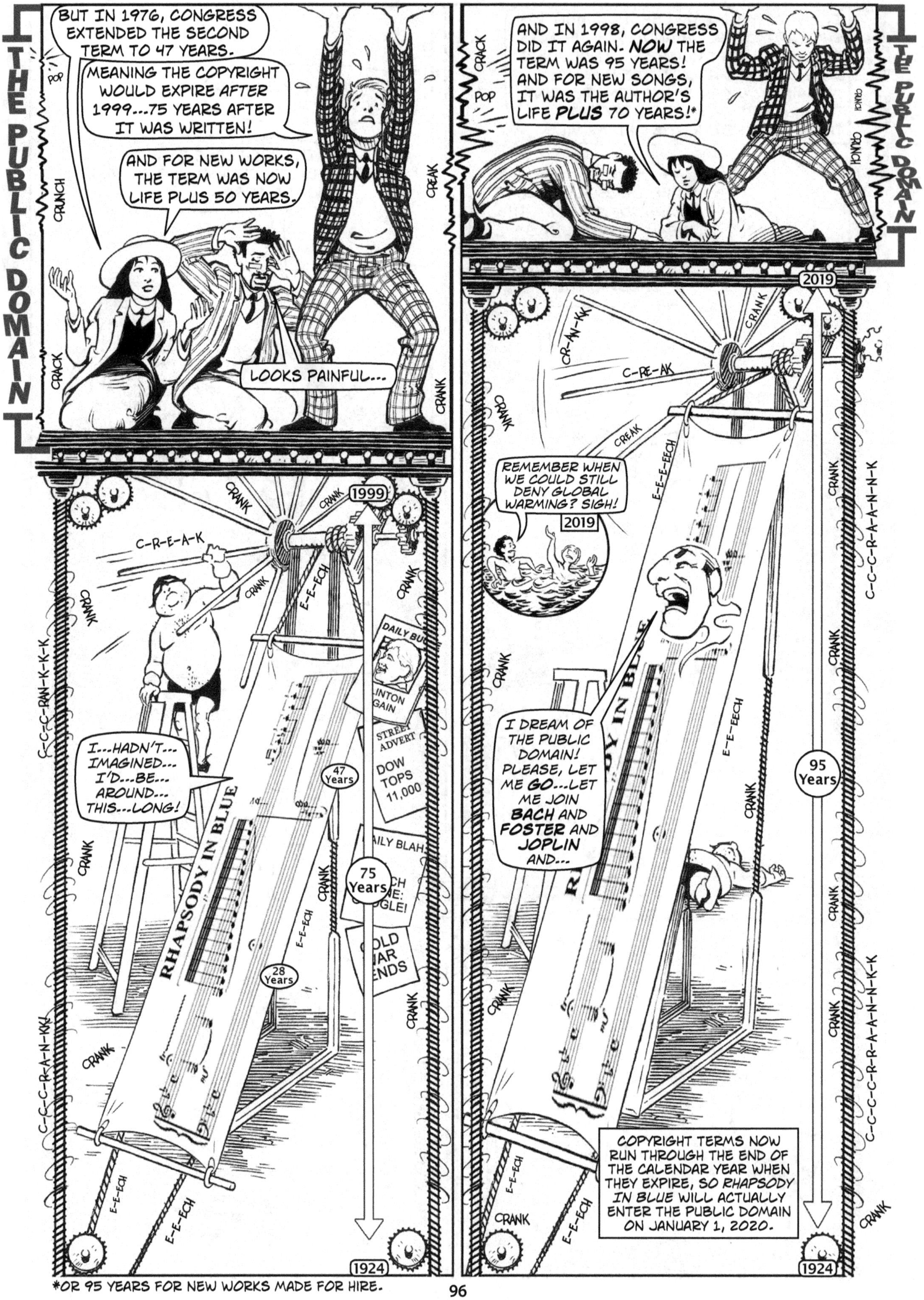

*OR 95 YEARS FOR NEW WORKS MADE FOR HIRE.

OK, THAT'S IT!

I'M CALLING IT.

WHAT?

THAT IMAGE OF GERSHWIN'S COPYRIGHT BEING STRETCHED ON A RACK — THAT'S A FLAGRANT FOUL RIGHT THERE. IT'S A LOADED IMAGE.

ARE YOU SAYING "WE'D ALL BE A GREAT DEAL BETTER FOR A LOT LESS SIMILE AND METAPHOR"?*

INFLAMMATORY ALLEGORY? DOPE TROPE?

NO, OF COURSE WE HAVE TO USE ANALOGIES. MAYBE THAT'S ALL LANGUAGE *IS* AT THE END OF THE DAY. ANYWAY, THIS IS A COMIC BOOK.

*APOLOGIES TO OGDEN NASH — EDS.

A LITTLE TOO PO-MO!!!

BUT THE IDEA THAT WE ARE TORTURING GERSHWIN'S COPYRIGHT BY STRETCHING IT...WHY? HE WAS A GREAT COMPOSER. PEOPLE STILL LOVE TO LISTEN TO HIS MUSIC. WHY SHOULDN'T HIS COPYRIGHTS GET EXTENDED AND EXTENDED? WHERE'S THE HARM? TO HIM OR US?

THAT'S A GREAT QUESTION. YOU COULD SAY THAT COPYRIGHT IS A DEAL, AND IF HE WAS WILLING TO WRITE THE SONG FOR 56 YEARS OF PROTECTION, IT'S UNFAIR FOR HIS ESTATE AND THE OTHER COPYRIGHT HOLDERS TO KEEP UPPING THE ANTE AFTERWARDS.

OR YOU COULD SAY THAT COPYRIGHT IS AN INCENTIVE...
R.I.P. A Composer
...AND EXTENDING THE TERMS OF PEOPLES' COPYRIGHTS AFTER THEY ARE DEAD ISN'T LIKELY TO MAKE THEM PRODUCE ANY MORE.
R.I.P. A Composer
WAHLWAHLWAHHHLL
SCREECH!
EMERGENCY
EMERGENCY
R.I.P. A Compose
GET OUT THE PADDLES!
R.I.P. A Composer
STILL NO RESPONSE.
OK. LET'S GIVE HIM ANOTHER 20 YEARS!
CLEAR!! CLEAR!!
RIP
R.I.P. A Composer
DON'T THEY KNOW THE DIFFERENCE BETWEEN COMPOSING AND DECOMPOSING?

PUT THAT WAY, IT DOES SEEM PRETTY SILLY.
YES BUT ITS EFFECTS WERE SERIOUS.
IMAGINE THE 20TH CENTURY HOLDINGS OF THE LIBRARY OF CONGRESS...
LIBRARY OF CONGRESS
NOW THESE ARE THE SONGS, POEMS, MOVIES AND BOOKS...
THAT WERE PUBLISHED BEFORE 1923...
PRE-1923 WORKS

THEY ARE FREE...
...YOU CAN STAGE THE PLAYS, REPRINT THE BOOKS, ADAPT THE MUSICALS, SING THE SONGS...
NOW THIS STUFF COMES FROM 1923 AND AFTER...
Post 1923
...IT'S STILL UNDER COPYRIGHT BUT WE CAN'T FIND THE COPYRIGHT HOLDER. THAT'S A HUGE PERCENTAGE OF SOME HOLDINGS – AS MUCH AS 50% OF FILM HOLDINGS, FOR EXAMPLE...
THEY CALL THEM "ORPHAN WORKS." EVEN IF YOU WANTED TO GET PERMISSION, OR TO PAY, FOR THE USE OF THE WORK, YOU CAN'T. EFFECTIVELY, THAT MEANS NO ONE CAN COPY THEM, PERFORM THEM, ADAPT THEM, PRESERVE THEM.
ORPHAN WORKS
ORPHAN WORKS

"THAT'S ABSURD!!"

"THAT'S COPYRIGHT."

"THESE ARE THE WORKS THAT ARE COPYRIGHTED AND STILL COMMERCIALLY AVAILABLE. GUESS HOW MANY OF THEM ARE MORE THAN 56 YEARS OLD...? REMEMBER, THAT USED TO BE THE COPYRIGHT TERM."

"NOW EVEN IF THE WORKS AREN'T ORPHANED, THE VAST MAJORITY OF THE OLDER ONES ARE COMMERCIALLY UNAVAILABLE. THEIR COPYRIGHT TERM GOT EXTENDED, BUT THEY GOT NO BENEFIT FROM IT."

404 OUT OF STOCK

"THAT'S BECAUSE MOST WORKS HAVE A SHORT COMMERCIAL LIFESPAN AND ONLY NEED A SHORT COPYRIGHT TERM. WHEN COPYRIGHT LASTED 28 YEARS, ONLY 15% BOTHERED TO RENEW FOR A SECOND TERM."

COPYRIGHTED & COMMERCIALLY AVAILABLE WORKS FROM THE 1950s AND BEFORE

COPYRIGHT TERM EXTENSION ACT BENEFICIARIES

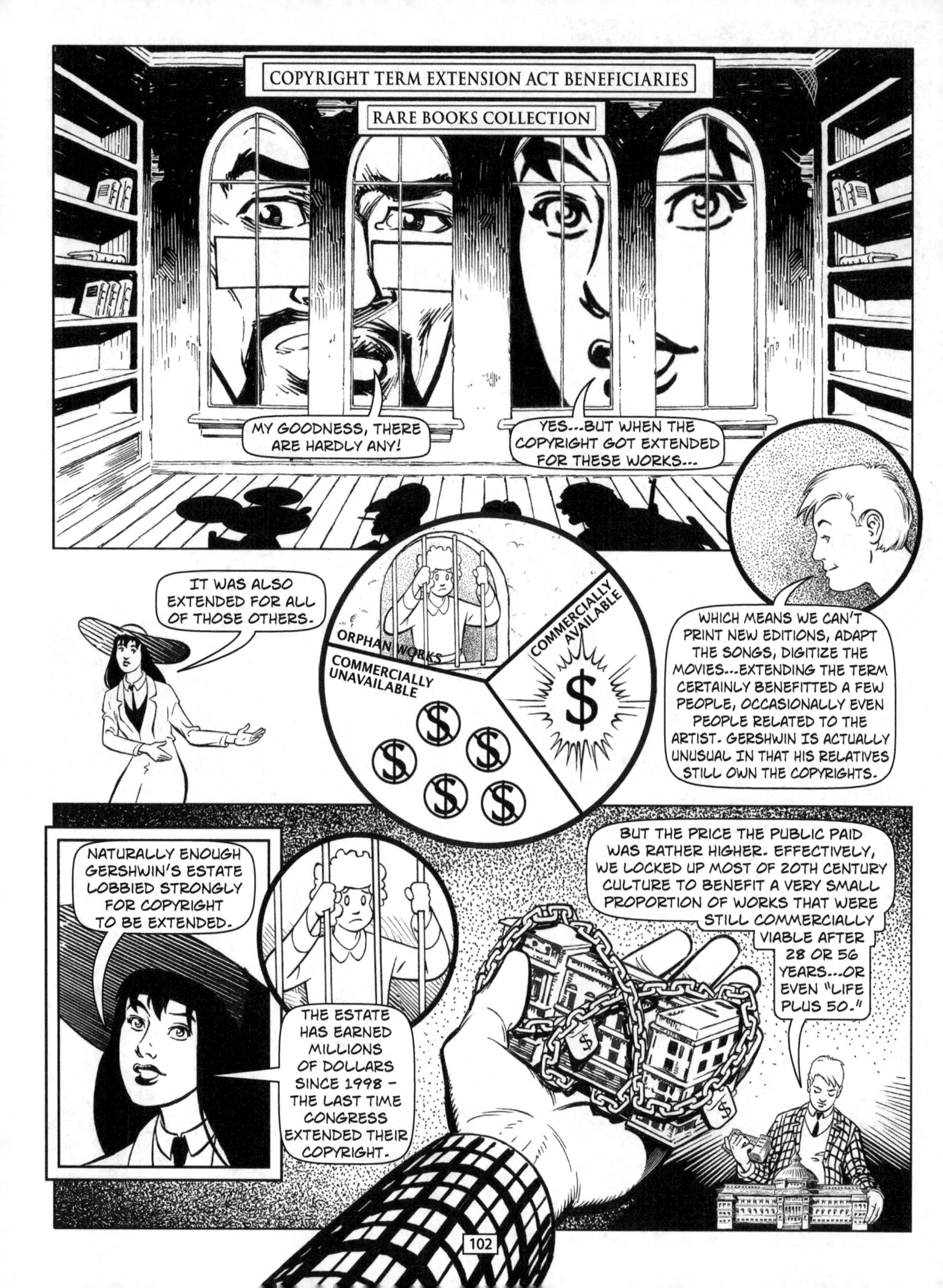

RARE BOOKS COLLECTION

MY GOODNESS, THERE ARE HARDLY ANY!

YES...BUT WHEN THE COPYRIGHT GOT EXTENDED FOR THESE WORKS...

IT WAS ALSO EXTENDED FOR ALL OF THOSE OTHERS.

ORPHAN WORKS / COMMERCIALLY UNAVAILABLE / COMMERCIALLY AVAILABLE

WHICH MEANS WE CAN'T PRINT NEW EDITIONS, ADAPT THE SONGS, DIGITIZE THE MOVIES...EXTENDING THE TERM CERTAINLY BENEFITTED A FEW PEOPLE, OCCASIONALLY EVEN PEOPLE RELATED TO THE ARTIST. GERSHWIN IS ACTUALLY UNUSUAL IN THAT HIS RELATIVES STILL OWN THE COPYRIGHTS.

NATURALLY ENOUGH GERSHWIN'S ESTATE LOBBIED STRONGLY FOR COPYRIGHT TO BE EXTENDED.

THE ESTATE HAS EARNED MILLIONS OF DOLLARS SINCE 1998 – THE LAST TIME CONGRESS EXTENDED THEIR COPYRIGHT.

BUT THE PRICE THE PUBLIC PAID WAS RATHER HIGHER. EFFECTIVELY, WE LOCKED UP MOST OF 20TH CENTURY CULTURE TO BENEFIT A VERY SMALL PROPORTION OF WORKS THAT WERE STILL COMMERCIALLY VIABLE AFTER 28 OR 56 YEARS...OR EVEN "LIFE PLUS 50."

IF YOU WANTED TO MOVE MONEY OUT OF THE POCKETS OF THE PUBLIC TO THE SUCCESSORS OF POPULAR CREATORS, IT'S THE MOST CULTURALLY INEFFICIENT WAY YOU COULD HAVE FOUND TO DO SO.

THE CONSTITUTION SAID THAT COPYRIGHTS SHOULD BE FOR "LIMITED TIMES." WHAT WE GOT WAS "REPEATEDLY EXTENDED TIMES." THE PAST GAVE US ITS WORKS TO USE, BUT WE DON'T SEEM TO BE DOING THE SAME FOR THE FUTURE...

...WOULD WE WANT TO PAY ROYALTIES TO USE SHAKESPEARE...?

...TO SING GREENSLEEVES...?

...OR THE STAR-SPANGLED BANNER...?

AND WE'D HAVE TO PAY THE BRITISH!

OK!! I GET IT, I GET IT. IT'S ABOUT ECONOMICS AND ACCESS TO OUR CULTURAL HERITAGE. YOU WANT LIMITED TERMS SO THE COMPOSERS AND DISTRIBUTORS GET PAID, BUT THEN EVERYONE GETS ACCESS TO THE WORK. AND YOU DON'T WANT ALL THOSE ORPHAN WORKS LOCKED UP FOR ANOTHER 20 YEARS WHEN WE EXTEND COPYRIGHT ON THE FEW OLD COMMERCIAL SUCCESSES.

NICE SUMMARY. BUT IT'S *NOT* JUST ABOUT PRICE OR ACCESS.

103

IT'S ABOUT CONTROL. FOR GOOD OR ILL. WHEN ALICE RANDALL — AN AFRICAN-AMERICAN WRITER — WANTED TO TELL THE STORY OF *GONE WITH THE WIND* FROM THE **SLAVES'** POINT OF VIEW, MARGARET MITCHELL'S HEIRS TRIED TO USE COPYRIGHT TO FORBID HER.*

IT'S ALL A MATTER OF PERSPECTIVE...

*SEE *BOUND BY LAW?* — EDS.

Suntrust v. Houghton Mifflin 11th Circuit

FAIR ENOUGH. BUT THERE WE ARE TALKING ABOUT CONTROL OVER BOOKS, OVER STORIES. HOW DOES CONTROL MATTER WHEN WE ARE TALKING ABOUT A SONG?

GREAT QUESTION... AND ONE THAT GERSHWIN'S STORY...ANSWERS NICELY.

GERSHWIN DIED IN 1937. HE WAS ONLY 38. BUT HIS FAMILY HAS CLOSELY GUARDED HIS WORKS.

The Telegraph

By Maureen Paton

... Marc Gershwin, the 58-year-old stockbroker son of the overlooked third Gershwin brother Arthur, and the 63-year-old Leopold Godowsky III, the classical composer and pianist son of the only Gershwin sister Frances (Frankie), jealously guard their artistic heritage and carefully vet all revivals of the Gershwin shows...

GEORGE GERSHWIN
1898 - 1937

WHAT DO THEY MEAN "VET"?
THE GERSHWIN HEIRS DECIDE WHO GETS TO PLAY GERSHWIN'S MUSIC AND EVEN HOW THEY DO IT.
?
TAKE THE MUSICAL PORGY AND BESS. THE GERSHWINS REFUSED ON PRINCIPLE TO ALLOW A VERSION IN SOUTH AFRICA DURING APARTHEID.
SUMMERTIME AND WE'RE CAGING MANDELA...
GOOD FOR THEM!
AGREED! AND THEY STOPPED A KARAOKE VERSION BY AN ENGLISH VICAR WHO WANTED TO CHANGE THE WORDS...
I'VE GOT PLENTY OF MUFFINS, AND MUFFINS GOT PLENTY OF ME!
THEY ONLY ALLOW PORGY TO BE STAGED WITH A BLACK CAST...
WELL, I GUESS THAT IS FAIR...CERTAINLY BETTER THAN A MINSTREL VERSION.
WHICH MEANT THAT WHEN A FINNISH COMPANY WANTED TO PERFORM PORGY THEY WERE OUT OF LUCK...
Porgy & Bess
Koekuvaukset
Gershwin
20 Afrikkalainen-
Suomen laulu toimijat
Avaa Koelaulut
Keskiviikko 10
Torstai 13
Laajennettu
FINLAND OPERA CO.
MARC GERSHWIN NEW YORK CITY NEW YORK U.S.A.
THEY WROTE, "BUT MR. GERSHWIN, THE PROBLEM IS WE HAVE NO BLACK ACTORS IN FINLAND."

A FINNISH GERSHWIN...?

FISH ARE FROZEN AND THE SNOW IS HIGH...

BESS, I BROUGHT YOU A HERRING!

THEY SAID NO TO FINNISH PORGY AND YES TO UNITED!? FINE. I'M GIVING UP MUSIC. I'LL GO AND WRITE AN OPERATING SYSTEM INSTEAD.

LUTEFISK ROW

BUZZARD, JATKAA YLI LENTOAAN PORGY ON NUORI TAAS...

BUT THEY DIDN'T ALWAYS SAY NO. THE GERSHWINS LICENSED RHAPSODY IN BLUE TO UNITED AIRLINES FOR $500,000.

THAT SAID, I DON'T THINK WORLD CULTURE LOST MUCH BY MISSING OUT ON 'PORGY GOES TO HELSINKI.'

IF PEOPLE LOVE THE MUSIC AND WANT TO SING IT, WHERE'S THE HARM?

YES, BUT THAT'S NOT OUR CALL TO MAKE. IT'S THE GERSHWINS'.

AND THAT'S EXACTLY THE POINT.

107

"I FEEL LIKE I WALKED INTO A *TRAP*. WHO SAID THOSE THINGS?"

"THEY ARE FROM THE AUGUST 1924 EDITION OF ETUDE MUSIC MAGAZINE...IT WAS ON..."THE JAZZ PROBLEM"!"

ETUDE MUSIC MAGAZINE

THE JAZZ PROBLEM
Opinions of Prominent Public Men and Musicians

AUGUST, 1924

SOME SAW JAZZ AS THREATENING AND DEBASED MUSIC...

TAKE GEORGE ADE, FOR EXAMPLE...

THE CRUDER FORM OF "JAZZ," A COLLECTION OF SQUEALS AND SQUAWKS AND WAILS AGAINST A CONCEALED BACK-STRUCTURE OF MELODY, BECAME UNBEARABLE TO ME SOON AFTER I BEGAN TO HEAR IT.

GEORGE ADE

IN ASSOCIATION WITH SOME OF THE MODERN DANCING AND THE SENTIMENT OF THE VERSES ON WHICH MANY OF THE "JAZZ" SONGS ARE FOUNDED, IT WOULD BE DIFFICULT TO FIND A COMBINATION MORE VULGAR OR DEBASING.

MRS. H.H.A. BEACH

TAKE MRS. H.-H.-A. BEACH AS ANOTHER...

SOUSA DEFENDED IT, THOUGH...

THERE IS NO REASON, WITH ITS EXHILARATING RHYTHM, ITS MELODIC INGENUITIES, WHY IT SHOULD NOT BECOME ONE OF THE ACCEPTED FORMS OF COMPOSITION.

LT. COM. JOHN PHILIP SOUSA

108

MUSIC MAGAZINE
...A FEW WERE FRANKLY RACIST ABOUT ANY STYLISTIC MINGLING.
JAZZ IS TO REAL MUSIC WHAT THE CARICATURE IS TO THE PORTRAIT... IF JAZZ ORIGINATED IN THE DANCE RHYTHMS OF THE NEGRO, IT WAS AT LEAST INTERESTING AS THE SELF-EXPRESSION OF A PRIMITIVE RACE. WHEN JAZZ WAS ADOPTED BY THE "HIGHLY CIVILIZED" WHITE RACE, IT TENDED TO DEGENERATE IT TOWARDS PRIMITIVITY.
FRANK DAMROSCH
THE JAZZ PROBLEM
Opinions of Prominent Public Men and Musicians
PEOPLE SAID STUFF LIKE THAT??!! THEY EVEN FEARED MUSICAL MISCEGENATION?
YES, INDEED. BUT OTHERS HAILED IT AS EMBLEMATIC AMERICAN MUSIC, A GREAT CONTRIBUTION TO THE NATIONAL REMIX.
JAZZ PROMPTED RACIAL ANXIETIES, BUT IT ALSO REACHED ACROSS THE COLOR BAR, BREAKING CULTURAL BARRIERS. IT'S HARDER TO STEREOTYPE PEOPLE WHO ARE YOUR ARTISTIC HEROES.
WHEN RAP MUSICIANS TODAY WANT TO JUSTIFY SAMPLING OTHER TUNES, THEY SOMETIMES COMPARE IT TO BORROWING IN JAZZ...
BUT JAZZ WAS JUST AS CONTROVERSIAL IN ITS HEYDAY!
MAKES YOU WONDER HOW PEOPLE WILL BE TALKING ABOUT RAP IN 100 YEARS...
YOUR HONOR, WHAT I AM DOING IS REALLY NO DIFFERENT THAN WHAT THE ESTEEMED SNOOP DOGG OR LIL WAYNE DID IN THE EARLY DAYS OF THE 21ST CENTURY...
YOU DARE COMPARE YOURSELF TO A CLASSICAL RAPPER!!!!!???

WAIT, ALL THIS STARTED BECAUSE WE WERE TALKING ABOUT A RAP GERSHWIN. SO YOUR POINT IS THAT THESE LONG COPYRIGHTS GIVE THE OWNERS A VETO OVER NEW WORKS BUILT ON THEIR MUSIC.

BUT YOU ARE A COMPOSER. DON'T YOU WANT ARTISTS TO HAVE GREATER CONTROL OVER THEIR WORK?

YES!

NO!

?

?

ART DEPENDS ON CONTROL! WE NEED MORE RIGHTS!

MUSIC MUST BE ALLOWED TO BUILD ON ITSELF! WE NEED MORE FREEDOM!

UM...CAN YOU EXPLAIN...?

IT'S OBVIOUS!

IT'S OBVIOUS!

NOT TO ME...

WE NEED MORE...

CONTROL!

FREEDOM!

I NEED GREATER CONTROL OVER MY WORK, TO MAKE A LIVING, TO PROTECT THE INTEGRITY OF MY ART...!
I NEED MORE FREEDOM TO BUILD ON THE PAST! MORE CONTROL IS THE LAST THING I NEED. LOOK AT ALL THE JAZZ THAT'S BUILT ON GERSHWIN'S *I GOT RHYTHM*. YOU THINK THOSE CHORD CHANGES SHOULD BE LICENSED?

YOU JUST DON'T WANT TO MAKE THE EFFORT TO CREATE ORIGINAL MUSIC!
YOU JUST WANT TO DENY EVERYONE ELSE THE FREEDOMS YOU HAD YOURSELF!

PIRATE!
INGRATE!
PLAGIARIST!
CONTROL FREAK!
YOU'RE NO REAL MUSICIAN!

NOW YOU'VE GONE TOO FAR!!!!
STARVING...COMPOSER ...GARRET!
SOULLESS... RECORD COMPANY ...ACCOUNTANTS!
ARTISTIC... INTEGRITY!
FREE... CULTURE!
PURITY!
PARODY!
SWOOSH!

YOU'LL...DESTROY...MUSIC...
AS...WE...KNOW...IT!!!
WELL, I HAVE CONFLICTING FEELINGS ABOUT IT.
WHY DO THE INTERESTING GUYS ALL HAVE IDENTITY ISSUES...?
SIGH!

I ALWAYS THOUGHT THE 'A TRAIN' WAS A PARALLEL DIMENSION.	DID THE JAZZ COMPOSERS SHARE YOUR "CONFLICTING FEELINGS"?	ACTUALLY, THEY DID. ON THE ONE HAND, AS AN ART FORM, JAZZ IS THE ULTIMATE REMIX. YOU'VE GOT ELEMENTS OF CLASSICAL MUSIC...
...CHORD CHANGES, CHROMATIC SCALES...	...RAGTIME, SWING, CARIBBEAN RHYTHMS, THE AFRICAN-INFLECTED SYNCOPATION...	SWIRL! SWIRL!
BUT ON ANOTHER LEVEL, BORROWING IS A CENTRAL PART OF INDIVIDUAL JAZZ PIECES. IT WASN'T JUST MIXING MUSICAL STYLES, IT WAS TAKING FRAGMENTS FROM OTHER SONGS AND BUILDING ON THEM OR IMPROVISING OVER THEM.	IS THAT PART OF THE DEFINITION OF JAZZ?	DEFINITION? THERE IS NO DEFINITION. DEFINING JAZZ IS LIKE DEFINING ART OR LOVE. AND WITHIN JAZZ, PEOPLE BORROWED AND IMPROVISED IN COMPLETELY DIFFERENT WAYS. PAUL WHITEMAN'S TIGHTLY SCRIPTED SETS DON'T SOUND ANYTHING LIKE WHAT DIZZY GILLESPIE OR COUNT BASIE WOULD DO WITH A SIMILAR CHORD SEQUENCE. BY WHICH YOU MEAN TO SAY, "YES"? I GUESS SO. BUT THAT DOESN'T MEAN THAT THE PEOPLE WHO WERE BORROWING ALWAYS APPRECIATED IT WHEN THEY WERE BORROWED FROM THEMSELVES.

THAT'S GERSHWIN'S *I GOT RHYTHM*. THE CHORD SEQUENCE BECAME SUCH A STANDARD PROGRESSION IN JAZZ THAT IT'S CALLED "THE RHYTHM CHANGES."

WHO WROTE SONGS BASED ON THOSE CHORDS?

WHO DIDN'T? THERE'S DIZZY GILLESPIE, CHARLIE PARKER AND DUKE ELLINGTON...THE CHORDS WERE THE BASE. AND NO ONE THOUGHT THAT GERSHWIN WAS ENTITLED TO ROYALTIES...

...OR CONTROL.

SEE WHAT THEY ARE BUILDING...? A NEW TUNE WOULD BE PUT ON TOP — CONTRAFACT, WE CALL IT — AND THEN THE MUSICIANS WOULD LAYER IMPROVISATION ON THAT...QUOTING FRAGMENTS FROM OTHER SONGS IN SOLOS, REFERRING BACK TO OTHER MUSICIANS...

HENRY LOUIS GATES CALLS IT "SIGNIFYIN'" — SHOWING YOU KNOW YOUR PLACE IN THE TRADITION, BUT SHOWING YOUR VIRTUOSITY, TOO.

BUT I THOUGHT YOU SAID THEY DIDN'T ALWAYS LIKE IT WHEN OTHERS BORROWED FROM THEM?

SOMETIMES THEY DIDN'T! WHEN DIZZY GILLESPIE'S DIZZY CRAWL WAS RECORDED BY COUNT BASIE AS ROCK-A-BYE BASIE, DIZZY WAS QUITE UPSET.	"I DIDN'T COPYRIGHT IT; IT WAS A HEAD ARRANGEMENT... ANYTIME YOU WRITE SOMETHING, COPYRIGHT IT OR LOOK OUT... A LOTTA TUNES GOT STOLEN BY THE BANDLEADERS TOO THAT WAY. I PROBABLY DID IT MYSELF A COUPLE OF TIMES, BUT NOT COMPLETELY....."

NOWADAYS IF DIZZY RECORDED IT, OR WROTE IT DOWN, IT WOULD BE COPYRIGHTED AUTOMATICALLY.

THAT'S GREAT!

AND WOULD YOU SAY THE SAME IF ALL THOSE MUSICIANS STARTED CLAIMING COPYRIGHT INFRINGEMENT FOR EACH SOLO...?

"...BUT AT THE SAME TIME, 'YOU CAN'T STEAL A GIFT.'"

?

!

LET'S CHANGE THE SUBJECT! WHAT WAS THE AUDIENCE LIKE FOR THESE SONGS?

THAT WAS THE OTHER ENORMOUS CHANGE. PATRONAGE GAVE US MUSIC DESIGNED FOR THE CATHEDRAL AND THE COURT...

AND THEN WE SAW THE RISE OF THE MASS MARKET. SHEET MUSIC FILLED THE DRAWING ROOMS WITH MELODY BUT THE "PLAYER" WAS THE CUSTOMER. THAT GAVE US MUSIC DESIGNED FOR A LAY AUDIENCE, BUT ALSO FOR AMATEUR PERFORMERS.

BUT, STARTING AROUND 1900, THE PLAYER PIANO AND THE GRAMOPHONE BROUGHT THE SOUND OF PROFESSIONAL MUSICIANS INTO MIDDLE CLASS LIVING ROOMS. SO WHY ARE WE STILL LOOKING AT A CATHEDRAL?

BECAUSE IT ISN'T A CATHEDRAL...

IT'S A *RADIO!!*

AND NOW...SUPPORTED BY ALKA-SELTZER, AND BUBBLING OVER WITH MIRTH AND MELODY, IT'S...THE NATIONAL BARN DANCE!!

---FEATURING THE YODELING DEZURIK SISTERS!!

YODELING? DEZURIK? SISTERS?

YODEL.... LAY-EE-OOH!!

ALSO KNOWN AS THE CACKLE SISTERS. TRICK YODELERS. THEY DID ANIMAL NOISES, TOO.

THAT WAS WHAT WAS PLAYING IN THE 1930s?

SURE, BUT SO WAS LOTS OF OTHER MATERIAL - FROM OPERA TO JAZZ. THE POINT WAS, THE BALANCE HAD SHIFTED AGAIN.

THE MUSIC MADE TO PLEASE THE KING IS DIFFERENT FROM THE MUSIC MADE TO SELL THE KING OF BEERS...

OR TO ATTRACT THE PEOPLE WHO DRINK THE BEER...I SEE. SO RADIO STATIONS WEREN'T SELLING MUSIC. THEY WERE SELLING THE AUDIENCE'S EARS TO ADVERTISERS.

YOU'LL NEVER BELIEVE THE DEAL I HAVE FOR YOU ON THESE BABIES...!

NICE...VERY NICE...

THAT'S A GRISLY IMAGE!

118

WHICH MEANT THAT, SUDDENLY, PEOPLE MIGHT BE EXPOSED TO DIFFERENT KINDS OF MUSIC — WITHOUT REGARD TO GEOGRAPHY — AS ADVERTISERS TRIED TO REACH THEIR TARGET AUDIENCE.

YOU COULD LISTEN TO THE NEW YORK PHILHARMONIC IN A BARBERSHOP...

OR JAZZ IN A PENTHOUSE OVERLOOKING CENTRAL PARK...

WHEN THEY GET TO THE "RONDO" IN THE PATHETIQUE I SOB LIKE A BABY, YOU KNOW...MY HAND JUST SHAKES...

SHAVE FASTER, THEN! ALLEGRO! MOLTO ALLEGRO!

AND NOW, FROM PAUL WHITEMAN AND HIS BOYS, IT'S "MISSISSIPPI MUD"!

WHICH CHANGED THE BALANCE OF POWER BETWEEN SONGWRITERS AND PERFORMERS. NOW A SINGLE ARTIST COULD REACH MILLIONS, COULD BUILD UP A FAN BASE.

EVEN FOR YODELING...AND THE ECONOMICS OF THE INDUSTRY WERE CHANGING, TOO. REMEMBER THE DEBATES BETWEEN PUBLISHERS AND THE RECORDING INDUSTRY?

I THOUGHT WE AGREED TO LICENSE THE WHOLE THING OFF!?

RIGHT, BUT THIS WAS A NEW MARKET. BROADCASTERS HAD TO PAY THEIR LIVE PERFORMERS. DID THEY HAVE TO PAY COMPOSERS? WAS THIS A "PUBLIC PERFORMANCE"?

WELL, DUH!

NOT REALLY. THE COMPOSERS' GROUP — ASCAP — COLLECTED MONEY FOR "FOR PROFIT" PUBLIC PERFORMANCES. BROADCASTERS POINTED OUT THAT THEY WERE GIVING THE MUSIC AWAY FOR FREE AND MIGHT EVEN BE GETTING THE COMPOSERS NEW CUSTOMERS!

THOSE ARE THE SAME ARGUMENTS THAT FILE SHARERS MADE!

EXACTLY!

BUT THE BROADCASTERS LOST. IN 1923 A COURT RULED THAT RADIO PERFORMANCES WERE "FOR PROFIT" SO THEY HAD TO PAY FEES.

"THE DEFENDANT IS NOT AN 'ELEEMOSYNARY INSTITUTION'...COPYRIGHT OWNERS AND THE MUSIC PUBLISHERS THEMSELVES ARE PERHAPS THE BEST JUDGES OF THE METHOD OF POPULARIZING MUSICAL SELECTIONS..."

THE NEGOTIATIONS WERE SO STORMY, THE BROADCASTERS FORMED THEIR OWN GROUP — BMI — AS AN ALTERNATIVE FOR COMPOSERS TO JOIN. THOSE ARE THE MAIN OPTIONS TO THIS DAY. I'M STILL TRYING TO WORK OUT WHICH ONE TO JOIN.

ASCAP WAS PRETTY EXCLUSIONARY.

ASCAP MEMBERS

DOESN'T LOOK LIKE A VERY DIVERSE GROUP!

STYLISTICALLY, TOO. NEW KINDS OF MUSIC DIDN'T GET EASY ACCEPTANCE. LOUIS ARMSTRONG DIDN'T GET MEMBERSHIP UNTIL 1939, YEARS AFTER HE HAD BECOME FAMOUS.

"I SEE SHEAVES OF GREEN, LARGE CHECKBOOKS TOO, BUT THEY'RE NOT FOR ME, THEY'RE JUST FOR YOU...AND I SAY TO MYSELF, WHAT AN UNDERHAND WORLD!"

DIDN'T JELLY ROLL MORTON MAKE IT A CRUSADE TO GET MEMBERSHIP?

"I'M GOING TO THE RIVER, BY AND BY...BECAUSE THE RIVER'S WET BUT ASCAP'S RUN DRY..."

YES, HE GOT IN THE SAME YEAR, BUT STILL DIDN'T GET MUCH. BUT ASCAP WASN'T DOING ITSELF ANY FAVORS BY KEEPING THE DOORS LOCKED. MUSICIANS WHO WROTE JAZZ, COUNTRY, GOSPEL, FOLK AND BLUES FLOCKED TO BMI...

GIVING BMI A BIG ADVANTAGE WHEN RHYTHM AND BLUES AND ROCK AND ROLL ARRIVED!

SO, TALKING OF BLUES...

I HAVE A QUESTION...

YE-E-S-S-S??

YOU SEE, I WROTE MY THESIS ON THE MUSIC OF ROBERT JOHNSON...
MAYBE THE MOST FAMOUS BLUES MUSICIAN OF THEM ALL AND A HUGE INFLUENCE ON ROCK AND ROLL...AND...UM...WELL...
YE-E-S-S-S??
COULD WE, LIKE, YOU KNOW, WELL, SORT OF...UMM...KIND OF, WELL... ...SEE HIM?
W-E-L-L...
LOOK WHO'S BACK!!
HONK
SKREECH!
!
NYC
I HAVE A REMOTE...
CLIMB IN!
POP!
POP!
NYC
ZOOM!
SOME PEOPLE THINK THEY'RE ABOVE THE RULES!
SKREECH!

SO WASN'T ROBERT JOHNSON THE ONE WHO WENT TO THE CROSSROADS AND SOLD HIS SOUL TO THE DEVIL FOR THE ABILITY TO PLAY THE GUITAR...?

THAT STORY AGAIN!!

W-H-A-T?!?

OH, THERE IS A LEGEND THAT ROBERT JOHNSON DISAPPEARED FOR A WHILE AND WHEN HE CAME BACK, THE OTHER MUSICIANS WERE AMAZED BY HIS SKILL ON THE GUITAR...

...THE TRUTH IS THAT JOHNSON WAS VERY SOPHISTICATED IN HIS MUSICAL INFLUENCES...RADIO BROUGHT A WEALTH OF STYLES...HE TRAVELLED MORE WIDELY THAN PEOPLE THINK*...WAS WORKING IN THE RICH TRADITION OF THE BLUES...THE TROPE OF THE SELF-TAUGHT DIABOLICALLY GIFTED INDIVIDUAL FITS THE NARRATIVE NEED TO HAVE A SINGLE ROMANTIC AUTHOR FOR THE BLUES...

WHOA!

*SEE ELIJAH WALD, ESCAPING THE DELTA: ROBERT JOHNSON AND THE INVENTION OF THE BLUES —EDS.

FAUX PRIMITIVISM...

...LIMINAL TRANSGRESSION...

CULTURAL DIREMPTION...

TIME OUT!!

SNAP!

WHAT?

YOU LOST US AROUND "RICH TRADITION OF THE BLUES"...

THOUGH I DO LOVE A SPOT OF 'CULTURAL DIREMPTION,' MYSELF...

I'M SORRY. I GUESS I WAS BACK IN GRAD SCHOOL. YOU'VE GOT TO UNDERSTAND THAT THE MYTHOLOGY...THAT'S REALLY THE ONLY WORD...OF ROBERT JOHNSON IS REALLY IMPORTANT TO PEOPLE. LOOK...

ERIC CLAPTON

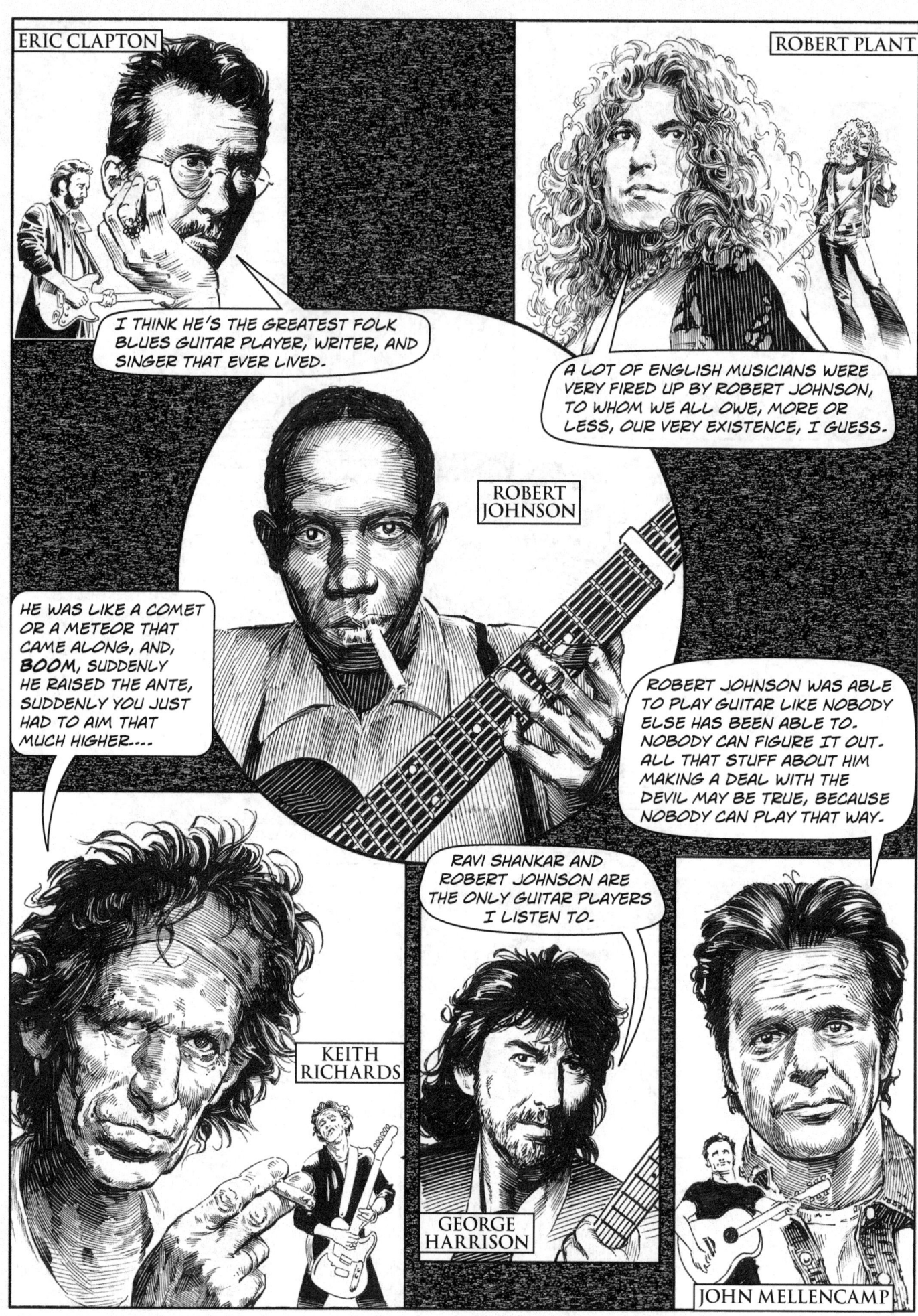

ROBERT PLANT

I THINK HE'S THE GREATEST FOLK BLUES GUITAR PLAYER, WRITER, AND SINGER THAT EVER LIVED.

A LOT OF ENGLISH MUSICIANS WERE VERY FIRED UP BY ROBERT JOHNSON, TO WHOM WE ALL OWE, MORE OR LESS, OUR VERY EXISTENCE, I GUESS.

ROBERT JOHNSON

HE WAS LIKE A COMET OR A METEOR THAT CAME ALONG, AND, **BOOM**, SUDDENLY HE RAISED THE ANTE, SUDDENLY YOU JUST HAD TO AIM THAT MUCH HIGHER....

ROBERT JOHNSON WAS ABLE TO PLAY GUITAR LIKE NOBODY ELSE HAS BEEN ABLE TO. NOBODY CAN FIGURE IT OUT. ALL THAT STUFF ABOUT HIM MAKING A DEAL WITH THE DEVIL MAY BE TRUE, BECAUSE NOBODY CAN PLAY THAT WAY.

RAVI SHANKAR AND ROBERT JOHNSON ARE THE ONLY GUITAR PLAYERS I LISTEN TO.

KEITH RICHARDS

GEORGE HARRISON

JOHN MELLENCAMP

124

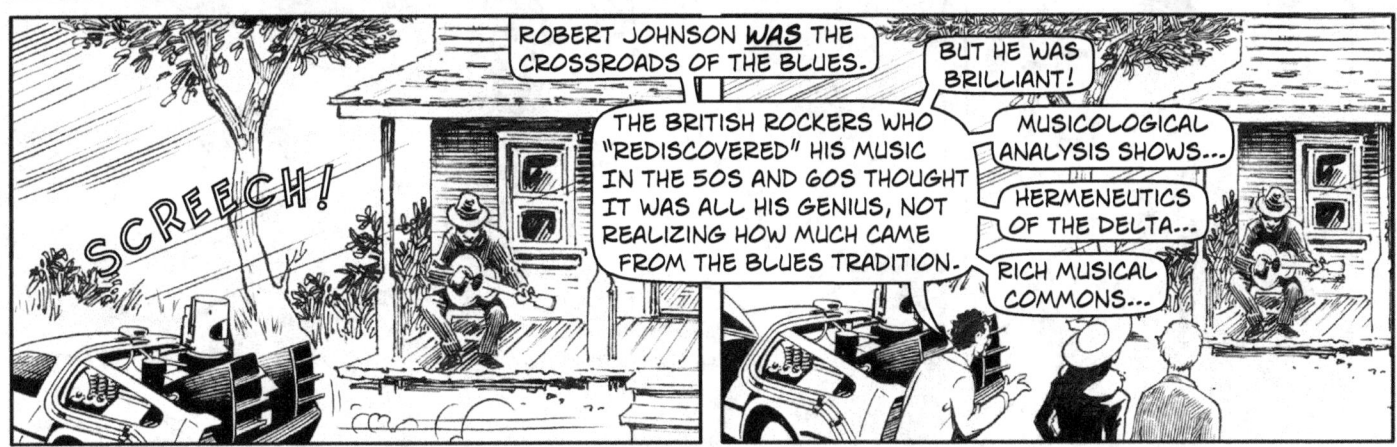

WHOOSH!!

"WHERE ARE WE?"
"AT A CROSSROADS..."

SCREECH!

"ROBERT JOHNSON *WAS* THE CROSSROADS OF THE BLUES."
"THE BRITISH ROCKERS WHO "REDISCOVERED" HIS MUSIC IN THE 50S AND 60S THOUGHT IT WAS ALL HIS GENIUS, NOT REALIZING HOW MUCH CAME FROM THE BLUES TRADITION."

"BUT HE WAS BRILLIANT!"
"MUSICOLOGICAL ANALYSIS SHOWS..."
"HERMENEUTICS OF THE DELTA..."
"RICH MUSICAL COMMONS..."

"YOU FOLKS AREN'T FROM AROUND HERE ARE YOU?"

"NO WE AREN'T MR. JOHNSON."
"DO WE KNOW EACH OTHER?"
"NOT EXACTLY, BUT WE ALL KNOW YOUR MUSIC. IN FACT, HE'S A STUDENT OF IT."
"UH... WELL... ER... I ...THAT IS..."
"REALLY? WHAT DO YOU THINK?"

THAT'S OK...NOT EVERYONE IS MADE FOR TALKING.
WANT TO JAM A LITTLE THEN?
JAM!?!
...WITH ROBERT JOHNSON. DEFINING MOMENT OF MY LIFE! BUT MUST NOT VIOLATE THE PRIME MUSICAL DIRECTIVE!
!
SK-R-R-A-N-G!

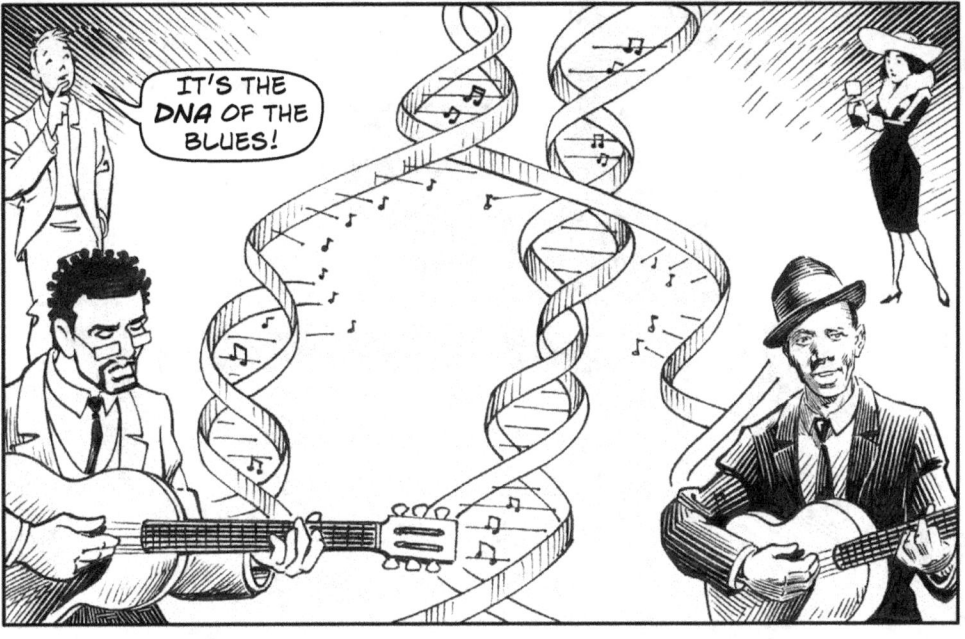

Panel 1: ?

Panel 2: I KNOW THAT ONE... I WENT TO THE CROSSROADS, FELL DOWN ON MY KNEES. I WENT TO CROSSROADS, FELL DOWN ON MY KNEES ASKED THE LORD ABOVE "HAVE MERCY NOW, SAVE POOR BOB, IF YOU PLEASE!"

Panel 3: E⁷...ROBERT JOHNSON!! ...A⁷...NOW BEND IT...D⁷... ROBERT JOHNSON!!!

Panel 4: IT'S THE *DNA* OF THE BLUES!

Panel 5: SAY...CHEESE!!!

Panel 6: CLICK! FLASH!

Panel 1:
"I THOUGHT YOU'D AT LEAST ASK HIM A QUESTION!"

"I HAD TOO MANY! THE MYSTERIES OF HIS LIFE. HIS MUSIC. HIS GUITAR TECHNIQUE. FINALLY, I WAS GOING TO ASK HIM HOW TO PLAY THE BLUES. BUT I THINK I KNOW WHAT HE WOULD HAVE SAID..."

Panel 2:
"WHAT JIMI HENDRIX SAID: 'BLUES IS EASY TO PLAY, BUT HARD TO FEEL.'"

Panel 4:
"YOU MAY BURY MY BODY, OOH
DOWN BY THE HIGHWAY SIDE,
SO MY OLD EVIL SPIRIT,
CAN CATCH A GREYHOUND BUS AND RIDE..."

ZOOM!

I SEE THE METAPHOR BUDGET HASN'T BEEN CUT...

THE NATURAL HISTORY MUSEUM OF THE BLUES

PRICE OF ADMISSION: YOUR **MIND**

ROBERT JOHNSON

NO!

YES!

SO THE POINT OF THIS IS THAT EVERYONE RIPPED OFF ROBERT JOHNSON? THAT THEY TOOK HIS STUFF AND IT BECAME PART OF ROCK 'N' ROLL?

THAT'S WHY ROBERT PLANT SAID THAT ROCKERS ACTUALLY OWED HIM FOR THEIR VERY EXISTENCE?

WELL, NO. BUT...!

YES, BUT...

LOOK...JOHNSON BECAME A SYMBOL OF THE BLUES — AND HE WAS A GENIUS. BUT HE WAS TAKING A TRADITION THAT WAS ALREADY AT LEAST 30 OR 40 YEARS OLD...

...A COLLECTIVE TRADITION, ROOTED IN THE AFRICAN-AMERICAN COMMUNITY OF THE MISSISSIPPI DELTA...

I'LL PLAY YOU SOME CHORDS!

C
F
G

AND IN THE MELODY, I AM SUBSTITUTING THESE FLATTENED NOTES — CALLED BLUE NOTES...HEAR THAT SOUND?

NOW ALL THIS...THE STRUCTURE, THE CHORD SEQUENCE, THE LYRICAL PATTERN, WITH ITS REPETITION AND CALL AND RESPONSE...

ALL THAT IS TRADITIONAL... PART OF A MUSICAL COMMONS THAT EVERYONE CAN TAKE FROM...

130

SON HOUSE
BLIND LEMON JEFFERSON
MISSISSIPPI JOHN HURT
HOWLIN' WOLF
BIG MAMA THORNTON
CHARLEY PATTON
MEMPHIS MINNIE
SKIP JAMES
REVEREND GARY DAVIS
MUDDY WATERS
LIGHTNIN' HOPKINS
SLEEPY JOHN ESTES
LITTLE WALTER

IT IS AS IF WE DIPPED A GLASS INTO THE RICH WATERS OF THE DELTA* AND FOUND IT TEEMING WITH MUSICAL LIFE...

*THESE WERE NOT ALL DELTA BLUES MUSICIANS — SOME WERE FROM TEXAS, SOUTH CAROLINA, TENNESSEE — BUT YOU GET OUR POINT. —EDS.

BUT THEN WE WANT TO SAY "WHO OWNS THIS"? OR "WHOSE SONG IS THIS"?...

...AND TO DO THAT WE HAVE TO *FREEZE* WHAT'S THERE... SEPARATE IT FROM WHAT'S GONE BEFORE...

FREEZE

TOSS

AND DOING THAT JUST CHANGES THE NATURE OF THE MUSIC.

ONE LUMP OF THE BLUES, SIR, OR TWO?

I'LL TAKE ALL YOU HAVE...

131

LEROY CARR "WHEN THE SUN GOES DOWN"

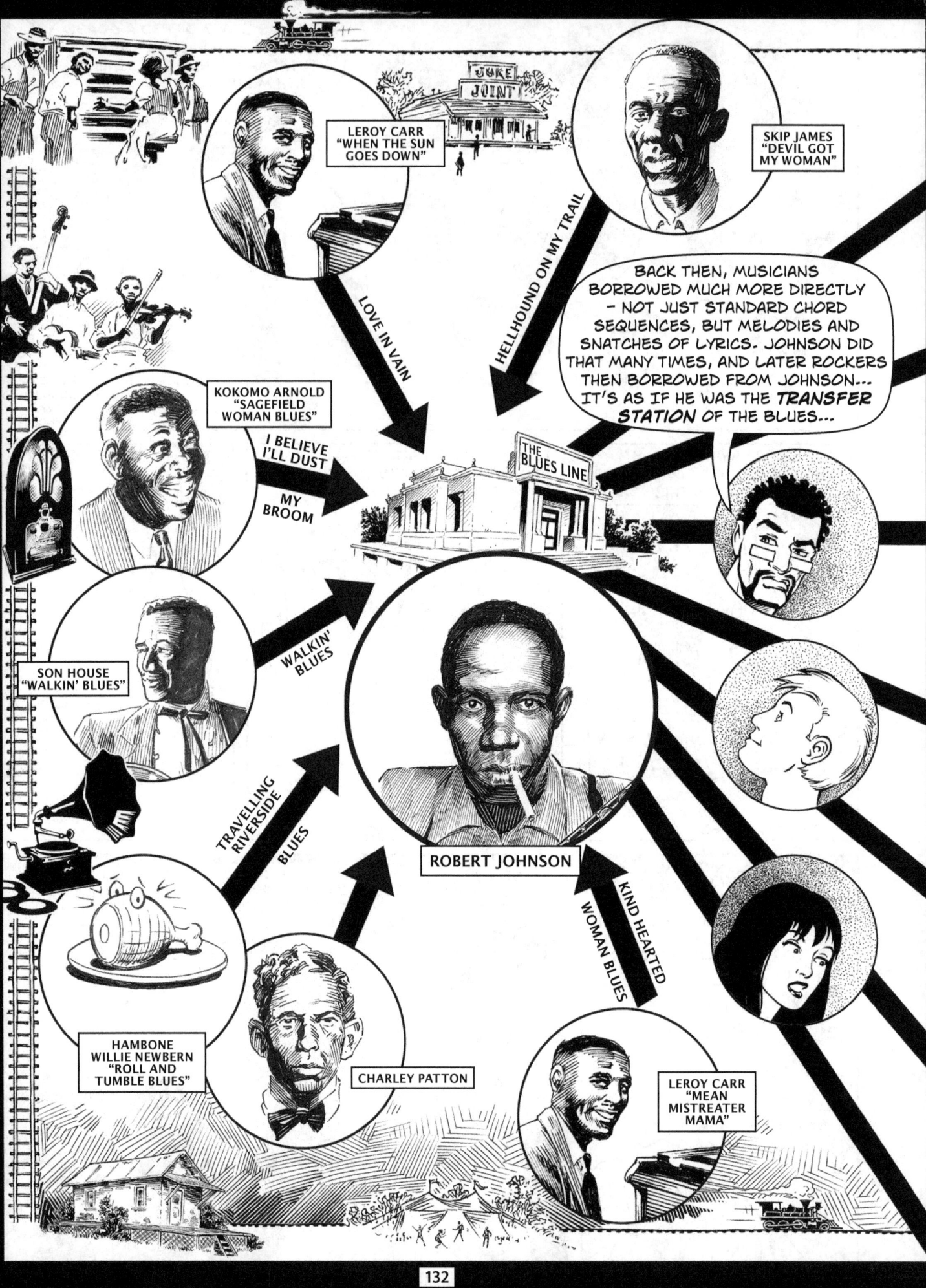

SKIP JAMES "DEVIL GOT MY WOMAN"

BACK THEN, MUSICIANS BORROWED MUCH MORE DIRECTLY – NOT JUST STANDARD CHORD SEQUENCES, BUT MELODIES AND SNATCHES OF LYRICS. JOHNSON DID THAT MANY TIMES, AND LATER ROCKERS THEN BORROWED FROM JOHNSON... IT'S AS IF HE WAS THE *TRANSFER STATION* OF THE BLUES...

LOVE IN VAIN

HELLHOUND ON MY TRAIL

KOKOMO ARNOLD "SAGEFIELD WOMAN BLUES"

I BELIEVE I'LL DUST MY BROOM

THE BLUES LINE

SON HOUSE "WALKIN' BLUES"

WALKIN' BLUES

TRAVELLING RIVERSIDE BLUES

ROBERT JOHNSON

KIND HEARTED WOMAN BLUES

HAMBONE WILLIE NEWBERN "ROLL AND TUMBLE BLUES"

CHARLEY PATTON

LEROY CARR "MEAN MISTREATER MAMA"

132

"HELLHOUND ON MY TRAIL" LINE → MOUNTAIN GOATS, RORY BLOCK, MANY OTHERS

"I BELIEVE I'LL DUST MY BROOM" LINE → YARDBIRDS, ZZ TOP, BEN HARPER, MANY OTHERS

"LOVE IN VAIN" LINE → ROLLING STONES, MANY OTHERS

He actually WAS the crossroads...

"WALKIN' BLUES" LINE → GRATEFUL DEAD, JOHNNY WINTER, HINDU LOVE GODS

"TRAVELLING RIVERSIDE BLUES" LINE → LED ZEPPELIN, MANY OTHERS

"CROSSROADS BLUES" LINE → CREAM, LYNYRD SKYNYRD, JOHN MAYER, MANY OTHERS

"KIND HEARTED WOMAN BLUES" LINE → BOB DYLAN, FLEETWOOD MAC, GEORGE THOROGOOD, MANY OTHERS

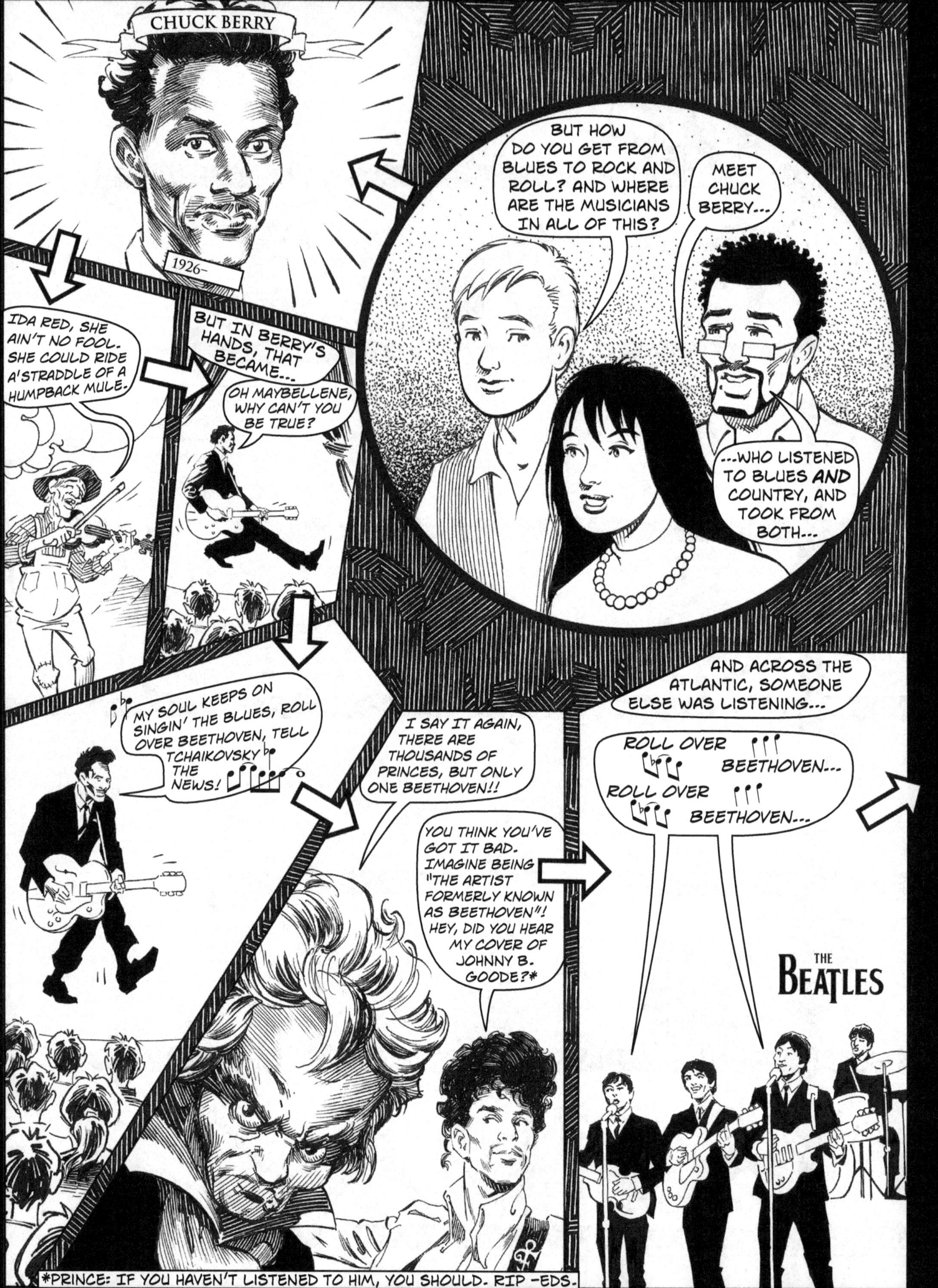

*PRINCE: IF YOU HAVEN'T LISTENED TO HIM, YOU SHOULD. RIP –EDS.

AND MEANWHILE, FEARS WERE GROWING OVER A DIFFERENT KIND OF REMIX...

CHUCK BERRY IS THE STEPHEN FOSTER OF ROCK AND ROLL. HE'S MIXING COUNTRY, RHYTHM AND BLUES...INVENTING A NEW GUITAR STYLE...AND CHANGING THE WORLD. SOME MUSICIANS WERE FRANK ABOUT THEIR DEBTS TO HIM.

...HE WAS A BROWN-EYED HANDSOME MAN...

IT'S VERY DIFFICULT FOR ME TO TALK ABOUT CHUCK BERRY 'CAUSE I'VE LIFTED EVERY LICK HE EVER PLAYED... THIS IS THE GENTLEMAN WHO STARTED IT ALL!

AYE KEITH, IF YOU TRIED TO GIVE ROCK AND ROLL ANOTHER NAME, YOU MIGHT CALL IT **CHUCK BERRY!**

BUT SOME ARTISTS JUST TOOK BERRY'S MUSIC FOR THE WHITE MUSIC MARKET OF THE TIME...THE BEACH BOYS WERE THREATENED WITH SUIT FOR COPYING SWEET LITTLE SIXTEEN AND CALLING IT SURFIN' USA.

YOU'D SEE 'EM WEARIN' THEIR BAGGIES. HUARACHE SANDALS TOO.

KEITH RICHARDS — JOHN LENNON

IT WASN'T ONLY JAZZ THAT MADE PEOPLE SCARED...

HERE'S GEORGE WALLACE'S SPEECH WRITER, ASA CARTER, ON ROCK AND ROLL...

"[ROCK AND ROLL IS THE] BASIC, HEAVY-BEAT MUSIC OF THE NEGROES. IT APPEALS TO THE BASE IN MAN; BRINGS OUT ANIMALISM AND VULGARITY..."

"[IT COMES FROM] THE HEART OF AFRICA, WHERE IT WAS USED TO INCITE WARRIORS TO SUCH FRENZY THAT BY NIGHTFALL NEIGHBORS WERE COOKED IN CARNAGE POTS!!"

> Court's *Brown* decision a "clear abuse of judicial power," they pledged not to obey it. At the end of the year six southern states had not yet allowed a single black child into a school attended by whites. Rock 'n' roll became a target of southern segrationists, who believed that race mixing led, inevitably, to miscegenation and that exposure to black culture promoted juvenile delinquency and sexual immorality. Asa Carter, former radio commentator, soft-drink salesman, and member of Ku Klux Klan Klavern No. 31, used the threat of rock 'n' roll to enhance his status as a leader of the White Councils in Alabama. Lumping together rock 'n' roll, bebop, blues, "congo rhythms," and "jungle music" Carter got the attention of *Newsweek*.

Altschuler, *All Shook Up: How Rock 'n' Roll Changed America*

WELL, I DIDN'T SEE THAT ONE COMING...

SEX AND DRUGS, SURE...

BUT NOW WE'RE SAYING ROCK AND ROLL CAN LEAD TO EATING PEOPLE?

ROCK AND ROLL = CANNIBALISM ?!?

136

THAT WASN'T ALL. CARTER WANTED ROCK AND ROLL *BANNED* BY THE STATE.

HIS FELLOW SEGREGATIONISTS CLAIMED ROCK WAS PART OF AN NAACP PLAN TO "MONGRELIZE AMERICA." IT WASN'T JUST *MUSICAL* MIXING THEY WERE WORRIED ABOUT. IT WAS AN ACTUAL BREACH OF THE *COLOR LINE*...

Segregationist Wants Ban on 'Rock and Roll'

BIRMINGHAM, Ala., March 29 (UP)—A segregation leader charged today that the National Association for the Advancement of Colored People had "infiltrated" Southern white teen-agers with "rock and roll music."

WHAT DID THE NAACP SAY TO THAT?

"SOME PEOPLE IN THE SOUTH ARE BLAMING US FOR EVERYTHING FROM MEASLES TO ATOMIC FALL-OUT."

ROY WILKINS, NAACP

REMEMBER PLATO TALKING ABOUT HOW DANGEROUS MUSIC WAS? HOW IT COULD BYPASS RATIONAL THOUGHT? SAYING MIXING MODES SHOULD BE BANNED? 2400 YEARS LATER NOTHING HAD CHANGED. ROCK WAS MIXING MUSIC, CULTURES, *RACES*. IT MADE SOME PEOPLE NERVOUS...

BUT APART FROM TOTAL LOONIES, DID ANYONE BELIEVE THIS STUFF?

I TOLD YOU IT WOULD LEAD TO *DANCING!*

UNFORTUNATELY, THESE "LOONIES" WERE RUNNING A BIG CHUNK OF THE COUNTRY! BUT, YES, OTHERS ACTUALLY DID AGREE. AT LEAST THE PART ABOUT "PRIMITIVE" MUSIC BEING ABLE TO BYPASS RATIONAL THOUGHT...

THEY WERE TALKING AS IF ROCK WERE A VIRUS, TAKING OVER ITS HOSTS!

...AND PEDDLING PARANOIA WAS A BIG BUSINESS...

ROCK and ROLL INFLAMES AND EXCITES YOUTH LIKE JUNGLE TOM-TOMS

HERE'S WHAT LAIT AND MORTIMER, JOURNALISTS WHO WROTE THE POPULAR CONFIDENTIAL SERIES, HAD TO SAY ABOUT THE "ROCK SCENE."

"...Tom-toms and hot jive and ritualistic orgies of erotic dancing, weed smoking and mass mania with African jungle background. Many music shops purvey dope; assignations are made in them. White girls are recruited for colored lovers... we know that many platter-spinners are hop heads. Many others are Reds, left-wingers or hecklers of social convention."

HOW DID BLACK ARTISTS DEAL WITH THIS KIND OF HYSTERIA?

WELL! I CERTAINLY WOULDN'T WANT TO CONSORT WITH "HECKLERS OF SOCIAL CONVENTION."

138

Panel 1: WELL, IF YOU DON'T WANT TO SEEM LIKE A THREAT — PARTICULARLY ONE THAT'S ATTRACTIVE TO WHITE GIRLS... THE BEST THING IS TO LOOK LIKE...

LITTLE RICHARD!

Panel 2: I'M THE ARCHITECT OF ROCK AND ROLL! ALSO, CHECK OUT MY EYELASHES!

Panel 3: WAS HE REALLY DOING THAT ON PURPOSE?

SURE.

Panel 4: "BY WEARING THIS MAKEUP, I COULD WORK AND PLAY WHITE CLUBS, AND THE WHITE PEOPLE DIDN'T MIND THE WHITE GIRLS SCREAMING OVER ME... THEY WAS WILLING TO ACCEPT ME, 'CAUSE THEY FIGURED I WOULDN'T BE NO HARM."

Panel 5: HA! LITTLE RICHARD WAS *HOT*!!!

Panel 6: REMEMBER THE WAY THAT SECULAR AND RELIGIOUS MUSIC BORROWED BACK AND FORTH IN THE RENAISSANCE?

YES, ALL THOSE LYRICS ABOUT SWEET PLEASANT BRUNETTES! HUMPH!

Panel 7: WELL, IT CERTAINLY DIDN'T STOP IN THE 15TH CENTURY. LITTLE RICHARD TOOK GOSPEL MUSIC WITH ITS WAILING AND MOANING AND TESTIFYING AND HE LAYERED RHYTHM AND BLUES ON TOP OF IT!

Panel 8: I'M THE INNOVATOR, I'M THE EMANCIPATOR, I'M THE ORIGINATOR, I'M THE ARCHITECT OF ROCK 'N' ROLL.

Panel 9: ONE OF HIS BIGGEST HITS CAME WHEN HE TOOK A PRETTY VULGAR SONG HE HAD PERFORMED BEFORE...

I'VE LEARNED MY LESSON ABOUT ASKING FOR THE WORDS!

...AND RELEASED IT WITH CLEANED-UP LYRICS...

A-WOP BOP-A-LOO-MOP A-LOP BOM-BOM!!

TUTTI FRUTTI   OH-RUTTI

...AND NOW A SECOND ROUND OF BORROWING WENT ON- WHITE MUSICIANS WOULD RELEASE "CLEANED UP" VERSIONS OF BLACK HITS....

...ELVIS PRESLEY AND PAT BOONE RELEASED COVERS OF TUTTI FRUTTI.

PAT BOONE?!!

YES, AND HIS VERSION OUTSOLD THE ORIGINAL!

NOW THAT'S A TRAVESTY!

HE'S THE INNOVATOR AND THE ORIGINATOR. I'M THE IMITATOR!

PAT "DON'T STEP ON MY BLUE SUEDE SHOES" BOONE

"THE WHITE KIDS WOULD HAVE PAT BOONE UP ON THE DRESSER AND ME IN THE DRAWER 'CAUSE THEY LIKED MY VERSION BETTER."

BUT WHY ALL THESE COVER VERSIONS? WHY WOULDN'T PEOPLE JUST LISTEN TO THE ORIGINALS?

SEGREGATION AFFECTED CONCERT HALLS, RADIO STATIONS, RECORD STORES...AND LISTENING HABITS. THAT MEANT THERE WAS A PREMIUM ON HAVING WHITE ARTISTS.

LET'S HEAR FROM SAM PHILLIPS, THE GUY WHO FIRST DISCOVERED AND PRODUCED ELVIS...

"IF I COULD FIND A WHITE MAN WHO SINGS WITH THE NEGRO FEEL, I'D MAKE A MILLION DOLLARS."

SO PEOPLE LIKE ELVIS JUST RIPPED OFF BLACK ARTISTS, TAKING THEIR TUNES AND "WHITE-WASHING" THEM?

SEGREGATION MEANT THAT A LOT OF BLACK ARTISTS COULDN'T REACH THE AUDIENCE THAT THEIR TALENT DESERVED. BUT THINGS WERE MORE COMPLEX THAN THAT.

LITTLE RICHARD SAID OF ELVIS: "HE WAS AN INTEGRATOR. ELVIS WAS A BLESSING. THEY WOULDN'T LET BLACK MUSIC THROUGH. HE OPENED THE DOOR FOR BLACK MUSIC..."

"HE BROKE THE ICE FOR ALL OF US."

THE REV. AL GREEN

DID PEOPLE REALLY SEE IT THAT WAY AT THE TIME?

SOME DID. HERE'S WHAT WALTER WHITE, EXECUTIVE SECRETARY OF THE NAACP, SAID ABOUT ROCK AND ROLL.

"[IT'S] A GREAT RACE LEVELER... A TREMENDOUS INSTRUMENT FOR BRINGING ABOUT A COMMON GROUND FOR INTEGRATION OF THE WHITE AND COLORED YOUTH."

STILL, ELVIS WAS REALLY FREE-RIDING ON THE SONGS OF OTHERS, WASN'T HE?

LAWDY MISS CLAAAWDY!

OF COURSE. BUT THERE'S MORE NUANCE TO IT. FIRST OF ALL, ELVIS ALWAYS GAVE CREDIT TO RHYTHM AND BLUES...

ROCK 'N' ROLL HAS BEEN AROUND FOR MANY YEARS.

IT USED TO BE CALLED RHYTHM & BLUES.

AND HE WASN'T JUST COPYING...HE WAS ONE OF THE FOUNDERS OF ROCKABILLY, FUSING COUNTRY WITH RHYTHM AND BLUES.

AH DON'T SOUND LIKE NOBODY!

AND THE BORROWING WENT TWO WAYS. TAKE *HOUND DOG*. IT WAS WRITTEN BY JERRY LEIBER AND MIKE STOLLER, TWO WHITE SONG WRITERS WHO LOVED BLACK MUSIC...

THEY WROTE SO MANY GREAT SONGS!

THE MUSICIAN AND PRODUCER JOHNNY OTIS HAD ASKED THEM TO WRITE A SONG FOR BIG MAMA THORNTON.

AFTER MEETING HER, THEY WERE INSPIRED, AND WROTE *HOUND DOG* IN MINUTES. SHE RECORDED IT...

YOU AIN'T NOTHIN' BUT A HOUND DOG...

...AND THEN *THAT* SONG WAS COVERED BY ELVIS WHO MADE CHANGES TO BOTH THE TEMPO AND THE LYRICS...

SO THE SONG CROSSED BACK AND FORTH ACROSS THE COLOR LINE...

...CRYIN' ALL THE TIME...

WOW! STEPHEN FOSTER WASN'T AN ISOLATED INCIDENT! THIS REALLY IS THE REMIX NATION!

I COULD NEVER MOVE MY HIPS LIKE THAT!

STEPHEN FOSTER

143

BUT I AM BETTING THAT BLACK ARTISTS DIDN'T GET A SHARE OF THE MONEY ALL THOSE COVER VERSIONS WERE MAKING...

AIN'T THAT THE TRUTH! BLACK ARTISTS WERE ROUTINELY EXPLOITED. IF BLACK COMPOSERS GOT COPYRIGHT AT ALL, THEY FREQUENTLY HAD TO SHARE IT WITH OTHERS LIKE DJs.

DJs!? THEY GOT COPYRIGHT FOR *PLAYING* A *SONG*!?

APPARENTLY. CHUCK BERRY HAD TO SHARE COPYRIGHT ON MAYBELLENE WITH THE DJ ALAN FREED AND ALSO WITH RUSS FRATTO....

MAYBELLENE, WHY CAN'T YOU BE TRUE, DJ GONNA OWN THE SONGS I USED TO DO!!

DID THAT HAPPEN TO WHITE ARTISTS, TOO?

IT DID. REMEMBER DICK CLARK?

AMERICAN BANDSTAND!!

THIS SONG IS GOING TO BE A HIT! IT'S GOT A GOOD BEAT AND I CAN *COPYRIGHT* IT!

THE BOTTOM LINE IS THAT MUSICIANS IN GENERAL HAD LITTLE BARGAINING POWER...

...BUT BLACK ARTISTS HAD THE LEAST OF ALL.

THEY STILL DON'T!

AMERICAN BANDSTAND

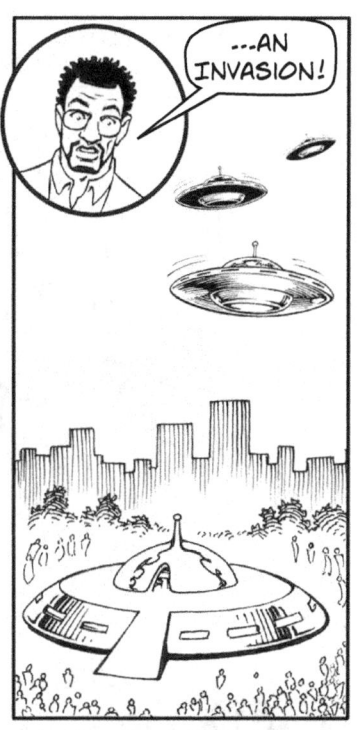

IRONICALLY, ONE REASON THAT BLACK MUSICIANS BEGAN TO GET MORE ATTENTION WAS...

...BECAUSE OF...

...AN INVASION!

THE BRITISH INVASION!!

NEW ACTS LIKE THE ROLLING STONES AND THE BEATLES WERE RAVENOUS FOR AMERICAN BLUES RECORDINGS. THEY WERE LISTENING TO MUDDY WATERS, JOHN LEE HOOKER, WILLIE DIXON, AND HOWLIN' WOLF...

I STILL FEEL BAD ABOUT TAKING THEIR NATIONAL ANTHEM...

I READ SOMEWHERE THAT THE STONES ACTUALLY CALLED THEMSELVES A BAND THAT PLAYS "AUTHENTIC CHICAGO RHYTHM AND BLUES MUSIC" IN A LETTER TO THE BBC.

YES, AND IRONICALLY THE BBC TURNED THEM DOWN BECAUSE THEY THOUGHT MICK JAGGER SOUNDED "TOO BLACK."

SAY IT LOUD! I'M BLACK AND I'M PROUD!!!!

WAIT! I'M WHITE AND FROM KENT...

"AND I FEEL FINE BORROWS FROM BOBBY PARKER'S R&B SONG WATCH YOUR STEP."

"YOU CAN HEAR IT IN THE BEATLES' SONGS ...YESTERDAY DRAWS ON A NAT KING COLE SONG CALLED ANSWER ME, MY LOVE."

"WAIT A MINUTE, I THOUGHT THAT WAS ELVIS COSTELLO..."

"PAUL WAS SO CUTE!"

"IN FACT, THE BEATLES EVOLVED FROM A "SKIFFLE" BAND CALLED THE QUARRYMEN. SKIFFLE HAD LINKS TO THE BLUES, TO JAZZ AND TO COUNTRY MUSIC."

"IT'S HARD TO BELIEVE JUST HOW MUCH ATTENTION THE BEATLES GOT. WHEN THEY WENT ON THE ED SULLIVAN SHOW IN '64, 75% OF TV WATCHERS TUNED IN!"

"AND SOME OF THAT ATTENTION GOT FOCUSED BACK ON THE BLACK – AND WHITE – AMERICAN ARTISTS THEY HAD BORROWED FROM, SOMETIMES TO THE MYSTIFICATION OF THE MUSIC PRESS."

"IS THERE ANYBODY BESIDES DYLAN YOU'VE GOTTEN SOMETHING FROM MUSICALLY?"

"OH, MILLIONS...LITTLE RICHARD, PRESLEY..."

"ANYONE CONTEMPORARY?"

"ARE THEY DEAD?"

"LIKE I* ALWAYS SAID ABOUT MUSIC JOURNALISM: PEOPLE WHO CAN'T WRITE, INTERVIEWING PEOPLE WHO CAN'T TALK, FOR PEOPLE WHO CAN'T READ..."

"OF COURSE, LENNON WAS A BRILLIANT TALKER... I MIGHT HAVE SAID A THING OR TWO MYSELF... HMMM..."

*WE THINK YOU MEAN 'LIKE ZAPPA SAID' —EDS.

147

BUT THE BEATLES WEREN'T JUST BORROWING FROM RHYTHM & BLUES, RIGHT?
Beatles
MAGICAL MYSTERY TOUR
MR. HARRISON? I'VE GOT SOME INDIAN RAGA FOR WITHIN YOU, WITHOUT YOU. I'LL JUST NEED A SIGNATURE HERE...

RIGHT. THIS IS SOME OF THAT BACH BOURÉE IN E MINOR FOR BLACKBIRD, INNIT? CAREFUL YOU LOT, IT'S FRAGILE...
Bourée
Abbey Road

20'S MUSIC HALL FOR YER HONEY PIE, SOME JOHN CAGE FOR YER REVOLUTION 9...
'EY JOHN...
'EY PAUL.
SOMETHING FOR YOU...
JOHN CAGE
MUSIC HALL

BIG INTERNATIONAL DELIVERY HERE FOR ALL YOU NEED IS LOVE – LET'S SEE, LA MARSEILLAISE, SOME OF BACH'S TWO-PART INVENTION IN F, GREENSLEEVES, SPOT OF IN THE MOOD...
I LOVED HOW THEY TOOK ALL THOSE SONGS FROM ALL OVER THE WORLD. IT SHOWED THAT ALL WE REALLY DO NEED IS...
YOU'LL NEED MORE THAN LOVE TO GET THAT BIT OF IN THE MOOD. IT'S OURS!
SOME LINES FROM CHUCK BERRY FOR COME TOGETHER...AND I'VE GOT SOME CREAM BADGE FOR MR. HARRISON'S HERE COMES THE SUN.
...HERE COME OLD FLATTOP...
ALSO, HERE COMES BIG SEVEN MUSIC CORPORATION WITH A LAWSUIT!
HANDLE WITH CARE
THIS SIL
UP

Panel 1
(No dialogue)

Panel 2
GATEWAY OF THE LAW

Panel 3
LOOK, MR. K, IF I'VE TOLD YOU ONCE, I'VE TOLD YOU A THOUSAND TIMES...

GATEWAY OF THE LAW

THE GUARDIAN OF THE LAW

Panel 4
OY! YOU CAN'T GO IN THERE!!!

GATEWAY OF THE LAW

?!

SQUEAK

THE GUARDIAN OF THE LAW

Panel 5
SO NOW IT'S TIME FOR *YOU* TO TELL *ME* ABOUT SOMETHING.

Panel 6
WE'VE TALKED ABOUT ATTEMPTS TO LIMIT BORROWING AND REMIX BY EVERYONE FROM PLATO AND THE HOLY ROMAN EMPIRE TO THOSE WHO THOUGHT JAZZ WOULD DEBASE THE WHITE MUSICAL HERITAGE.

BUT WHAT ABOUT THE LAW?

WHAT KIND OF LINES DOES *IT* DRAW?

IS ANY PART OF WHAT THE BEATLES WERE DOING — WHAT ALL ROCKERS DO — IS ANY PART OF THAT ILLEGAL?

THAT'S A GREAT QUESTION. BUT FIRST WE NEED TO CLEAR UP SOME BASICS...
NEVER EXPECT A STRAIGHT ANSWER FROM A LAWYER, DUH!
BOOKS, MOVIES, MUSIC, FILMS...ALL THESE THINGS ARE COVERED BY COPYRIGHT.
A SHORT HISTORY OF THE U.S.A.
COPYRIGHT'S DOMAIN
...THEY ARE COVERED BY COPYRIGHT AS SOON AS THEY ARE FIXED...THE PEN LEAVES THE PAPER, THE MUSIC IS WRITTEN DOWN OR SAVED ON YOUR HARD DRIVE, THE FILM IS SHOT... YOU DON'T NEED TO DO ANYTHING TO GET THE COPYRIGHT.
COOL!
BUT THE FIRST THING YOU HAVE TO UNDERSTAND IS WHAT COPYRIGHT COVERS...AND DOESN'T.
MUSIC
PICTURES
A SHORT HISTORY OF THE U.S.A. BY A.N. AUTHOR
BOOKS
HERE, I AM GIVING YOU THIS BOOK, IT'S YOURS NOW...
COOL!
A SHORT HISTORY OF THE U.S.A. BY A.N. AUTHOR

YOU OWN THE PHYSICAL OBJECT... THESE PIECES OF PAPER...THIS BINDING. YOU COULD BURN IT, OR SELL IT, OR GIVE IT AWAY...

AND THE AUTHOR HAS NO RIGHT TO STOP YOU...

That didn't last long.

...AND EVEN INSIDE THE BOOK THERE ARE LOTS OF THINGS THE AUTHOR DOESN'T OWN...

AAAHHHHHH!

FACTS

IDEAS

CHRISTOPHER COLUMBUS 1492

ALL MEN ARE CREATED EQUAL

LOUISIANA PURCHASE 1803

DE TOQUEVILLE'S 1787 PIVOTAL

DECLARATION OF INDEPENDENCE, NOT U.S. CONSTITUTION EXPRESSES IDEALS OF AMERICA

153

Panel 1:
WHAT **WAS** THAT!!??! AND IS THAT THING GOING TO DO IT AGAIN?

THOSE WERE THE FACTS AND IDEAS IN THAT BOOK, THEY AREN'T COPYRIGHTABLE ...THEY GO IMMEDIATELY INTO THE PUBLIC DOMAIN.

Panel 2:
COPYRIGHT COVERS THE AUTHOR'S **EXPRESSION**, NOT THE IDEAS OR FACTS THEMSELVES.

SO, BOY MEETS GIRL...

Panel 3:
...OR EVEN BOY MEETS GIRL AT COLLEGE, FALLS IN LOVE, GIRL DIES...

...ISN'T COPYRIGHTABLE... BUT ERICH SEGAL'S LOVE STORY ...HIS EXPRESSION OF THOSE IDEAS...**IS** COPYRIGHTED.

Panel 4:
Ali MacGraw ◦ Ryan O'Neal
Love Story
Love means never having to say you're sorry.

...HOW I CRIED AT THAT MOVIE!

Panel 5:
WAIT A MINUTE. WHAT ABOUT THAT POSTER? ISN'T **IT** COPYRIGHTED? DO YOU HAVE PERMISSION TO USE THAT PICTURE?

NO, IT'S A FAIR USE.* FAIR USE MEANS THAT YOU CAN TAKE THE AUTHOR'S EXPRESSION WHEN YOU USE IT FOR SUCH PURPOSES AS CRITICISM OR COMMENTARY, PARTICULARLY IF YOUR USE IS **TRANSFORMATIVE**.

*FOR MORE ON FAIR USE, SEE BOUND BY LAW? – EDS.

Panel 6:
...LIKE A QUOTATION IN A CRITICAL BOOK REVIEW...

HARSH!

REVIEW
A Short History of the U.S.A.
Wish it had been shorter.
[Quote here]

BUT HOW DOES ALL THIS APPLY TO MUSIC?
Rhapsody In Blue
HERE'S OUR OLD FRIEND RHAPSODY IN BLUE! IMAGINE YOU WERE GERSHWIN, OR HIS HEIRS. YOU WOULD HAVE A COPYRIGHT OVER THIS AS A MUSICAL COMPOSITION.
BUT WHAT DOES THAT MEAN? WHAT POWERS DOES THE COMPOSITION COPYRIGHT GIVE ME?
Rhapsody In Blue
GEORGE GERSHWIN
...TO ANSWER THAT WE'LL HAVE TO LOOK AT THE COPYRIGHT STATUTE...
THE LAST TIME SOMEONE DID THIS IN A MOVIE, REALLY BAD STUFF HAPPENED...
WAIT! NO!! DON'T OPEN THAT!!
17 United States Code
17 U.S.C. §§101 et seq.
MEET YOUR EXCLUSIVE RIGHTS. THINK OF THEM AS POWERS TO STOP PEOPLE FROM DOING THESE PARTICULAR THINGS...
...OR THE POWER TO GIVE PERMISSION WHEN YOU WANT, TO THE PERSON YOU WANT...

HERE ARE THE ONES THAT MATTER MOST FOR COMPOSITIONS...

SHORTER THAN I'D EXPECTED.

17 U.S.C. §106. Exclusive Rights in Copyrighted Works

Subject to sections 107 through 118, the owner of copyright under this title has the exclusive rights to do and to authorize any of the following:

(1) to reproduce the copyrighted work in copies or phonorecords;
(2) to prepare derivative works based on the copyrighted work;
(3) to distribute copies or phonorecords of the copyrighted work to the public by sale or other transfer of ownership, or by rental, lease, or lending;
(4) in the case of literary, musical, dramatic, and choreographic works, pantomimes, and motion pictures and other audiovisual works, to perform the copyrighted work publicly; and
(5) in the case of literary, musical, dramatic, and choreographic works, pantomimes, and pictorial, graphic, or sculptural works, including the individual images of a motion picture or other audiovisual work, to display the copyright work publicly.

BUT TOO MUCH LEGALESE. CAN YOU DECODE?

AND THESE WERE YOUR SUPER POWERS.

HMM...WELL HOW ABOUT THINKING OF THIS AS IF IT WERE A COMIC BOOK?*

*IMAGINE THAT! — EDS.

(1) TO REPRODUCE THE COPYRIGHTED WORK

THE ANTI-COPYING POWER!!!

156

I DECIDE WHO MAKES COPIES OF MY WORK!
RHAPSODY IN BLUE
iTunes
Rhapsody In Blue
---THE ANTI-ADAPTATION POWER!!!
§ 106 (2)
NO DERIVATIVES WITHOUT MY SAY-SO!!
RHAPSODY IN RED!
RAP CITY IN BLUE TOOK GERSHWIN'S GLISSANDO AN' MY RHYMES TO ORLANDO, DISNEYWORLD! MOUSE IN THE HOUSE!
RHAPSODY IN RED

AND NO DISTRIBUTING COPIES OF IT...

BORIS' BACK-ALLEY SHEET MUSIC 50 RUBLES

...OR PUBLICLY PERFORMING IT EITHER!!!

I *CONTROL* COPYING, ADAPTATION, PERFORMANCE AND DISTRIBUTION!!!

I AM THE *KING* OF THE COPYRIGHT WORLD!!!

AHEM---THERE'S JUST ONE THING...

WHAT?

ALL OTHER COPYRIGHT HOLDERS HAVE THE SAME POWERS OVER *YOU*!
SO THEY CAN STOP ME FROM MAKING ANY KIND OF ADAPTATION? ANY REFERENCE, QUOTATION, PARODY? IS THIS TOTAL CONTROL?
NOT AT ALL. SOMETIMES PEOPLE TALK AS THOUGH COPYRIGHT WAS AN ABSOLUTE PROPERTY RIGHT...
...BUT ACTUALLY IT IS POROUS, FULL OF EXCEPTIONS...
THE FIRST IS TERM LIMITS. BEETHOVEN, MOZART, BACH - MOST OF THE MUSIC BEFORE 1923 IS FAIR GAME, EITHER BECAUSE THERE WAS NEVER A COPYRIGHT OR IT HAS EXPIRED.
TWIST
TWIST
SO PAUL MCCARTNEY COULD USE BACH'S *BOURÉE* IN *BLACKBIRD*. WHEN BACH WROTE IT, THERE WASN'T A COPYRIGHT. EVEN IF THERE HAD BEEN, IT WOULD HAVE EXPIRED LONG AGO.
WHEW!!
SAME WITH THE CLASSICAL RAGAS THE BEATLES USED.
OR *PACHELBEL'S CANON*. THAT'S BEEN USED BY EVERYONE FROM CATCH 22 TO COLDIO.
...COOLIO...
AH!

COPYRIGHT ONLY COVERS "ORIGINAL" EXPRESSION... THERE HAS TO BE SOME CREATIVE CHOICE BY THE AUTHOR...
AND SOME MUSICAL CHOICES – A PERFECT FIFTH, AN OCTAVE JUMP – WOULD BE SO BASIC AND OBVIOUS THAT THEY AREN'T ORIGINAL. THAT MEANS NO ONE CAN OWN THEM.
UNORIGINAL ITEMS
TWIST
TWIST
ZZZT!
FLIP!
"HAVING CHOSEN THE FAMILIAR THEME OF A BROKEN-HEARTED LOVER SEEKING SOLACE IN COUNTRY MUSIC, THE CHOICE OF A BARROOM WITH A JUKEBOX AS THE SETTING IN WHICH TO UNFOLD THIS IDEA SIMPLY CANNOT BE ATTRIBUTED TO ANY UNIQUE CREATIVITY ON THE PART OF THE SONGWRITER."
Black v. Gosdin, 740 F. Supp. 1288 (M.D. Tenn. 1990)
SCÈNES À FAIRE
WHAT ABOUT FACTS AND IDEAS? YOU SAID THOSE AREN'T COPYRIGHTABLE. BUT WHAT COUNTS AS A MUSICAL IDEA???
NOT MUCH – MAYBE "MINOR KEY REQUIEMS ARE SOLEMN." JUDGES VIEW MUSIC AS BEING ALL "EXPRESSION." BUT SOME THINGS ARE STILL TOO BASIC TO BE PROTECTED BY COPYRIGHT.
IF THEY ARE INHERENT TO THE GENRE, OR THEY'VE BECOME STANDARD, THEY'RE CALLED "SCÈNES À FAIRE"... LIKE COMMONPLACE MOTIFS OR A TYPICAL GUITAR RHYTHM...
MUSIQUE A FAIRE
GENRE
TRITE
COMMON-PLACE
MUSICAL BUILDING BLOCKS
TWIST
CRANK
CRANK
CRANK
SO ROCKERS CAN GO ON USING THE I, IV, V CHORD SEQUENCE?
YES! YOU NEED THEM FOR THE 12 BAR BLUES...
...THAT'S THE HARMONIC STRUCTURE IN *TUTTI FRUTTI*, *HOUND DOG*, AND *MAYBELLENE*!
YOU'LL HAVE MY I, IV, V WHEN YOU TAKE IT FROM MY COLD, DEAD FRETTING HAND.

Panel 1: AND NOT ALL COPYING COUNTS AS COPYRIGHT INFRINGEMENT — SIMILARITIES BETWEEN SONGS HAVE TO BE "SUBSTANTIAL." IF THE AMOUNT IS SMALL ENOUGH, THE LAW DOESN'T CARE...

DE MINIMIS NON CURAT LEX

Panel 2: "MEANIE MEECE"?

LATIN AGAIN. "THE LAW DOES NOT CONCERN ITSELF WITH TRIFLES."

Panel 3: SO WHEN THE BEASTIE BOYS USED A FLUTE SOLO BY JAMES NEWTON, THE COURT SAID THAT TAKING SIX SECONDS — THREE NOTES OVER A SINGLE SUSTAINED NOTE — WAS JUST TOO LITTLE TO COUNT AS COPYING.

Newton v. Diamond, 388 F.3d 1189 (9th Cir. 2004)

Panel 4: THOUGH THE RECORD COMPANY GOT PAID, BECAUSE THE BEASTIES LICENSED THE SOUND RECORDING. AS WE'LL SEE IN A MOMENT, THAT'S AN ENTIRELY DIFFERENT COPYRIGHT.

HOW DOES **FAIR USE** PLAY OUT IN MUSIC?

THAT MUST BE THE KEY TO IT ALL, RIGHT? THINK OF ALL THE BORROWING WE'VE ALREADY SEEN! CHURCH MUSICIANS TAKING TROUBADOURS' TUNES, TCHAIKOVSKY TAKING THE FRENCH AND RUSSIAN NATIONAL ANTHEMS, DVORAK GRABBING FOLK SONGS, JAZZ MUSICIANS QUOTING FROM OTHER SONGS. IF SOMEONE DID THOSE THINGS TODAY, IT WOULD ALL BE FAIR USE, RIGHT?

ER... NOT...EXACTLY ...CLEAR...

Campbell v. Acuff-Rose, 510 U.S. 569 (1994)

ONE OF THE MOST IMPORTANT FAIR USE CASES IS ABOUT MUSIC...

WHEN 2 LIVE CREW MADE A VERSION OF ROY ORBISON'S OH PRETTY WOMAN, THE SUPREME COURT SAID IT COULD BE FAIR USE.

"2 LIVE CREW JUXTAPOSES THE ROMANTIC MUSINGS OF A MAN WHOSE FANTASY COMES TRUE, WITH DEGRADING TAUNTS, A BAWDY DEMAND FOR SEX, AND A SIGH OF RELIEF FROM PATERNAL RESPONSIBILITY."
– Justice David Souter

THEY COULD TAKE HIS SONG?

WITHOUT PERMISSION?

THE COURT SAID THAT AS A PARODY, 2 LIVE CREW'S VERSION HAD A STRONG FAIR USE CLAIM...

EVEN THOUGH IT WAS COMMERCIALLY SOLD AND TOOK A SIGNIFICANT PART OF BOTH THE LYRICS AND MUSIC!

BECAUSE A PARODY **HAS** TO USE THE ORIGINAL WORK IN ORDER TO PARODY IT!

163

MUSIC!
MUSIC!
OK, I GET IT. BUT IF WE HAVE ALL THESE GREAT SPACES FOR CREATIVE FREEDOM, WHAT'S THE PROBLEM?
THE THEORY IS GREAT...
BUT IN PRACTICE ...SOMETIMES IT DOESN'T SEEM TO WORK OUT IN THE MUSICAL CONTEXT. TAKE FAIR USE AGAIN...

OTHER THAN THE PARODY CASES, THERE'S A MYSTERIOUS SILENCE.
IN OTHER AREAS LIKE LITERATURE OR SCHOLARSHIP, WE HAVE LOTS OF EXAMPLES OF FAIR USE BEYOND PARODY – CRITICISM, QUOTATION, "TRANSFORMATIVE" USES...
MUSICAL FAIR USE: THE DOG THAT DIDN'T BARK!!!
BUT IN MUSIC, THOSE KINDS OF FAIR USE ARGUMENTS HAVE NOT BEEN MADE TO THE COURTS...
THE HIGHLY TRANSFORMATIVE USE OF A SAMPLED PIECE OF MUSIC IN A RAP SONG...
Welcome to GarageBand for iOS
...OR THE FRAGMENTARY QUOTE OF THE MUSIC OF THE TIME IN A SYMPHONY ABOUT THE CIVIL RIGHTS MOVEMENT...
EYES ON THE PRIZE: THE SYMPHONY
...ARE EXCELLENT CASES FOR FAIR USE, BUT THE MUSIC-SPECIFIC CASE LAW ISN'T THERE, EVEN SO.
...AND THE PRACTICE IN THE INDUSTRY SEEMS TO BE TO PAY TO LICENSE MATERIAL EVEN WHEN A GOOD FAIR USE ARGUMENT EXISTS.
IT'S NEARLY AS BAD AS THOSE RIDICULOUS DEMANDS FOR LICENSES IN DOCUMENTARY FILMS!!*
...BUT THAT'S CRAZY! BY THAT LOGIC, JAZZ MUSICIANS SHOULD HAVE TO ASK FOR A LICENSE FOR EVERY TUNE THEY INCLUDE IN A SOLO.
*SEE BOUND BY LAW? – EDS.
I THINK I WANT TO RIFF SOME. BETTER CALL THE LAWYER...
MUSICAL INTERRUPTUS
CUT!
?
?
HEY, IT'S MILES. CAN YOU GET ME A LICENSE FOR 12 NOTES OF GERSHWIN AND A DASH OF RODGERS AND HAMMERSTEIN? I'LL NEED IT ABOUT 8 BARS FROM NOW... WAIT! HOW MUCH??!?

YOU'RE RIGHT. THAT'S RIDICULOUS. WITHOUT QUOTATION THERE IS NO JAZZ. REQUIRING LICENSES WOULD DESTROY THE MUSIC.
COPYRIGHT IS SUPPOSED TO ENCOURAGE CREATIVITY, NOT DESTROY IT.
SO...
BUT FEDERAL JUDGES LISTEN TO JAZZ – OR KNOW IT IS CULTURALLY "RESPECTABLE."
WOULD THEY HAVE THE SAME INTUITIONS ABOUT RAP? OR SOMEONE LIKE GIRL TALK WHOSE MUSIC IS ENTIRELY MADE UP OF SAMPLES?
LOVE THE LAYERED REMIXES IN *NIGHT RIPPER*...
BUT I THINK HE WAS BETTER IN *UNSTOPPABLE*...
WE DON'T KNOW, BECAUSE THE CASES AREN'T BROUGHT OR FAIR USE ISN'T CLAIMED.

SOME SAY IT'S BECAUSE RECORD LABELS ARE AFRAID OF EXPANSIVE FAIR USE DECISIONS, SO THEY WON'T CLAIM FAIR USE AGAINST EACH OTHER...

FAIR USE: THE MONSTER FROM THE BLACK LAGOON

SPECIAL PREMIERE! Badge Required

WELCOME MUSIC EXECUTIVES!

...OR THAT CLAIMING FAIR USE MEANS ADMITTING YOU COPIED IN THE FIRST PLACE. HIGH RISK! THE MUSIC BUSINESS ACTS AS THOUGH PERMISSION WERE ALWAYS NEEDED...

END RESULT? EVEN THOUGH LOTS OF MUSICAL BORROWING *COULD* BE FAIR USE, IN PRACTICE, LICENSES ARE GENERALLY DEMANDED.

SOLD — MUSICAL COMMONS — UNDER NEW MGMT

NO TRESPASSING

KEEP OUT

WE'VE HANDED THE FUTURE OF MUSIC OVER TO *LAWYERS* AND *ACCOUNTANTS* ...AAARRGHH!!

THAT'S IT!

SMASH!!

YOU'VE GONE TOO FAR. I AM OUT OF HERE, HUMANS!

MUSICAL INSPIRATION

167

LOOK, I AM SORRY BUT ALL THIS CAN'T BE TRUE.
LOOK AT THE HISTORY OF HIP HOP...
PUBLIC ENEMY PUT HUNDREDS OF SAMPLES ON THEIR ALBUMS.
THEY TOOK EVERYTHING FROM THE BAR-KAYS TO MALCOLM X TO RUFUS THOMAS, PLAYED WITH IT, DISTORTED IT. THAT'S HOW YOU GET THAT AMAZING "WALL OF SOUND" IN '80s RAP.
PUBLIC ENEMY
SOUNDSCAPE
IT TAKES A NATION OF MILLIONS TO MAKE OUR SOUND
"WE WERE TAKING A HORN HIT HERE, A GUITAR RIFF THERE, WE MIGHT TAKE A LITTLE SPEECH, A KICKING SNARE FROM SOMEWHERE ELSE. IT WAS ALL BITS AND PIECES."
HANK SHOCKLEE
BITS AND PIECES STRUNG TOGETHER ON MACHINES LIKE THIS, WHICH COULD ONLY RECORD SAMPLES A FEW SECONDS LONG!
E-mu Syster
ARE YOU TELLING ME ALL OF THOSE SAMPLES WERE LICENSED?! THAT'S IMPOSSIBLE.
IT IS IMPOSSIBLE. HOW MANY BANDS SOUND LIKE THEM TODAY?

WHEN SAMPLERS STARTED TAKING FRAGMENTS OF PRIOR SONGS, THE PRACTICE WAS IN LEGAL LIMBO. THEY ONLY CLEARED RIGHTS TO REALLY LARGE SAMPLES.
"THE ONLY TIME COPYRIGHT WAS AN ISSUE WAS IF YOU ACTUALLY TOOK THE ENTIRE RHYTHM OF A SONG..."
BUT THEN HIP HOP STARTED TO GET PROFITABLE AND THE CLAIMS OF COPYRIGHT INFRINGEMENT BEGAN.
YO JIMMY!
YO LEROY
THE BEASTIE BOYS GOT SUED FOR TAKING THE PHRASE "YO LEROY" AND SOME BACKBEAT FROM A 1977 SONG BY THE JIMMY CASTOR BUNCH AND USING IT IN *HOLD IT NOW, HIT IT*.
BUT WE DIDN'T GET A COURT DECISION UNTIL A CASE CALLED *GRAND UPRIGHT*.
WOW! HE GOT THEIR NAMES RIGHT!
BIZ MARKIE HAD SAMPLED A LOT OF GILBERT O'SULLIVAN'S *ALONE AGAIN (NATURALLY)* – TAKING MOST OF THE PIANO INTRODUCTION. HE ALSO SANG A FRAGMENT OF THE LYRICS HIMSELF.
COOL HAT!
BIZ
HIS LAWYERS CONTACTED O'SULLIVAN'S AGENT BEFORE THE RELEASE OF THE RECORD, BUT HADN'T OBTAINED THE RIGHTS BEFORE RELEASE. O'SULLIVAN SUED, AND WON.
NOW THAT YOU'VE TAUGHT ME ALL ABOUT COPYRIGHT, THAT STRIKES ME AS AN INTERESTING CASE! WHAT DID THE JUDGE SAY ABOUT FAIR USE – THE ARGUMENT THAT SAMPLING WAS JUST LIKE JAZZ QUOTATION? OR DE MINIMIS? WERE THE BITS TAKEN JUST STANDARD – SCÈNES À FAIRE? AND HOW ABOUT...
ER...ACTUALLY, THE JUDGE'S OPINION WAS A *LITTLE* MORE LIMITED THAN THAT.

170

KEMBREW McLEOD: "There's a noticeable difference in Public Enemy's sound between 1988 and 1991...

...Did this have to do with the lawsuits and enforcement of copyright laws at the turn of the decade?"

CHUCK D: "Public Enemy's music was affected more than anybody's because we were taking thousands of sounds...

Let's take it down now!

...If you separated the sounds, they wouldn't have been anything — they were unrecognizable. The sounds were all collaged together to make a sonic wall."

"Public Enemy was affected because it is too expensive to defend against a claim. So we had to change our whole style — the style of *It Takes a Nation* and *Fear of a Black Planet* — by 1991."

*CAUGHT: CAN WE GET A WITNESS, FROM "IT TAKES A NATION OF MILLIONS TO HOLD US BACK"

THIS IS REALLY VERY DAPPER!

N.W.A. HAD TAKEN TWO SECONDS OF A GUITAR SOLO FROM GEORGE CLINTON'S GET OFF YOUR ASS AND JAM. THE SAMPLE WAS OF THREE NOTES — AN ARPEGGIATED CHORD.

...OTHERWISE KNOWN AS THE DEEDLY, DEEDLY, DEEDLY OF THE FIRST GUITAR SOLO EVERY KID LEARNS TO PLAY.

✹SIGH✹

I'M SURPRISED GEORGE CLINTON OBJECTED!

OH, DIDN'T YOU KNOW HE DOESN'T *OWN* THE COPYRIGHTS TO HIS MUSIC!

GEORGE CLINTON

A COMPANY CALLED BRIDGEPORT MUSIC BOUGHT UP THE RIGHTS TO CLINTON'S MUSIC. THEY'RE THE ONES WHO SUED.

YOU SOUND EXACTLY LIKE JOHN FOGERTY!

BUT I AM JOHN FOGERTY.

DEFENDANT STANDS CONVICTED OUT OF HIS OWN MOUTH!

IS IT NORMAL FOR ARTISTS NOT TO OWN THE COPYRIGHTS IN THEIR SONGS?

OH YES! THAT'S WHY I JUST *LOVE* RECORD CONTRACTS. IN FACT IN FANTASY v. FOGERTY, JOHN FOGERTY WAS SUED FOR INFRINGING THE COPYRIGHT IN ONE OF HIS OWN SONGS.

DON'T WORRY. THE JURY HELD THAT IT WASN'T COPYRIGHT INFRINGEMENT.

WHEW!

Panel 1: SO N.W.A. HAD TAKEN 3 NOTES AND 2 SECONDS OF GEORGE CLINTON AND SAMPLED IT IN 100 MILES AND RUNNIN'?

Panel 2: THEY ACTUALLY CHANGED IT QUITE A BIT. THEY LOWERED THE PITCH AND LOOPED IT SO IT SOUNDED LIKE A POLICE SIREN IN THE BACKGROUND OF THE TRACK.

Panel 3: OK. I AM GOING TO SHOW OFF MY COPYRIGHT KNOWLEDGE. THE CHIEF JUSTICE OF THE SUPREME COURT SAYS JUDGES SHOULD BE LIKE UMPIRES AND JUST CALL BALLS AND STRIKES. SO, I AM GOING TO BE A COPYRIGHT UMPIRE AND CALL THIS ONE.

YOU'RE OUT!

Panel 4: THE ARPEGGIATED CHORD IS A STANDARD PART OF SO MANY ROCK SONGS, SO IT IS EITHER NOT ORIGINAL, OR AN UN-PROTECTABLE STOCK PHRASE. IT WOULD NOT BE COPYRIGHTABLE IN THE FIRST PLACE!

STEEE-RIKE ONE!

WHUMP!

Panel 5: THREE NOTES IS DE MINIMIS – TOO SMALL TO COUNT AS COPYING. THIS IS JUST LIKE THE CASE OF THE BEASTIES TAKING A TINY SAMPLE OF NEWTON'S FLUTE!

STEEE-RIKE TWO!

Panel 6: AND FINALLY, EVEN IF THE DEEDLY, DEEDLY WERE ORIGINAL AND THREE NOTES WERE ENOUGH OF A COPY, N.W.A. TRANSFORMED IT DRAMATICALLY, SO IT WOULD PROBABLY BE FAIR USE UNDER SECTION 107!

Panel 7: STEEE-RIKE THREE! AND YOU ARE OUT OF HERE, BRIDGEPORT! NO COPYRIGHT INFRINGEMENT! LEGAL BORROWING!!

Panel 8: HOW AM I DOING?

ERRR...

Panel 1: "WELL, YOU *SHOULD* BE RIGHT..." "BUT THAT'S NOT QUITE HOW IT CAME OUT."

Panel 2: "THE CASE FOCUSED ON THE *DE MINIMIS* CLAIM...THAT IS WAS JUST TOO LITTLE TO COUNT AS ACTIONABLE COPYING."

Panel 3: "...BUT THERE IS ONE EXTRA THING YOU NEED TO KNOW...YOU SEE THERE ARE ACTUALLY *TWO* COPYRIGHTS IN ANY RECORDED MUSIC..."

SOUND RECORDING COPYRIGHT

MUSIC COMPOSITION COPYRIGHT

"THERE IS THE COPYRIGHT OVER THE COMPOSITION...WE ALREADY TALKED ABOUT THAT."

"...BUT IN 1972 CONGRESS ADDED A COPYRIGHT OVER THE SOUND RECORDING AS WELL."

Panel 4: "SO, IF I RECORD KNOCKIN' ON HEAVEN'S DOOR, BOB DYLAN OWNS THE COPYRIGHT OVER THE SONG. I HAVE TO PAY HIM ROYALTIES..."

Panel 5: "OK...SOUNDS PRETTY SENSIBLE. BUT HOW DOES THIS CHANGE ANYTHING? SURELY THE SAME RULES APPLY TO COPYING THE COMPOSITION AND THE SOUND RECORDING? THREE NOTES IS STILL ONLY THREE NOTES!"

"SO YOU WOULD THINK. BUT THE *BRIDGEPORT* COURT DISAGREED."

Panel 6: "...BUT *I* OWN THE COPYRIGHT OVER THAT PARTICULAR RECORDING OF IT. SOMEONE WHO WANTS TO USE IT HAS TO GET PERMISSION FROM BOTH OF US."

Bridgeport Music v. Dimension Films,
410 F.3d 792 (6th Cir. 2005) (Judge Ralph B. Guy, Jr.)
"THAT LEADS US DIRECTLY TO THE ISSUE IN THIS CASE. IF YOU CANNOT PIRATE THE WHOLE SOUND RECORDING, CAN YOU 'LIFT' OR 'SAMPLE' SOMETHING LESS THAN THE WHOLE. OUR ANSWER TO THAT QUESTION IS IN THE NEGATIVE...."
"GET A LICENSE OR DO NOT SAMPLE. WE DO NOT SEE THIS AS STIFLING CREATIVITY IN ANY SIGNIFICANT WAY...."
"FOR THE SOUND RECORDING COPYRIGHT HOLDER, IT IS NOT THE 'SONG' BUT THE SOUNDS THAT ARE FIXED IN THE MEDIUM OF HIS CHOICE. WHEN THOSE SOUNDS ARE SAMPLED THEY ARE TAKEN DIRECTLY FROM THAT FIXED MEDIUM. IT IS A PHYSICAL TAKING RATHER THAN AN INTELLECTUAL ONE."
SERIES, SERIES
SERIES
NO SERIES!
PHYSICAL TAKING!!? IF YOU TAKE MY SHOES, I DON'T HAVE MY SHOES. IF YOU TAKE THE BEAT OF MY SONG, I DON'T LOSE THE SONG!!
SO TAKING ANY AMOUNT OF A SOUND RECORDING COULD BE A COPYRIGHT INFRINGEMENT?!!!
WELL, THE COURT DID SAY THAT THERE WOULD PROBABLY HAVE TO BE TWO NOTES, OTHERWISE IT WOULD NOT BE A "SERIES."
KIND OF THEM.

BUT WHY? WHY MAKE THE RULES SO DIFFERENT FOR BORROWING FROM A RECORDING AND BORROWING FROM A COMPOSITION? IF THEY SAID "GET A LICENSE OR DO NOT SOLO," EVERYONE WOULD THINK IT WAS CRAZY!!
PART OF THE REASON WAS THAT THE COURT READ THE STATUTE IN A WAY THAT NO COURT HAD EVER DONE BEFORE. BUT THE OTHER REASON WAS THAT THEY THOUGHT THIS WOULD BE A REALLY CLEAR RULE, WHAT LAWYERS CALL A BRIGHT LINE.
OKAY BUDDY, STEP OVER THAT AT YOUR OWN RISK!!
#@*!
"GET A LICENSE OR DO NOT SAMPLE!" WELL, IT IS CERTAINLY CLEAR...
...THOUGH NOT VERY BRIGHT!
NO DE MINIMIS DEFENSE NO FAIR USE
THE COURT INITIALLY SUGGESTED THERE WAS NO FAIR USE EITHER. THEN AFTER A STORM OF PROTEST, THEY ISSUED A NEW OPINION SAYING THEY TOOK NO POSITION ON FAIR USE.
BUT IF WE STILL HAVE TO JUDGE FAIR USE, THEN WHERE IS THE BRIGHT LINE?
FAIR USE? I NEVER MENTIONED FAIR USE...
NO DE MINIMIS NO FAIR USE
THAT WILL STILL HAVE TO BE DONE CASE BY CASE.
EXACTLY.

VMG Salsoul v. Madonna Louise Ciccone,
824 F.3d 871 (9th Cir. 2016) (Judge Susan P. Graber)
IN 2016, A FEDERAL APPEALS COURT IN CALIFORNIA REJECTED THIS "BRIGHT LINE" RULE AND SAID THAT THE "DE MINIMIS" EXCEPTION DOES APPLY TO SAMPLING.
STRIKE A CHORD!
MADONNA'S SONG VOGUE SAMPLED A .23 SECOND "HORN HIT" FROM A SONG KNOWN AS LOVE BREAK, AND CHANGED IT TO CREATE A DIFFERENT SOUND.
THE COURT SAID THIS WAS DE MINIMIS – NO ONE WOULD HAVE RECOGNIZED THE SAMPLE'S SOURCE.
DUH? LESS THAN A QUARTER SECOND OF MUSIC?! OF COURSE! BUT I GUESS BRIDGEPORT WOULD STILL HAVE SAID "GET A LICENSE OR DO NOT SAMPLE"?
YES...AND THE JUDGE WENT SOME LENGTHS TO REFUTE BRIDGEPORT'S REASONING.
SO...NOW SAMPLING A TINY AMOUNT IS CLEARLY LEGAL?
"[MY] COMMON-SENSE CONCLUSION IS BORNE OUT BY DRY ANALYSIS...."
NO. AS OF 2016, WE HAVE TWO APPEALS COURTS DISAGREEING. THERE IS NO CLEAR NATIONAL RULE.
"Get a license or do not sample." (6th Cir. 2005)
"The 'de minimis' exception applies to infringement actions concerning copyrighted sound recordings, just as it applies to all other copyright infringement actions." (9th Cir. 2016)
BRIDGEPORT ONLY REINFORCED AN INDUSTRY PRACTICE OF LICENSING EVERYTHING. WILL THIS DECISION CHANGE THAT? TOO SOON TO TELL.

"MOST COMMERCIALLY SUCCESSFUL SAMPLERS PAY FOR A FEW BIG SAMPLES AND LOOP THEM..."

"...SOME STAY UNDERGROUND, HOPING THE SAMPLES WON'T BE RECOGNIZED..."

"...WHILE A FEW JUST THUMB THEIR NOSES AT THE LAW."

"SO THE LAW HAS CHANGED THE CREATIVE PROCESS..."

"BUT I AM UNCOMFORTABLE. MUSICIANS OUGHT TO GET PAID FOR THEIR WORK. LOOK AT JAMES BROWN, HIS WORK WAS SAMPLED BY PRETTY MUCH EVERYONE!"

"ANYTHING THEY TAKE OFF MY RECORD IS MINE. CAN I TAKE A BUTTON OFF YOUR SHIRT AND PUT IT ON MINE? CAN I TAKE A TOENAIL OFF YOUR FOOT — IS THAT ALL RIGHT WITH YOU?"

SO THE MUSIC THAT BEGAN WITH DJ KOOL HERC, WEAVING SONGS TOGETHER...
COME ON NOW B-BOYS AND B-GIRLS!!
...AND GOT EVEN MORE COMPLEX WITH SAMPLERS LIKE DE LA SOUL AND PUBLIC ENEMY...
...THAT MUSIC IS MUCH SIMPLER NOW.
THINK OF A SONG LIKE PUFF DADDY'S *I'LL BE MISSING YOU*. IT'S ONE HUGE SAMPLE OF THE POLICE'S *EVERY BREATH YOU TAKE*...
AND IT'S NOT JUST *CREATIVITY*, IT'S *ACCESS* -- YOU CAN'T STREAM OR BUY DE LA SOUL'S EARLY ALBUMS ONLINE BECAUSE OF SAMPLE CLEARANCE PROBLEMS.
PE
PE
WE'RE IN THE LIBRARY OF CONGRESS, BUT WE'RE NOT ON iTUNES. PEOPLE KEEP ASKING "YO, WHERE'S THE OLD STUFF?"
EMU SYSTEMS

I'D BE HONORED IF ANYONE SAMPLED MY MUSIC!

I'D BE AMAZED IF ANYONE WANTED TO SAMPLE YOUR MUSIC.

WELL, I DON'T KNOW. WHY CAN'T THESE HIPPITY HOP CHAPS JUST MAKE THEIR OWN MUSIC.

I LIKE BIG CARROTS AND I CANNOT LIE, YOU OTHER BUNNIES CAN'T DENY.

WOULD YOU SAY THAT ABOUT JAZZ?

WHAT DO YOU MEAN?

HIPPITY HOP!

DON'T JAZZ MUSICIANS TAKE FROM OTHER PEOPLE?

THAT'S TOTALLY DIFFERENT...

HOW?

WELL, IT'S A GREAT AMERICAN TRADITION...

WHICH STOPS WITH JAZZ, APPARENTLY?

NO — JAZZ MUSICIANS ARE TRANSFORMING THE TUNES, AND PLAYING THE MUSIC THEMSELVES...IT'S IMPROV...

BUT THEY ARE COPYING IT RIGHT? SOUNDS "LAZY" TO ME...

I THINK HE HAS A POINT. SAMPLING IS LAZY. IF THIS IS THE FUTURE OF MUSIC, WE ARE ALL IN TROUBLE. THERE'S NO REAL CREATIVITY HERE.

WHAT A BUNCH OF BALONEY. HIP HOP IS REALLY CREATIVE...THE BORROWING IS JUST LIKE JAZZ. YOU BORROW TO SHOW YOU KNOW YOUR ROOTS, BUT ALSO TO SHOW YOUR VIRTUOSITY IN THE WAY YOU USE THE SAMPLE.

THAT'S JUST NONSENSE. HAVE YOU LISTENED TO THIS STUFF? AUTOTUNED SINGING BY PEOPLE WHO CAN'T SING, ON TOP OF TUNES THEY DIDN'T WRITE, ALL OVER A BEAT STOLEN FROM SOME GREAT BLACK ARTIST FROM THE PAST WHO DIDN'T GET PAID.

"STOLEN?" THEN WHY ISN'T JAZZ STEALING? YOU'RE ONE OF THOSE PEOPLE WHO NEVER LOVES AN ART FORM UNTIL IT'S DEAD.

YOU WANT TO CALL THIS MUSIC? IN YOUR WORLD I GUESS KARAOKE IS HIGH ART! "I LOVE HOW HE TRANSFORMED MY WAY. SO POST-MODERN!"

NOW THAT NO-ONE LISTENS TO JAZZ, YOU CAN ROMANTICIZE IT. BACK IN THE DAY YOU WOULD HAVE BEEN CONDEMNING IT AS "STOLEN SQUEALS AND SQUAWKS" BY PEOPLE TOO LAZY TO WRITE REAL MUSIC.

YOU ARE SERIOUSLY COMPARING WHAT MILES DAVIS DOES IN A SOLO TO WHAT PUFF DADDY DID TO EVERY BREATH YOU TAKE?
HE WAS WRITING A SONG FOR A FRIEND WHO DIED, OK? AND ARE YOU SERIOUSLY SAYING THAT RAKIM'S WORDS, OR EVEN KANYE WEST'S, DON'T RANK AS BRILLIANT LYRICS...AS ART?
I DO ADMIT GOOD RAP IS GREAT POETRY...
I ADMIT I DON'T LIKE AUTOTUNE MUCH...AND SOME SAMPLING IS PRETTY LAZY.
MAYBE IT ALL COMES BACK TO THIS: "BORROWING IS PERMISSIBLE BUT ONE MUST RETURN THE OBJECT BORROWED WITH INTEREST....IMITATIONS... PRETTIER AND BETTER THAN THE PIECES FROM WHICH THEY ARE DERIVED."
THAT'S NOT CHUCK D, THAT'S "DER VOLLKOMMENE CAPELLMEISTER" FROM 1739. AND ON THAT WE CAN AGREE!
DOES HE CONTRADICT HIMSELF, VERY WELL THEN, HE CONTRADICTS HIMSELF, HE IS LARGE, HE CONTAINS MULTITUDES...

OK, SO THAT'S THE AESTHETIC RULE. CREATIVE BORROWING, NOT SLAVISH IMITATION. BUT WHAT SHOULD THE LAW SAY?

I'D LET THEM SAMPLE FREELY. IT'S NOT LIKE THEY OWN THEIR OWN COPYRIGHTS ANYWAY, MOST OF THE TIME! ARTISTS PAY FOR SAMPLES, BUT MOST DON'T GET PAID WHEN THEIR WORK IS USED — THE FEES GO TO LAWYERS AND INTERMEDIARIES...

NO, THOSE SAMPLES ARE CHARGED TO YOU WHILE FEES FROM PEOPLE WHO SAMPLED YOU GO TO US. LOOKS LIKE YOU SHOULD "RECOUP" YOUR ADVANCE BY THE YEAR 2987.

THIS IS SOME KIND OF TWISTED...

WE CAN'T MAKE ALL SAMPLING FREE.

WHEN BIZ MARKIE OR MR. COMBS TAKES A LARGE CHUNK OF A SONG TO MAKE A NEW COMMERCIAL PRODUCT THEY SHOULD PAY FOR THE PRIVILEGE.

YES. BUT EVERY JAZZ MUSICIAN WHO USES CHORDS FROM I GOT RHYTHM DOESN'T NEED A LICENSE...

....IS JUST TOO SMALL TO BOTHER ABOUT.

AT SOME POINT WE HAVE TO SAY THAT SOME LEVEL OF BORROWING...

EVEN JAMES BROWN BORROWED FROM GOSPEL SONGS, AND FROM RAY CHARLES' SOUL MUSIC.

REQUIRING PERMISSION FOR TRIVIAL BORROWING STOPS COPYRIGHT FROM FULFILLING ITS GOAL...

...TO ENCOURAGE CREATIVITY!

MIX AND MATCH AS YOU WILL!

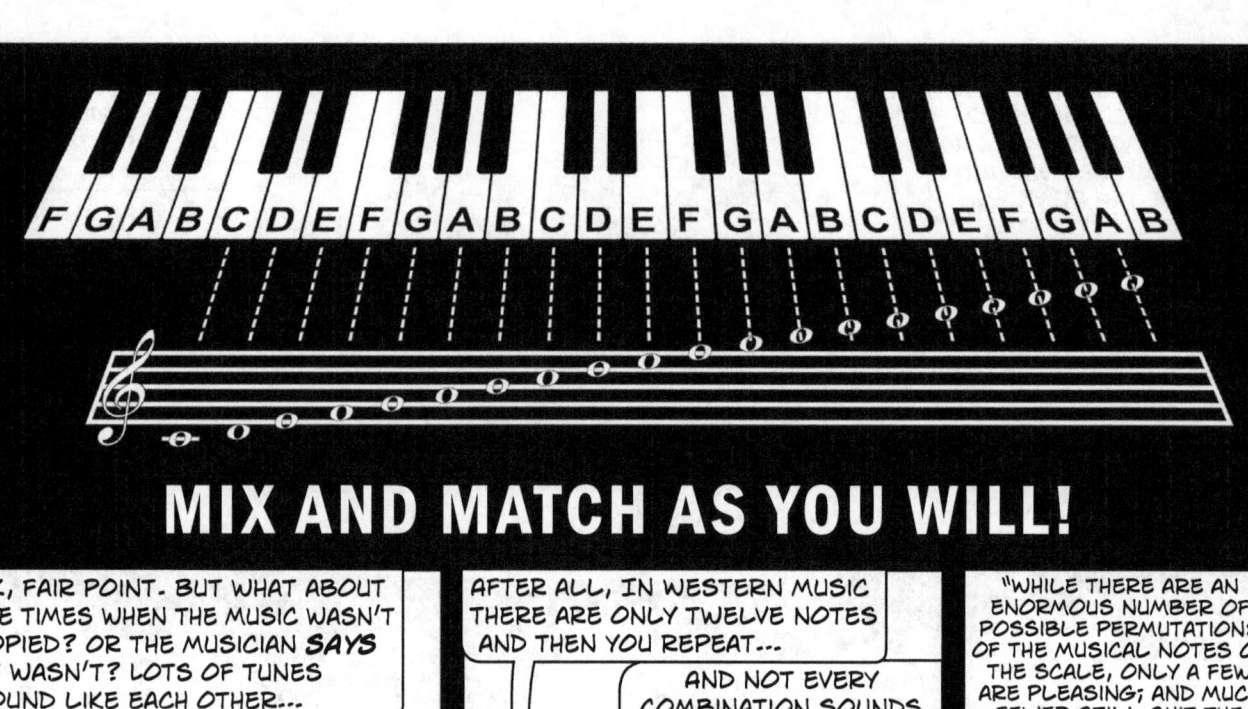

OK, FAIR POINT. BUT WHAT ABOUT THE TIMES WHEN THE MUSIC WASN'T COPIED? OR THE MUSICIAN *SAYS* IT WASN'T? LOTS OF TUNES SOUND LIKE EACH OTHER...

AFTER ALL, IN WESTERN MUSIC THERE ARE ONLY TWELVE NOTES AND THEN YOU REPEAT...

AND NOT EVERY COMBINATION SOUNDS GOOD. OR AS JUDGE LEARNED HAND PUT IT...

"WHILE THERE ARE AN ENORMOUS NUMBER OF POSSIBLE PERMUTATIONS OF THE MUSICAL NOTES OF THE SCALE, ONLY A FEW ARE PLEASING; AND MUCH FEWER STILL SUIT THE INFANTILE DEMANDS OF THE POPULAR EAR."

"RECURRENCE IS NOT THEREFORE AN INEVITABLE BADGE OF PLAGIARISM."

Darrell v. Joe Morris Music, 113 F.2d 80 (2d Cir. 1940)

A GUY WHOSE NAME IS *LEARNED HAND* WAS DISSING POPULAR TASTE!?? WHAT ABOUT PARENTS' TASTE IN KIDS' NAMES?

LEARNED WAS HIS MOTHER'S MAIDEN NAME, ACTUALLY...AND HIS REAL FIRST NAME WAS BILLINGS. BUT WE DIGRESS...

JUDGE BILLINGS HAND??

SO WHAT HAPPENS WHEN THE MUSICIAN CREATES THE MELODY HIMSELF? THAT'S NOT COPYRIGHT INFRINGEMENT, RIGHT? EVEN IF THE TUNES ARE IDENTICAL?

RIGHT — LAWYERS CALL THAT "INDEPENDENT CREATION" AND IT'S A DEFENSE.

Ma-ry had a lit-tle lamb, lit-tle lamb, lit-tle lamb

MY MASTERPIECE!

Ma-ry had a lit-tle lamb, lit-tle lamb, lit-tle lamb

BUT HOW DO YOU PROVE YOU DIDN'T COPY SOMEONE ELSE'S TUNE?

THAT TURNS OUT TO BE HARD...BASICALLY THE COURTS LOOK TO WHETHER YOU HAD ACCESS TO THE OTHER PERSON'S SONG, AND WHETHER YOUR SONG IS "SUBSTANTIALLY SIMILAR."

WHICH TAKES US BACK TO THE QUESTION YOU ASKED ABOUT THE BEATLES. SPECIFICALLY, GEORGE HARRISON.

THAT WAS *PAGES* AGO!

187

REMEMBER THE SONG BY THE CHIFFONS, HE'S SO FINE?

♪ HE'S SO FINE ♪ [DO-LANG-DO-LANG-DO-LANG]

I SO WANTED TO BE "THE BOY WITH THE WAVY HAIR" THEY WERE TALKING ABOUT.

HENCE THAT HAIRSTYLE?

♪ WISH HE WERE MINE ♪ [DO-LANG-DO-LANG-DO-LANG] ...I DON'T KNOW HOW I'M GOING TO DO IT, BUT I'M GONNA MAKE HIM MINE...

AND REMEMBER GEORGE HARRISON'S MY SWEET LORD?

MY SWEET LORD, MMM MY LORD... ...I REALLY WANT TO SEE YOU, REALLY WANT TO BE WITH YOU...

WELL, I ADMIT THEY SOUND PRETTY SIMILAR...BUT I DON'T THINK GEORGE HARRISON WOULD HAVE **DELIBERATELY** COPIED THE CHIFFONS...

THE JUDGE AGREED WITH YOU!

SO HARRISON WON?

NOT EXACTLY...

188

Bright Tunes Music v. Harrisongs Music,
420 F. Supp. 177 (S.D.N.Y. 1976)

A court ruled George Harrison infringed copyright by subconsciously copying The Chiffons' song *He's So Fine* in *My Sweet Lord*.

"HIS SUBCONSCIOUS KNEW IT ALREADY HAD WORKED IN A SONG HIS CONSCIOUS MIND DID NOT REMEMBER.... DID HARRISON DELIBERATELY USE THE MUSIC OF *HE'S SO FINE*? I DO NOT BELIEVE HE DID SO DELIBERATELY. NEVERTHELESS, IT IS CLEAR THAT *MY SWEET LORD* IS THE VERY SAME SONG AS *HE'S SO FINE* WITH DIFFERENT WORDS, AND HARRISON HAD ACCESS TO *HE'S SO FINE*. THIS IS, UNDER THE LAW, INFRINGEMENT OF COPYRIGHT, AND IS NO LESS SO EVEN THOUGH SUBCONSCIOUSLY ACCOMPLISHED."

JUDGE RICHARD OWEN

MY LITTLE SUBCONSCIOUS IS ALL GROWN UP AND INFRINGING COPYRIGHT!

SOMETIMES A DO-LANG IS ONLY A DO-LANG.

THAT SOUNDS SO FINE BUT I THINK IT'S MINE... DO-LANG-DO-LANG-DO-LANG...

I WAS JUST VAMPING SOME CHORDS AND NEXT THING YOU KNOW... HAL-LE-*SUE*-YA!

"WAIT, THEY CAN FIND YOU **SUBCONSCIOUSLY COPIED** SOMEONE'S SONG? IS THAT ONLY IF THE SONG IS REALLY RECENT AND VERY POPULAR?"

"ASK MICHAEL BOLTON!"

Three Boys Music v. Michael Bolton, 212 F.3d 477 (9th Cir. 2000)

A court upheld a $5.4 million jury verdict against singer Michael Bolton for subconsciously copying an Isley Brothers' song that he might have heard in his youth.

JUDGE DOROTHY NELSON: "IT IS ENTIRELY PLAUSIBLE THAT TWO CONNECTICUT TEENAGERS OBSESSED WITH RHYTHM AND BLUES MUSIC COULD REMEMBER AN ISLEY BROTHERS' SONG THAT WAS PLAYED ON THE RADIO AND TELEVISION FOR A FEW WEEKS, AND SUBCONSCIOUSLY COPY IT TWENTY YEARS LATER."

LOVE IS A WONDERFUL THING...SO WONDERFUL THAT THERE ARE 129 OTHER SONGS WITH THIS N-A-M-E!

...LOVE IS A WONDERFUL THING...

BOLTON SAID HE HAD NEVER HEARD THE ISLEY BROTHERS' SONG, WHICH DIDN'T TOP THE CHARTS AND WASN'T RELEASED ON ALBUM OR CD UNTIL AFTER BOLTON'S SONG WAS WRITTEN...

SO IF I WRITE A SONG THAT SOUNDS LIKE ANOTHER SONG, I CAN BE ACCUSED OF COPYRIGHT INFRINGEMENT IF I *COULD* HAVE HEARD IT AND *COULD* HAVE SUBCONSCIOUSLY COPIED IT?

NOT QUITE. COURTS DON'T PRESUME YOU HEARD THE OTHER SONG UNLESS THE TWO ARE "STRIKINGLY" SIMILAR. BUT EVIDENCE OF ACCESS CAN BE PRETTY REMOTE. THINK OF MICHAEL BOLTON!

SO I AM SUPPOSED TO LIVE IN A MUSICAL "CLEAN ROOM"...?!

AND MUSICIANS ARE SUPPOSED TO FLEE ANY POSSIBLE MUSICAL INSPIRATION?!

LOOK OUT! HE'S GOT A BOOMBOX! RUN!!!!!

OH, OH, IT'S HAPPENING AGAIN...

THAT'S ABSURD!

NO IT'S NOT!

IF JUDGES DIDN'T PRESUME COPYING IN CASES LIKE THIS, ANYONE COULD GET AWAY WITH RIPPING OFF MY MUSIC BY CLAIMING TO HAVE WRITTEN IT INDEPENDENTLY!

OH, IT'S YOUR MUSIC NOW!? AND YOU'RE WILLING TO RUN THE RISK THAT SOMEONE COULD ACCUSE YOU OF RIPPING THEM OFF? EVEN WHEN YOU DIDN'T?

MY GENIUS IS UNIQUE...

...AND UNRELATED TO MUSIC YOU'VE HEARD BEFORE? NOT LIMITED BY GENRE AND TRADITION SO IT MIGHT SOUND SIMILAR? YEAH, I'M SURE...

IT'S COMPLICATED...

IT'S COMPLICATED...

THIS IS SCARY. I AM KIND OF LIKING THESE MOMENTS NOW.

SO IF YOU ARE ALL SO SMART, HOW COME PEOPLE SAY OUR SONG "BLURRED LINES" IS ILLEGAL?
THEY SAY WE VIOLATED MARVIN GAYE'S COPYRIGHT OVER "GOT TO GIVE IT UP"!
I'M A HUGE MARVIN GAYE FAN! I KNOW BOTH OF THOSE SONGS. THEY DO SOUND SIMILAR, BUT THAT'S BECAUSE...
OH, **THAT** SONG. WITH THE MESSED-UP LYRICS. AND SUCH A "CLASSY" VIDEO.
...I WAS CHANNELING THAT LATE '70S FEELING!! IS IT ILLEGAL TO EVOKE A GROOVE?
SO, WHAT DOES COPYRIGHT LAW SAY?

WELL, FIRST, THIS ISN'T ONE OF THOSE SAMPLING CASES INVOLVING THE "SOUND RECORDING" RIGHT. IT'S JUST ABOUT THE MUSICAL COMPOSITION.
GOT TO GIVE IT UP
Moderately
Words and Music by MARVIN GAYE
UNDER THE LAW, SOME OF THE THINGS THAT MAKE THE SONGS SOUND SIMILAR – THE COWBELL, THE PARTY NOISE, THE FALSETTO – AREN'T PART OF THE "COMPOSITION" BECAUSE THEY WEREN'T IN THE SHEET MUSIC. SO THEY'RE OFF THE TABLE.
SO THE REGULAR RULES APPLY...
I'VE GOT THIS!
SURE, THERE ARE SIMILARITIES BETWEEN THE SONGS. BUT LOTS OF SONGS SOUND THE SAME. IT'S ONLY COPYRIGHT INFRINGEMENT IF "BLURRED LINES" TOOK ENOUGH COPYRIGHT-PROTECTED MATERIAL FROM "GOT TO GIVE IT UP" TO MAKE THE SONGS SUBSTANTIALLY SIMILAR.

LIKE YOU SAID, WE'RE ONLY TALKING ABOUT THE COMPOSITION, SO THINGS LIKE THE COWBELL AREN'T LEGALLY RELEVANT.
BLURRED LINES
COWBELL ALWAYS RELEVANT! 'MORE COWBELL,' I SAY!!
COPYRIGHT DOESN'T COVER ANYTHING THAT ISN'T "ORIGINAL" – MARVIN GAYE GOT A COPYRIGHT OVER WHAT HE CREATED. NOT THE STUFF HE BORROWED FROM OTHER SONGS.
YEAH, LIKE THE STUFF FROM JOHNNIE TAYLOR'S "DISCO LADY" – GAYE USED THAT!
AND COPYRIGHT DOESN'T COVER "SCÈNES À FAIRE." ALL OF THOSE DEFINING STOCK ELEMENTS OF FUNK, DISCO, OR MOTOWN...MARVIN GAYE, PHARRELL WILLIAMS, MARK RONSON, EVEN MILEY CYRUS WOULD BE FREE TO BUILD UPON THEM.
MILEY CYRUS?!
MOST OF WHAT MAKES THE SONGS SOUND SIMILAR IS STUFF THE LAW LEAVES FREE! WHAT'S LEFT ARE SCATTERED, MARGINAL SIMILARITIES. NO COPYRIGHT INFRINGEMENT!
OH YEAH? A JURY SAID WE OWED OVER $7.3 MILLION FOR COPYRIGHT INFRINGEMENT!
OK, WHAT HAPPENED *THIS* TIME?

WELL THIS WAS A JURY VERDICT...

THOUGH A JUDGE DID DECIDE THE CASE WAS WORTH SENDING TO THE JURY.

THE JURY WAS TOLD TO LOOK FOR "INTRINSIC SIMILARITY," AND TO BASE THEIR DECISION ON THE "TOTAL CONCEPT AND FEEL" OF THE SONGS.

JURY INSTRUCTION NO. 43
Intrinsic similarity is shown if an ordinary, reasonable listener would consider that the total concept and feel of the Gaye Parties' work and the Thicke Parties' work are substantially similar ...

WAIT. HOW CAN YOU COMPARE "TOTAL CONCEPT AND FEEL" WITHOUT INCLUDING ALL OF THE UN-PROTECTABLE MATERIAL I JUST MENTIONED? THAT'S WHACK!

IT IS, INDUBITABLY, "WHACK"!!

"YOUR HONOR, I WOULD SUBMIT THAT THE 9TH CIRCUIT'S APPLICATION OF THE INTRINSIC SIMILARITY TEST IS WHACK! ALSO, POSSIBLY BOGUS."

YEAH. WE SAY WE ARE FILTERING OUT ALL THE UNPROTECTED STUFF, AND THEN LET IT ALL BACK IN BY ASKING ABOUT "TOTAL CONCEPT AND FEEL."

THICKE'S TESTIMONY DIDN'T HELP. PARTICULARLY THE STUFF ABOUT BOOZE AND VICODIN.

IT WAS A TOUGH TIME! AND FEEL FREE TO CUT SONGS WRITTEN UNDER THE INFLUENCE OUT OF YOUR MUSIC LIBRARY. PLAYLISTS WILL BE SHORT!

THE JUDGE DID REDUCE THE $7.3 MILLION TO AROUND $5.3 MILLION, PLUS 50% OF FUTURE PUBLISHING REVENUE.

THICKE AND WILLIAMS ARE APPEALING.

JURIES SOMETIMES COME OUT THE OTHER WAY. A JURY FOUND LED ZEPPELIN'S *STAIRWAY TO HEAVEN* WASN'T SUBSTANTIALLY SIMILAR TO SPIRIT'S *TAURUS*. THERE, THE JUDGE CAREFULLY LIMITED THE EVIDENCE TO SIMILARITIES IN THE COMPOSITIONS, NOT THE RECORDINGS, AND THE JURY INSTRUCTIONS EXCLUDED "UNORIGINAL" MATERIAL.

POCKET CHANGE!

F
F#
G
G#
A

WELL, LIKE I SAID, I'M A HUGE GAYE FAN. AT LEAST HIS HEIRS GOT SOMETHING...
YOU KNOW WE'VE GOT TO FIND A WAY TO BRING SOME UNDERSTANDING HERE TODAY...
THEY COPIED "GOT TO GIVE IT UP" AND THE JURY HEARD IT! ...RIGHT NOW, I FEEL FREE. FREE FROM...PHARRELL WILLIAMS AND ROBIN THICKE'S CHAINS AND WHAT THEY TRIED TO KEEP ON US AND THE LIES THAT WERE TOLD.
IT SPEAKS VOLUMES ABOUT WHO WE ARE AS A COUNTRY THAT, NO MATTER WHO YOU ARE, IF YOU DO SOMETHING WRONG THERE ARE CONSEQUENCES.
NONA GAYE
RICHARD BUSCH (the Gayes' lawyer)
SO I UNDERSTAND THE IMPULSE TO SYMPATHIZE WITH HIM. I DO THINK THEY SHOULD MAYBE HAVE CREDITED HIS INFLUENCE...
BUT THAT DOESN'T MEAN THERE WAS COPYRIGHT INFRINGEMENT! WAS THIS VERDICT GOOD FOR MUSIC?
WELL IT PROMPTED SOME STRONG REACTIONS FROM MUSICIANS AND COMMENTATORS...
LA WEEKLY Great, Now "Blurred Lines" Has ruined the entire music industry
The Washington Post It's okay if you hate Robin Thicke. But the 'Blurred Lines' verdict is bad for pop music.
Slate Squelching Creativity
THE NEW YORKER Why the "Blurred Lines" copyright verdict should be thrown out
Chicago Tribune 'Blurred Lines' copyright verdict creates bad law for musicians
#CHILLINGEFFECTS?

Stevie Wonder: I don't think it's a steal from Marvin Gaye. I think that the groove is very similar but you have to remember he is a big fan of Marvin Gaye's so that's okay. But it's not the same song.

Adam Levine: It still baffles me that that case went the way that it did. Hopefully someday it will get overturned and an aspiring songwriter won't feel as though they can't emulate their heroes.

John Legend: You don't want to get into that thing where all of us are suing each other all the time because this and that song feels like another song. I'm a little concerned that this verdict might be a slippery slope.

Professor Christopher Sprigman: The jury's verdict...takes what should be familiar elements of a genre, available to all, and privatizes them.

Professor E. Michael Harrington: If this were to become a standard, it's going to be one of the greatest growth industries of all time, suing people who sound like someone else.

So what do you two think?

Pharrell Williams: The verdict handicaps any creator out there who is making something that might be inspired by something else. If we lose our freedom to be inspired, we're going to look up one day and the entertainment industry as we know it will be frozen in litigation.

Robin Thicke: I know the difference between inspiration and theft. You can't help but be inspired by all of the greatness that came before you. In popular music, you know, there's only so many chords being used.

COPYRIGHT IS SUPPOSED TO LEAVE ROOM FOR MUSICIANS TO BUILD ON THEIR INSPIRATIONS. I'M FEELING LESS CONFIDENT ABOUT THAT NOW.

ME TOO. WHAT'S BORROWED HERE IS A FEEL. LIKE I SAID BEFORE, NO INFRINGEMENT!

COPYRIGHT'S RULES — SUCH AS "SCÈNES À FAIRE" — TRY TO DRAW A LINE BETWEEN CREATIVE FREEDOM AND INFRINGEMENT.

BUT VERDICTS LIKE THIS COULD LEAD TO...

BLURRED LINES!

WHAT WOULD HAVE HAPPENED TO MUSIC IF WE HAD HAD TODAY'S RESTRICTIONS ON BORROWING?
THAT'S A GOOD QUESTION, AND ONE WE CAN EXPLORE THROUGH THE STORY OF A SINGLE SONG...
IT IS BEAUTIFUL!
HAUNTING...
Pull
Allegiez moy, doulce plaisant brunette, desous la boudinette
SOOTHE ME, SWEET PLEASANT BRUNETTE JUST BELOW...
THE FUNNY THING IS, THE FIRST AND LAST LINES OF EACH VERSE ARE ACTUALLY TAKEN FROM POPULAR SONGS...SECULAR SONGS.
STRANGE TO DESCRIBE THE VIRGIN MARY AS A "SWEET, PLEASING BRUNETTE."
WELL, THAT LINE IS STRIKING - THE POPULAR SONG IT IS TAKEN FROM GOES LIKE THIS...
WOW!! STEPHEN FOSTER WASN'T AN ISOLATED INCIDENT! THIS REALLY IS THE REMIX NATION!
I COULD NEVER MOVE MY HIPS LIKE THAT!
STEPHEN FOSTER
Pull
Pull
Pull
YANK!

I GOT A MASHUP
~ A SONG'S TALE ~

IN 2005 A HURRICANE MADE LANDFALL IN NEW ORLEANS. ITS NAME WAS KATRINA.*

[*FOR THE FULL STORY SEE HTTP://BOYLE.YUPNET.ORG/CHAPTER-6-GOT-MASHUP.]

DAMIEN RANDLE AND MICAH NICKERSON WERE TWO HOUSTON HIP HOP ARTISTS. THE DUO WAS CALLED THE "LEGENDARY K.O."...

AFTER HURRICANE KATRINA, THEY WERE VOLUNTEERING IN THE HOUSTON ASTRODOME...

Katrina Looters

..."WIDESPREAD LOOTING"...

THEY DIDN'T LIKE WHAT THEY SAW. BOTH THE SLOWNESS OF THE RESPONSE AND THE WAY THE DISASTER WAS COVERED MADE THEM PROFOUNDLY UNHAPPY.

THIS IS MESSED UP...

202

ONE NIGHT, THE RAPPER KANYE WEST APPEARED ON A TELETHON FOR VICTIMS OF KATRINA.

OVERCOME BY EMOTION, WEST UTTERED THE WORDS THAT WOULD IGNITE A CONTROVERSY AROUND THE COUNTRY.

I HATE THE WAY THEY PORTRAY US IN THE MEDIA.

IF YOU SEE A BLACK FAMILY, IT SAYS "THEY'RE LOOTING"...

YOU SEE A WHITE FAMILY, IT SAYS "THEY'RE LOOKING FOR FOOD."

AND YOU KNOW, IT'S BEEN FIVE DAYS BECAUSE MOST OF THE PEOPLE ARE BLACK.

...THEY'VE GIVEN THEM PERMISSION TO GO DOWN AND SHOOT US...

GEORGE BUSH DOESN'T CARE ABOUT BLACK PEOPLE.

IN 2016, MR. WEST SAID HE WOULD HAVE VOTED FOR DONALD TRUMP FOR PRESIDENT, HAD HE VOTED. MR. BUSH MIGHT FIND HIS CONCERN FOR RACIAL JUSTICE STRANGELY EPISODIC. —EDS.

THE LEGENDARY K.-O. SHARED WEST'S OUTRAGE.

AND THEY WEREN'T JUST VOLUNTEERS, THEY WERE ALSO HIP HOP ARTISTS.

SO THEY DECIDED TO WRITE A SONG ABOUT IT.

A SONG CALLED...

GEORGE BUSH DOESN'T CARE ABOUT BLACK PEOPLE

GEORGE W. BUSH SAID IN HIS MEMOIR THAT BEING CALLED A RACIST WAS THE WORST MOMENT OF HIS PRESIDENCY.
WAIT, WAIT, WAIT!!
DIDN'T A LOT OF PEOPLE OBJECT TO THOSE COMMENTS?
THE ISSUE ISN'T WHETHER OR NOT YOU AGREE WITH KANYE'S CLAIM.
WE ARE TALKING ABOUT WHAT THE RULES ARE FOR MAKING SONGS... FOR ANYONE WITH ANY MESSAGE.
"I DISAGREE WITH YOUR SONG, BUT WILL DEFEND TO THE DEATH YOUR RIGHT TO SING IT."

WANTING TO REFERENCE WEST'S WORDS, THE LEGENDARY K.O. REMIXED GOLD DIGGER...

CUTIE DA BOMB MET HER AT A BEAUTY SALON WITH A BABY LOUIS VUITTON UNDER HER UNDER ARM

CAN'T USE THE CELL PHONE, I KEEP GETTIN' STATIC DYIN' 'CAUSE THEY LYIN' INSTEAD OF TELLIN' US THE TRUTH OTHER DAY THE HELICOPTERS GOT MY NEIGHBORS OFF THE ROOF?

...CHANGED THE WORDS...

...EXCHANGED VERSES BY INSTANT MESSAGE...

FIFTEEN MINUTES LATER IT WAS UP ONLINE. WITHIN DAYS, HUNDREDS OF THOUSANDS OF PEOPLE HAD HEARD IT.

THEN FILMMAKERS MADE VIDEO VERSIONS OF THE SONG, TAKING IMAGES FROM THE NEWS COVERAGE AND ADDING K.O.'S MUSIC TO IT...

...MANY MORE PEOPLE SAW THOSE.

A SONG WRITTEN IN MINUTES, FOR PENNIES, WAS REACHING A HUGE AUDIENCE.

THE NEW YORK TIMES PUBLISHED AN ARTICLE ABOUT IT...

Art Born of Outrage in the Internet Age
By JOHN LELAND

IN the 18th century, songwriters responded to current events by writing new lyrics to existing melodies.

"Benjamin Franklin used to write broadside ballads every time a disaster struck," said Elijah Wald, a music historian, and sell the printed lyrics in the street that afternoon.

This tradition of responding culturally to terrible events had almost been forgotten, Mr. Wald said, but in the wake of Hurricane Katrina, it may be making a comeback with the obvious difference that, where Franklin would have sold a few song sheets to his fellow Philadelphians, the Internet allows artists today to reach the whole world.

For example, an unlicensed rap song describing the frustration of African-American evacuees has been made available free on the Internet.

The song, "George Bush Doesn't Care About Black People," by the Houston duo called the Legendary K.O., vividly recounts the plight of those who endured the hurricane, occasionally using crude language in the process.

It has already been downloaded by as many as a half-million people. The videos have been seen by thousands.

"A. J. Liebling famously commented that freedom of the press belongs to those who own one," said Mike Godwin, legal director of Public Knowledge, a First Amendment group. "Well, we all own one now."

207

BUT THE CHAIN OF BORROWING THAT ENDED WITH THE LEGENDARY K.O. WENT BACK A LOT FURTHER THAN KANYE WEST...

KANYE WEST HAD BORROWED FROM AN OLDER TUNE...RAY CHARLES' I GOT A WOMAN.
I GOT A WOMAN... THAT'S GOOD TO ME...
NOW I AIN'T SAYING SHE A GOLD DIGGER...
SHE GIVE ME MONEY, WHEN I'M IN NEED...
SHE TAKE MY MONEY WHEN I'M IN NEED...
CHARLES' MESSAGE WAS RATHER DIFFERENT FROM GOLD DIGGER'S.
WEST TELLS THE STORY OF A GOLD DIGGER WHO STEALS MONEY.
SHE'S A KIND OF FRIEND INDEED...
YEAH, SHE'S A TRIFLIN' FRIEND INDEED...
KANYE SAMPLED CHARLES' SONG.
BUT HE ALSO TOOK THE MELODY AND HAD JAMIE FOXX SING SOME VERY DIFFERENT WORDS.
WEST BORROWED FROM THIS SONG FOR A REASON.

I GOT A WOMAN HAD BEEN HAILED AS ONE OF THE FIRST SOUL SONGS.

SOUL TAKES THE ECSTATIC MUSIC OF GOSPEL...

...AND FUSES IT WITH THE EARTHY SOUNDS OF THE BLUES.

IN PLACE OF DIVINE PRAISE...

...SOUL SUBSTITUTED A MESSAGE OF PROFANE DESIRE.

IT'S A MIRROR IMAGE OF THE TROUBADOURS!
??
THAT "SWEET, PLEASANT BRUNETTE" SONG!
SOUL IS A GENRE CROSS-FADE!
CHARLES TOOK GOSPEL AND REPLACED GOD WITH A WOMAN.
DIVINE LONGING
EROTIC DESIRE
THE CHURCH COMPOSERS TOOK THE BAWDY TROUBADOUR SONGS OF THE DAY AND MADE THEM ODES TO THE VIRGIN MARY!
THERE SECULAR MUSIC BECAME SACRED, HERE SACRED BECOMES SECULAR. *VERY* SECULAR!

CHARLES HAD ALWAYS BUILT HIS SONGS ON OTHER MUSIC — HE MADE NO BONES ABOUT IT.

AT THE START OF HIS CAREER, HE MODELED HIMSELF ON NAT KING COLE.

FUNNY THING, BUT DURING ALL THESE YEARS I WAS IMITATING NAT COLE, I NEVER THOUGHT TWICE ABOUT IT, NEVER FELT BAD ABOUT COPYING THE CAT'S LICKS. TO ME IT WAS PRACTICALLY A SCIENCE. I WORKED AT IT, I ENJOYED IT, I WAS PROUD OF IT, AND I LOVED DOING IT...

...IT WAS SOMETHING LIKE WHEN A YOUNG LAWYER — JUST OUT OF SCHOOL — RESPECTS AN OLDER LAWYER. HE TRIES TO GET INSIDE HIS MIND, HE STUDIES TO SEE HOW HE WRITES UP ALL HIS CASES, AND HE'S GOING TO SOUND A WHOLE LOT LIKE THE OLDER MAN — AT LEAST TILL HE FIGURES OUT HOW TO GET HIS OWN SHIT TOGETHER. TODAY I HEAR SOME SINGERS WHO I THINK SOUND LIKE ME. JOE COCKER, FOR INSTANCE. MAN, I KNOW THAT CAT MUST SLEEP WITH MY RECORDS. BUT I DON'T MIND. I'M FLATTERED; I UNDERSTAND. AFTER ALL, I DID THE SAME THING.

BUT THE PROCESS OF BORROWING WENT FURTHER THAN THAT. CHARLES HAD ALWAYS LIVED IN TWO MUSICAL WORLDS.

THERE WAS THE RAY CHARLES OF THE SUNDAY CHURCH SERVICE, THE WORLD OF ECSTATIC TESTIMONY, WITH THE ORGAN PROVIDING THE BACKBEAT TO A CHOIR BELTING OUT GOSPEL FAVORITES...

AND THERE WAS THE WORLD OF THE AFTER HOURS CLUB WITH RHYTHM AND BLUES SONGS BLARING INTO THE SMOKY AIR.

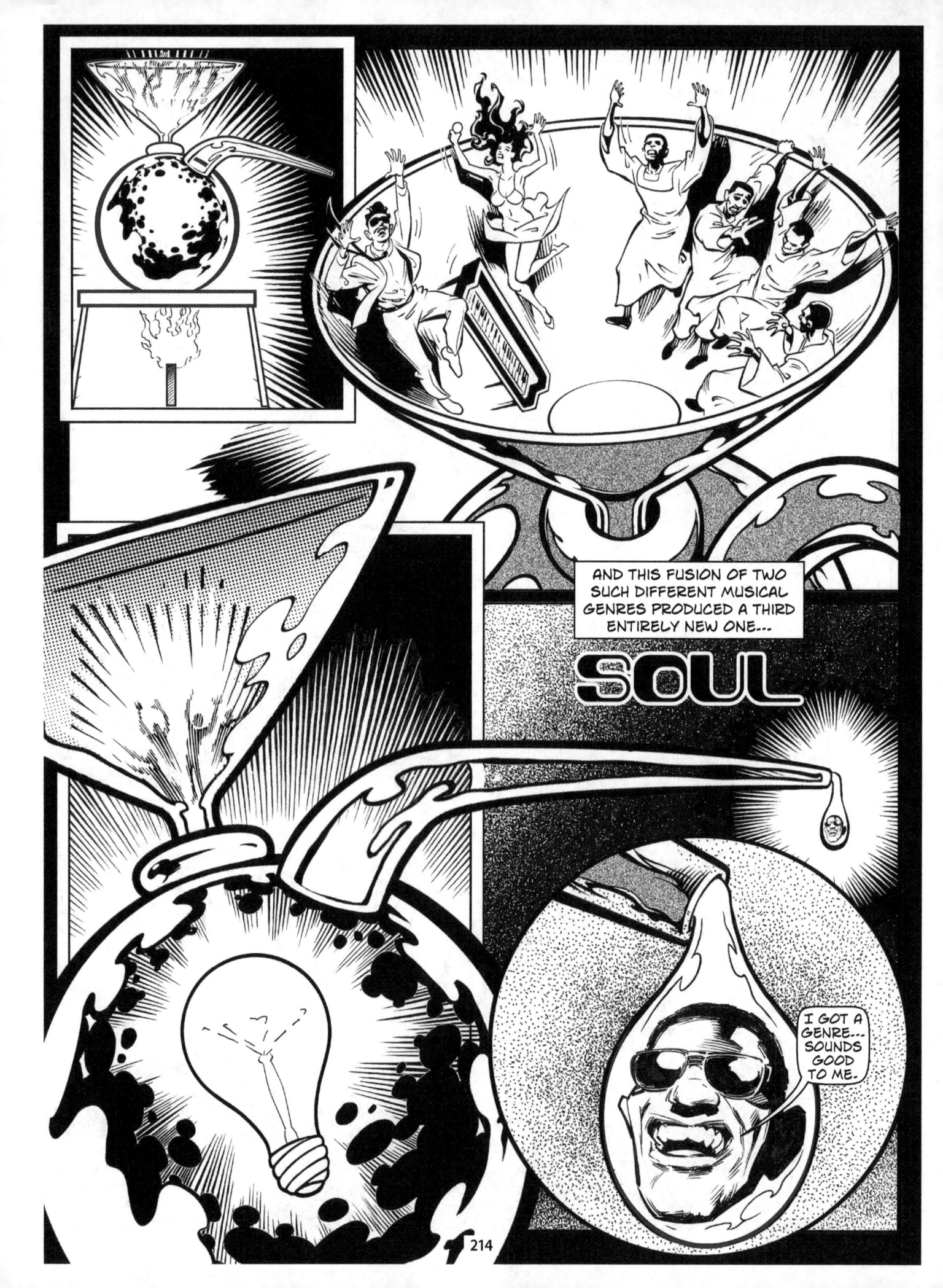

AND THIS FUSION OF TWO SUCH DIFFERENT MUSICAL GENRES PRODUCED A THIRD ENTIRELY NEW ONE...

SOUL

I GOT A GENRE... SOUNDS GOOD TO ME.

THE INFLUENCES THAT CHARLES DREW ON TO CREATE HIS MUSIC WEREN'T JUST GENERAL TRADITIONS. THEY WERE VERY, VERY SPECIFIC.

"I LIKE THAT SONG."

IN 1954, DRIVING FROM GIG TO GIG, CHARLES AND HIS TRUMPETER RENALD RICHARD WERE LISTENING TO THE RADIO. A GOSPEL SONG CAME ON.

LIKING WHAT THEY HEARD, THEY BOTH STARTED TO SING ALONG, CHANGING THE WORDS TO SUIT THEIR MOOD.

"I GOT A WOMAN..."

"YEAH, SHE LIVES ACROSS TOWN..."

"SHE'S GOOD TO ME..."

THAT SONG IS SAID TO BE THE ORIGIN OF CHARLES' SMASH HIT, "I GOT A WOMAN."

"SO YOU *CAN* GET YOUR KICKS ON ROUTE 66."

KEEPS ME UP KEEPS ME STRONG TEACH ME RIGHT WHEN I DOING WRONG WELL, I'VE GOT A SAVIOR OH WHAT A SAVIOR YES I HAVE
WHAT WAS THE SONG?!
ROUTE US 66
SHE GIMME MONEY WHEN I'M IN NEED YEAH SHE'S A KIND OF FRIEND INDEED I GOT A WOMAN WAY OVER TOWN THAT'S GOOD TO ME
SOME SCHOLARS THINK IT IS THE 1950 TUNE "I GOT A SAVIOR" FROM THE HAROLD BAILEY GOSPEL SINGERS, PROBABLY WRITTEN BY CLARA WARD.
IT IS NOT JUST THE TITLE THAT IS SIMILAR. THE CENTRAL MELODY IS ALMOST EXACTLY THE SAME.
WE KNOW CHARLES LIKED TO SUBSTITUTE LOVE FOR RELIGION. HE TOOK CLARA WARD'S ARRANGEMENT OF THE GOSPEL CLASSIC "THIS LITTLE LIGHT OF MINE" AND TURNED IT INTO "THIS LITTLE GIRL OF MINE." "I GOT A SAVIOR" BECAME "I GOT A WOMAN."
The Billboard
Reviews of New Spiritual Records
SOUTHERN TONES
It Must Be Jesus
DUKE 205—The good things that Jesus does for men is the theme of this swinging spiritual. The lead singer sparks the group on to an ever more hectic tempo, working up to a pitch of great excitement. (Lion, BMI)
BUT THERE IS ALSO "IT MUST BE JESUS" BY THE SOUTHERN TONES, A POPULAR GOSPEL SONG FROM 1954, WHICH HAS ITS OWN MUSICAL SIMILARITIES TO "I GOT A WOMAN"! HE PROBABLY TOOK FROM BOTH.

THIS MERGER OF GOSPEL AND BLUES, SUBSTITUTING THE WOMAN FOR GOD, WAS CONTROVERSIAL... "SEX, SIN, AND SYNCOPATION." SOME GOSPEL SINGERS FOUND IT OFFENSIVE, EVEN SACRILEGIOUS.

CLARA WARD, WHOSE SONGS AND ARRANGEMENTS CHARLES HAD BORROWED FROM, THOUGHT THAT IT WAS A DISRESPECTFUL ATTACK ON GOSPEL MUSIC. BIG BILL BROONZY SPOKE OUT AGAINST IT TOO. FOR CHARLES, THE MUSIC JUST REFLECTED HIS LIFE.

CLARA WARD

BIG BILL BROONZY

HE'S CRYING SANCTIFIED. HE'S MIXING THE BLUES WITH THE SPIRITUALS. I KNOW THAT'S WRONG. HE SHOULD BE SINGING IN A CHURCH.

I WAS RAISED IN THE CHURCH AND WAS AROUND BLUES AND WOULD HEAR ALL THESE MUSICIANS ON THE JUKEBOXES AND THEN I WOULD GO TO REVIVAL MEETINGS ON SUNDAY MORNING. SO I WOULD GET BOTH SIDES OF MUSIC. A LOT OF PEOPLE AT THE TIME THOUGHT IT WAS SACRILEGIOUS, BUT ALL I WAS DOING WAS SINGING THE WAY I FELT.

IF I WROTE A SONG ABOUT JESUS AND SOME GUY TURNED IT INTO A SONG ABOUT HIS GIRLFRIEND, I'D BE PRETTY UPSET TOO!

AND YET WITHOUT THAT BACK AND FORTH, FROM THE TROUBADOURS ON FORWARD, THINK HOW MUCH MUSIC WE WOULD LOSE...

AND WHAT RAY CHARLES DID WAS SIMPLY BRILLIANT... HE TOOK GOSPEL AND BLUES, AND CREATED SOUL. IT WASN'T ORIGINAL BUT IT *WAS* SOMETHING NEW.

SOUL

MUAHAHAH!

217

SO. YOU GUYS ARE THE EXPERTS. IS THAT LEGAL?
WOULD IT BE LEGAL TODAY? PROBABLY NOT. CHARLES WAS TAKING BIG CHUNKS OF MELODY, REWORDING SONGS...YOU COULD CLAIM ALL CHARLES' SONGS WERE "FAIR USES"...
...PARODIES OF THE GOSPEL ORIGINALS...
IT WOULD BE A TOUGH – AND EXPENSIVE – FIGHT.
BUT BORROWING FROM GOSPEL AND BLUES IS WHAT SOUL'S ALL ABOUT!
THEFT
BACK THEN, PEOPLE JUST DIDN'T THINK THAT COPYRIGHT REGULATED MUSIC THIS FINELY – ON THE ATOMIC LEVEL. BUSINESS PEOPLE DIDN'T SUE.
SO YOU'RE TELLING ME THAT TODAY CLARA WARD COULD HAVE STOPPED RAY CHARLES?
YUP.
AND SHE PROBABLY WOULD HAVE.
WHAT ABOUT KANYE? COULD HE HAVE USED COPYRIGHT TO STOP THE LEGENDARY K.O. FROM SAMPLING HIM?
WELL, PEOPLE WOULD HAVE RIDICULED HIM IF HE HAD. BUT LEGALLY SPEAKING?
THAT'S A TOUGH ONE. THE SUBJECT MATTER IS TIMELY AND POLITICALLY CHARGED, THE NEW VERSION IS HEAVILY TRANSFORMED AND K.O. WEREN'T MAKING IT COMMERCIALLY.
THOSE THINGS ALL CUT STRONGLY IN FAVOR OF FAIR USE.
MR. WEST'S REPRESENTATIVES LATER TRIED TO USE COPYRIGHT TO BLOCK THE LEGENDARY KO'S MATERIAL FROM THE INTERNET. IRONY? –EDS.
BUT YOU CAN HARDLY SAY IT IS A PARODY OF GOLD DIGGER. IT IS MORE OF A SATIRE, USING KANYE'S SONG TO MAKE A DIFFERENT POINT...
...SATIRES CAN CERTAINLY BE FAIR USES BUT A PARODY WOULD HAVE BEEN AN EASIER CASE...
AND SOME COURTS HAVE SAID THAT GETTING SOMETHING WITHOUT PAYING THE CUSTOMARY PRICE IS "COMMERCIAL." K.O. DIDN'T PAY TO CLEAR THOSE SAMPLES...

BOTTOM LINE, I'D SAY THAT WHAT THEY ARE DOING IS PROTECTED FAIR USE, BUT SOME LAWYERS MIGHT DISAGREE, THINKING K.O. WERE JUST FREE-RIDING ON KANYE'S FAME AND THE POPULARITY OF HIS NEW SONG...

...JUST AS BEN FRANKLIN DID, WHEN HE REWORDED A POPULAR SONG OF HIS DAY.

OK. I AM HAVING LEGAL TMI. TOO. MUCH. INFORMATION.

T.M.I.

BASICALLY, WHAT YOU ARE TELLING ME IS THAT THE STORY OF THIS ONE SONG — THIS HUNDRED YEAR LONG CHAIN OF BORROWING AND TRANSPOSING — SHOWS HOW MANY OF THE CREATIVE PRACTICES MUSIC HAS ALWAYS USED MIGHT BE ILLEGAL TODAY? RIGHT?

RIGHT.

219

WAIT THIS ISN'T *FORBIDDING* IT, JUST SAYING PEOPLE HAVE TO PAY FOR IT. THAT'S LIKE SAYING GROCERY STORES ARE "FORBIDDING" FOOD BY CHARGING FOR IT!
OF COURSE COMPOSERS SHOULD GET PAID! LARGE-SCALE BORROWING GOES OVER THE LINE! BUT PAY FOR EVERY JAZZ SOLO, OR FOLK SONG IN A CLASSICAL COMPOSITION? EVERY TINY SAMPLE? WOULD THAT GET US MORE MUSIC? ACTUALLY IT WOULD BE A GREAT MUSICAL DISAPPEARING ACT!
...AND REMEMBER, THOSE WHO ARE BORROWED FROM, ALSO BORROW THEMSELVES! WE NEED THE RIGHT *BALANCE* BETWEEN WHAT'S OWNED AND WHAT'S FREE.
ANY RULE THAT MAKES JAZZ ILLEGAL IS CLEARLY WRONG. HMMM.
LOOK BACK AT THE WHOLE COMIC.
THIS IS A COMIC?
IMAGINE WE HAD TODAY'S COPYRIGHT SYSTEM FROM THE BIRTH OF MUSIC. MUCH OF THE MUSIC WE'VE BEEN TALKING ABOUT WOULDN'T EXIST.
THE SOURCES WOULD STILL HAVE BEEN UNDER COPYRIGHT - TODAY'S COPYRIGHT TERMS ARE SO LONG - AND THE BORROWING WOULD NOT FALL INTO AN EXCEPTION.
SHOULDN'T HAVE WRITTEN ABOUT SWEET AND PLEASANT BRUNETTES.
BUT THE CHURCH COMPOSERS BORROWED FROM US!!
Convicted of Borrowing

IT TURNS OUT THEY CAN'T HANDEL THE TRUTH.
IT TURNS OUT THERE ISN'T EVEN ONE BEETHOVEN!
Stravinsky
Berio
KIND OF GONE.
MILES DAVIS
COLUMBIA Lp
Kind of Gone
NONATHOLOGY.
Charlie Parker
Ornithology
Nonathology
NEVER MIND DEALS WITH THE DEVIL, JUST DON'T MAKE DEALS WITH THE LAWYERS!!
BLACKBIRD NOT SINGING IN THE DEAD OF NIGHT...
SO WHAT WOULD THAT LEAVE US WITH? SILENCE?

> This comic will resume in 4'33".
>
> Yours,
> John Cage.

> I THINK CAGE'S SILENCE IS A FLAGRANT RIPOFF OF WE MICE. EVER HEARD THE PHRASE 'QUIET AS A MOUSE'? WE SHOULD *SUE* HIM!

| NO, OF COURSE NOT! | WE'RE HUMAN, WE MAKE MUSIC. THAT'S WHAT WE DO... | ...LEGAL OR NOT. AND SOMETIMES FORBIDDING BORROWING WILL MAKE MUSICIANS MORE ORIGINAL. | ...BUT DOES IT MAKE IT HARDER TO BUILD ON WHAT CAME BEFORE? |

"IF I HAVE SEEN FURTHER, IT IS BECAUSE I HAVE STOOD ON THE SHOULDERS OF..."

"...NO ONE?"

OK, OK. YOUR POINT IS, WILL WE GET THE NEXT GENRE, THE NEXT SOUL OR JAZZ, THE NEXT RAY CHARLES OR K.O., OR WILL THE RULES STAND IN THE WAY? RIGHT?

RIGHT!

GUYS, WAKE UP! WHO CARES WHAT THE LAW SAYS, NOW WE'VE GOT THE INTERNET! LOOK AT YOUTUBE!

CATS DOING THE HARLEM SHAKE?

YOU CAN'T MAKE IT THROUGH A DAY WITHOUT HAVING A VIDEO OF CATS DOING THE HARLEM SHAKE ON THE PIANO, OR PRISONERS RE-ENACTING CALL ME MAYBE IN TAGALOG!

SERIOUSLY, THINK OF YOUR FAVORITES! THE LITERAL VIDEO OF TOTAL ECLIPSE OF THE HEART. KANYE WEST'S MONSTER SUNG BY THE MUPPETS.* BABY GOT BACK DONE AS A GILBERT AND SULLIVAN MUSICAL.

*CURRENTLY BLOCKED ON YOUTUBE. —EDS.

THIS IS THE ERA OF REMIX! WORRYING ABOUT THERE BEING TOO LITTLE MUSICAL BORROWING TODAY IS LIKE...

...WORRYING ABOUT A DROUGHT WHILE YOU ARE IN THE MIDDLE OF A RAINSTORM...

...AND NOT A DROP TO DRINK.

...WORRYING THAT THERE WON'T BE ENOUGH CELEBRITY GOSSIP...

224

...WORRYING THAT THERE WON'T BE ENOUGH FACTIONALISM IN CONGRESS...
I LOVE YOU, MAN.
IT'S THE LEAST OF OUR WORRIES!
WELL, YOU HAVE A POINT.
THE IRONY IS THAT AS THE LAW BECAME MORE CONTROLLING, AS IT HAS REGULATED MUSIC MORE TIGHTLY...
THE TECHNOLOGY DID THE OPPOSITE! A TEENAGER CAN NOW DO THINGS ON A LAPTOP THAT ONLY A HIGH END RECORDING STUDIO COULD HAVE DONE IN 1980.
Motown
Spector Wall of Sound
Abbey Road
Electric Lady
Select Your Studio!

SO WHO CARES WHAT THE LAW SAYS? LOOKING JUST AT REMIX, WE HAVE MORE PRACTICAL CULTURAL FREEDOM THAN EVER.
RIGHT!
EXCEPT IT ISN'T THAT SIMPLE.
REMEMBER THE LEGENDARY K.O.'S SONG?
SURE - AND YOU CAN'T TELL ME MILLIONS OF PEOPLE DIDN'T HEAR IT ONLINE.
YES THEY DID. IF THEY HAD AN INTERNET CONNECTION. BUT ON TV? ON MAINSTREAM RADIO? NO, THE LAW OPERATES LIKE A FILTER, A MEMBRANE, TO KEEP LEGALLY QUESTIONABLE MATERIAL OUT.
WHICH MEANS THAT THE HURRICANE KATRINA REFUGEES, THE PEOPLE EXILED TO THE HOUSTON ASTRODOME...
WERE VERY UNLIKELY TO BE ABLE TO HEAR THE SONG WRITTEN ABOUT THEM...
WE HAVE TWO REALMS OF CULTURE NOW. ONE, INFORMAL, FLEETING, AND ONLINE. THE VIDEO GOES UP AND YOU SEND IT TO YOUR FRIENDS BUT A YEAR LATER ALL YOU FIND IS...
IT'S THE VIDEO FORMERLY KNOWN AS "MASHUP"!!
THIS VIDEO HAS BEEN BLOCKED BY THE RIGHTSHOLDER
THE OTHER KIND OF MUSIC IS LEGAL, LICENSED, PERVASIVE AND PERMANENT. IT LASTS.
MUSICAL HERITAGE
GOT A NEW ONE FOR THE COLLECTION. NAME'S BIEBER.
THE HEAVENS WEEP...
The Grey Album
Let it Be, No Cry
DJ Earworm 25
Paid for my Doorbe
Sweet Dreams are Made of Seven Nation Army
IF ALL YOU CREATE ARE FLEETING LITTLE BUBBLES OF CLEVER REMIX, HOW CAN ANYONE BUILD ON WHAT YOU DO?

RAY CHARLES STARTED BY STRAIGHT COPYING... BUT HE DID MORE THAN THAT, HE BUILT A WHOLE TRADITION AND THEN OTHER ARTISTS BUILT ON WHAT HE'D DONE.
I SHOULD BE THE ONE ON THE BOTTOM!
TRY IT.
AND IT WAS LEGAL. PEOPLE COULD HEAR IT ON TV AND THE RADIO. MUSICIANS COULD BUILD THEIR CAREERS AROUND IT WITHOUT WORRYING THEIR SONGS WOULD BE BREAKING THE LAW.
SURE, MUSICIANS WILL ALWAYS MAKE MUSIC, WILL ALWAYS BREAK THE RULES, BUT IT BECOMES MUCH HARDER.
SO YOU ARE SAYING, YOU CAN MAKE AN INDIVIDUAL MASHUP ON YOUTUBE, BUT WHAT ABOUT A WHOLE GENRE LIKE SOUL OR JAZZ?
HE'S RIGHT. AT THE VERY LEAST, IT IS MUCH HARDER.
AND MAYBE WE DON'T WANT ONLY TO ENCOURAGE THE MAGPIE-CLEVER CUT AND PASTE OF THE INTERNET MEME...
I MAY ONLY BE A BIRD, BUT EVEN I KNOW THIS IS A MIXED METAPHOR.
"WHITHER VIRTUOSITY...?"
...OR THE AUTO-TUNED POP SONG THAT LICENSES A SINGLE RIFF FROM AN 80'S HIT...
...AND BEATS IT TO DEATH.
PLAY IT AGAIN, SAM.*
...AND AGAIN...
...AND AGAIN...
...AND AGAIN...
WAS YOU EVER BIT BY A DEAD B FLAT?
I BET I'VE BEEN BIT A HUNDRED TIMES THAT WAY.
...AND AGAIN.
*YES CLEVER-CLOGS, WE KNOW THEY DIDN'T USE THAT ACTUAL LINE IN THE MOVIE. HAPPY NOW? -EDS.

BUT DOESN'T ALL THIS IGNORE THE 800 POUND GORILLA IN THE ROOM?

??

DOWNLOADING!

DOWNLOADING!!!

I'VE HEARD THAT DOWNLOADING HAS ALL BUT DESTROYED THE MUSIC INDUSTRY.

HOW CAN YOU FUSS ABOUT A FEW RULES AFFECTING BORROWING LITTLE PIECES OF MUSIC, WHEN MILLIONS OF PEOPLE ARE STEALING WHOLE SONGS!!

DOWNLOADING IS THE 800 POUND GORILLA AND NO ONE COULD IGNORE IT.

ARE NORMAL GORILLAS EVER ALLOWED IN THE ROOM?

WIKIPEDIA SAYS THE AVERAGE MALE GORILLA WEIGHS 300-400 POUNDS! WHY THIS 800 POUND STANDARD?! I AM THINKING BODY IMAGE PROBLEMS!

NOW ALL YOU HAVE TO DO IS TELL ME WHICH SIDE IS TELLING THE TRUTH ABOUT DOWNLOADING...!

WELL, THE FIRST THING TO SAY IS, IN THE UNITED STATES, *IT IS ILLEGAL.*

NOT ALL DOWNLOADING OF COURSE. IF YOU ARE BACKING UP YOUR OWN MUSIC, OR SHARING MUSIC UNDER A CREATIVE COMMONS LICENSE, OR MAKING A FAIR USE OF A COPYRIGHTED WORK, THAT IS OK.

BUT LARGE SCALE "SHARING" OF COPYRIGHTED MUSIC WITHOUT PERMISSION? ILLEGAL IN THE U.S.

AND WHILE IT IS ONE THING TO BREAK THE LAW IF YOU THINK IT IS UNJUST AND YOU ARE PROTESTING AGAINST IT AND WILLING TO TAKE THE CONSEQUENCES...

WE SERVE WHITES only

...YOU CAN'T CLAIM CIVIL DISOBEDIENCE IF ALL YOU WANT IS ANONYMOUS AND ILLEGAL ACCESS TO MUSIC FOR FREE!

OK! A CLEAR ANSWER! BUT HOW BAD ARE ITS EFFECTS?

WELL, THAT'S A LITTLE MORE COMPLEX...

LET'S HEAR FROM THE TWO SIDES ON THE ISSUE.

MEGA UPLOAD
WE ALL LOVE MUSIC, DON'T WE? IF ANYTHING HURTS MUSIC, WE SHOULD BE AGAINST IT, RIGHT? PIRACY HURTS MUSICIANS. IT WOULD HARM *ANYONE* IF WHAT THEY MAKE IS STOLEN. PIRACY THREATENS MUSICAL CREATIVITY!
YES, DIGITAL MARKETS ARE GROWING, *THANKS TO US!* BUT OVERALL SALES ARE DOWN AND THAT IS HURTING THE ECONOMY. THINK OF ALL THE PEOPLE – FROM RECORD STORE CLERKS TO SESSION MUSICIANS – WHOSE JOBS DEPEND ON THE MUSIC INDUSTRY.
72%

BUT IN THE WORLD OF MUSIC, THE SKY ISN'T FALLING, IT'S RISING!* SURE THERE ARE LOSSES TO THE OLD BUSINESS MODELS, BUT IF YOU FACTOR IN THE EXTRAORDINARY GROWTH OF LIVE PERFORMANCES, THE OVERALL MUSIC BUSINESS IS ACTUALLY BIGGER THAN EVER! MORE PEOPLE ARE MAKING MUSIC AND DIGITAL MARKETS ARE BOOMING!
DON'T CONFUSE YOUR BUSINESS MODEL WITH THE MUSIC BUSINESS! THE MAJORITY OF MUSICIANS HAVE NEVER RECEIVED MUCH FROM THE SALE OF COPYRIGHTED MUSIC. THERE ARE NEW BUSINESS MODELS OUT THERE. WE'VE EVEN USED THE INTERNET TO CROWDSOURCE PATRONAGE!
Alternative Business Models
HEIGH HO, HEIGH HO, IT'S OFF TO KICKSTARTER WE GO!
SO NOW IT'S BACK TO MUSICIANS BEGGING FOR "TIPS" AND FLATTERING PATRONS? AND THIS IS PROGRESS?
*SEE MASNICK & HO, THE SKY IS RISING. EDS.

AND WHAT'S THE BASELINE WE ARE MEASURING AGAINST?

PEOPLE DON'T MAKE AS MUCH MONEY OUT OF RECORDS. BUT I HAVE A TAKE ON THAT — PEOPLE ONLY MADE MONEY OUT OF RECORDS FOR A VERY, VERY SMALL TIME.

WHEN THE ROLLING STONES STARTED OUT, WE DIDN'T MAKE ANY MONEY OUT OF RECORDS BECAUSE RECORD COMPANIES WOULDN'T PAY YOU! THEY DIDN'T PAY ANYONE!

THEN, THERE WAS A SMALL PERIOD FROM 1970 TO 1997, WHERE PEOPLE DID GET PAID, AND THEY GOT PAID VERY HANDSOMELY AND EVERYONE MADE MONEY. BUT NOW THAT PERIOD HAS GONE.

SO IF YOU LOOK AT THE HISTORY OF RECORDED MUSIC FROM 1900 TO NOW, THERE WAS A 25 YEAR PERIOD WHERE ARTISTS DID VERY WELL, BUT THE REST OF THE TIME THEY DIDN'T.

WE'RE BACK IN THE AGE OF THE TROUBADOUR?

AND WHAT'S THE ALTERNATIVE?

WE DO HAVE RAMPANT ILLEGAL COPYING. MUST WE DRAMATICALLY INCREASE SURVEILLANCE AND ENFORCEMENT TO STOP IT?
WILL IT BE THE WORLD OF...
TOTAL CONTROL
WINSTON SMITH!!
YOU TRIED TO PLAY A SONG ON SOMEONE ELSE'S TELESCREEN...
YOU SANG A SONG IN THE SHOWER...
YOU THOUGHT OF A SONG.
IG BROTHER
S WATCHING YOU.
THAT'S THREE STRIKES, MR. SMITH. TO RECEIVE YOUR PUNISHMENT...
PROCEED TO ROOM 1201.
NOT ROOM 1201!!!
SMITH, W.
ART REQUIRES CONTROL, TOTAL CONTROL!
ALSO, THAT NEW TREATY DOESN'T CHANGE DOMESTIC LAW AND WE HAVE ALWAYS BEEN AT WAR WITH OCEANIA.
DRM

NOTE FOR THE IRONY-CHALLENGED: WE ARE SAYING THIS WOULD BE **BAD**. -EDS.

SO OUR CHOICES ARE "NO LAW OR NO PRIVACY?" NO, THANK YOU!
BOTH OF THOSE SOUND *TERRIBLE*!
WE CAN IMAGINE BETTER FUTURES THAN THOSE!
RIGHT NOW, ARTISTS ARE PIECING TOGETHER WAYS OF MAKING A LIVING...
MORE PEOPLE THAN EVER ARE MAKING MUSIC AND MAKING MONEY AT IT...
...BUT MOST OF THEM ARE DOING IT ON THE "PRO-AM MODEL." MUSIC ISN'T THEIR ONLY GIG. IS THAT...
...GOOD?
...AESTHETICALLY SUSTAINABLE? FEWER VIRTUOSO RECORDING MUSICIANS WHO SPEND A YEAR ON AN ALBUM?
...FEWER PEOPLE WHO WRITE SONGS FULL TIME?
IS THAT WHAT WE WANT?
MAYBE...AND MAYBE NOT!
ADS
VIDEO GAMES AND RINGTONES
LIVE PERFORMANCE
DOWNLOADS
STREAMING ROYALTIES
MERCH
STREAMING ROYALTIES
ALLOWING MORE PEOPLE TO BE CREATORS...THAT'S *THRILLING*!! WE SHOULD CELEBRATE IT, BUT...
...A SYSTEM THAT MAKES IT HARD FOR THEM TO BE CREATORS FULL TIME... NOT SO MUCH.

WELL, THERE IT IS. OVER 2000 YEARS OF MUSICAL HISTORY. WHAT HAVE WE LEARNED?

AN EXAM! I LOVE EXAMS!!

I'LL TAKE A STAB AT IT. MUSIC IS DIFFERENT. WE LOVE IT, BUT IT HITS US DEEP, DEEP.

WHICH MAKES US WANT TO CONTROL IT...

...FOR PHILOSOPHICAL REASONS...

...OR RELIGIOUS AND POLITICAL ONES...

"ONE EMPIRE! ONE RELIGION! ONE MUSICAL TRADITION!"

...AND WE POLICE MUSIC, TRYING TO PREVENT THE MINGLING OF CULTURES...

...OR THE MINGLING OF AESTHETICS... HIGH AND LOW, SACRED AND SECULAR, RELIGIOUS AND PROFANE...

...OR THE MINGLING OF RACES...

MUSIC BECOMES ANOTHER BATTLEGROUND FOR PREJUDICES ABOUT RACE AND CULTURE...

AND BECAUSE MUSIC TOUCHES US SO DEEP...

...THOSE FIGHTS ARE PASSIONATE!

AND SO WE FIGHT OVER THE TECHNOLOGIES...

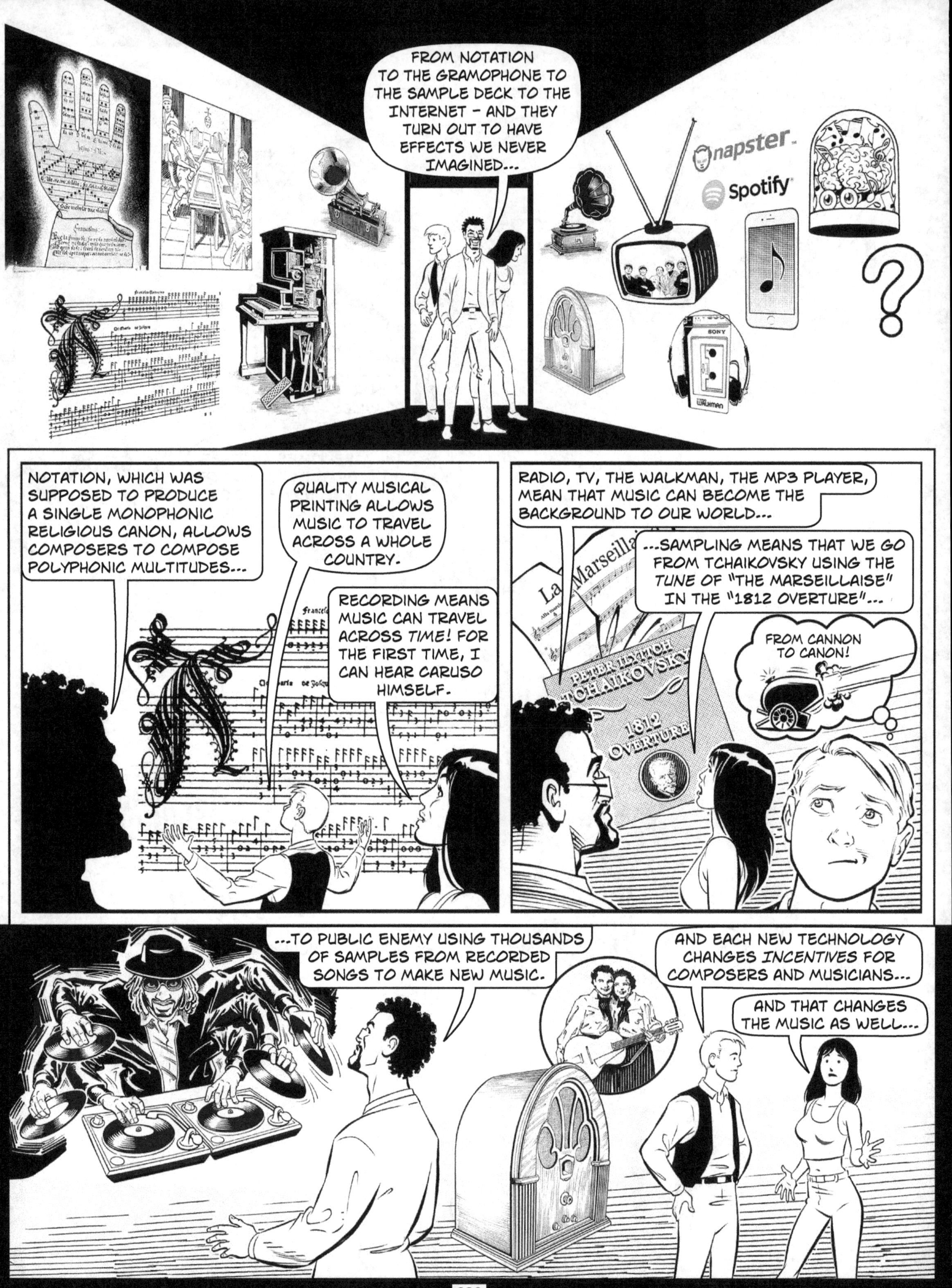
FROM NOTATION TO THE GRAMOPHONE TO THE SAMPLE DECK TO THE INTERNET – AND THEY TURN OUT TO HAVE EFFECTS WE NEVER IMAGINED...
napster
Spotify
SONY
WALKMAN
NOTATION, WHICH WAS SUPPOSED TO PRODUCE A SINGLE MONOPHONIC RELIGIOUS CANON, ALLOWS COMPOSERS TO COMPOSE POLYPHONIC MULTITUDES...
QUALITY MUSICAL PRINTING ALLOWS MUSIC TO TRAVEL ACROSS A WHOLE COUNTRY.
RECORDING MEANS MUSIC CAN TRAVEL ACROSS *TIME*! FOR THE FIRST TIME, I CAN HEAR CARUSO HIMSELF.
RADIO, TV, THE WALKMAN, THE MP3 PLAYER, MEAN THAT MUSIC CAN BECOME THE BACKGROUND TO OUR WORLD...
...SAMPLING MEANS THAT WE GO FROM TCHAIKOVSKY USING THE *TUNE* OF "THE MARSEILLAISE" IN THE "1812 OVERTURE"...
FROM CANNON TO CANON!
PETER ILYITCH TCHAIKOVSKY
1812 OVERTURE
...TO PUBLIC ENEMY USING THOUSANDS OF SAMPLES FROM RECORDED SONGS TO MAKE NEW MUSIC.
AND EACH NEW TECHNOLOGY CHANGES *INCENTIVES* FOR COMPOSERS AND MUSICIANS...
AND THAT CHANGES THE MUSIC AS WELL...

IN A WORLD WHERE MUSIC COULDN'T BE RECORDED, OR SHEET MUSIC SOLD, COMPOSERS DEPENDED ON PATRONAGE...

THE MUSIC WRITTEN TO PLEASE THE KING IS DIFFERENT THAN THE MUSIC ON A RADIO PROGRAM ADVERTISING 'THE KING OF BEERS...'

TRY PLEASING EMPEROR JOSEPH II! TALK ABOUT PICKY!!

...OR RECORDED BY THE YOUNG GERSHWIN ON A PIANO ROLL THAT PLAYED IN 10,000 SUBURBAN LIVING ROOMS.

AND THE WAY MUSICIANS EARN MONEY CHANGES.

DO I NEED A GREATER PRESENCE ON SOCIAL MEDIA?

#LUTELUST
@TROUBADOURFORHIRE

ROYALTY STATEMENT
$

ADS
VIDEO GAMES AND RINGTONES
LIVE PERFORMANCE
DOWNLOADS
MERCH
STREAMING ROYALTIES

THE LAW
AND THEN THERE IS THE LAW.
FOR THE FIRST 2400 YEARS OF THE STORY, PROPERTY LAW WAS FOREIGN TO MUSIC.
AND THE LAW AND TECHNOLOGY WEREN'T NEATLY SYNCHRONIZED, PROBABLY A GOOD THING. WE DIDN'T GET RIGHTS OVER "COPIES" UNTIL CENTURIES AFTER GUTENBERG.
REVOLUTIONARY TECHNOLOGY OVER HERE!? HELLO??!!
MUSIC COPYRIGHT: SOPHOCLES TO THE STATUTE OF ANNE
BUT STARTING IN THE 18TH CENTURY, WE STARTED USING COPYRIGHT AS A WAY OF ENCOURAGING MUSIC.
A BRILLIANT IDEA! IT GIVES RIGHTS TO CREATORS. BALANCES CONTROL WITH LIMITATIONS, POWERS WITH FREEDOMS...
ENCOURAGES THE CREATION OF NEW STUFF BY THIS CAREFUL PATTERN OF RIGHTS AND EXCEPTIONS...
...PROPERTY...
...AND THE PUBLIC DOMAIN.
THE CONCEPT IS MAGNIFICENT.
THE REALITY, LESS SO?
THE RIGHTS EXPAND IN EVERY DIMENSION. THE PERMISSIONS CULTURE CUTS AWAY AT THE PUBLIC DOMAIN.

AND NOW IN PLACE OF THIS CREATIVE FRENZY OF BORROWING AND INFLUENCE...
New Shiloh Baptist Church

...WE HAVE THE THREAT OF LEGAL GRIDLOCK, RIGHT AS THE TECHNOLOGIES GIVE US FREEDOMS WE'VE NEVER HAD.
CLEARLY ***ILLEGAL*** COPYING FLOURISHES – ILLICIT DOWNLOADING. BUT BORROWING THAT SHOULD BE ***LEGAL*** IS BLOCKED.
New Shiloh
Baptist Churc

243

WHAT ABOUT YOUR MUSIC BACKGROUND? CLASSICAL, I WOULD GUESS?
NO - PRETTY MUCH ALL PUNK ROCK. EARLY SEX PISTOLS KIND OF STUFF.
YEAH, I WAS THE FRONT MAN FOR A BAND CALLED MEAT & THE TENDERIZERS. I WAS "MEAT."

IT WAS SIMPLE STUFF. TWO CHORDS MAINLY. BUT I KNEW THOSE TWO CHORDS *WELL*!!

WHAT HAPPENED?

OH, SID VICIOUS DIED — THAT WAS A BLOW — WE STAGGERED ON.

BUT WHEN THE CLASH LOST THEIR ORIGINAL LINEUP... IT...

...IT WAS TOO MUCH.

I KNEW...

IT WAS TIME TO HANG IT UP.

I PUT IT BEHIND ME AND APPLIED...

TO LAW SCHOOL.

I HAVEN'T TOUCHED AN INSTRUMENT SINCE.

THAT'S SO SAD!!

IS IT REALLY SAD? I GAVE UP SOMETHING BUT I LEARNED ALL THIS...
NOW WHEN I LISTEN TO RAY CHARLES, OR LITTLE RICHARD...
...OR BEETHOVEN...
...OR A MASS...OR ROBERT JOHNSON!
...I KNOW WHERE IT ALL CAME FROM.
THERE'S SO MUCH BEAUTY THERE. SO MUCH HISTORY.

BARRIERS AND PREJUDICES, DISRUPTION AND OUTRAGE, BUT THE MUSIC ROLLS ON, GENERATION AFTER GENERATION.

"THE STAFF OF MUSIC IS LONG, BUT IT BENDS TOWARDS HARMONY?"

SOMETHING LIKE THAT.

"AND IF YOU'RE GIVEN THAT HISTORY, THAT HERITAGE, IT SEEMS IMPORTANT..., IMPORTANT..."

"...NOT TO SCREW IT UP!"

"YOU CAN'T AVOID THE VOID."

"ZIGGY PLAYED GUITAR..."

THESE SHADOWS HAVE DANCED FOR YOU FOR A FRAGMENT OF TIME.

PERHAPS SOMETHING IN THEIR WORDS HAS CAUGHT YOUR ATTENTION, TAUGHT YOU SOMETHING, GIVEN YOU AN IDEA?

BUT NOW THEIR MOMENT IN THE LIGHT IS OVER.

UNTIL THE NEXT TIME WE MEET, ALL THAT IS LEFT IS...

...THE OPPOSITE OF MUSIC...

NOT YET...

WAIT...

SILENCE.

About the Book
Or "*Pictures* of Dancing About Architecture"*

Music touches us deeply. A banal sentence. Remember when you were a teenager and the only thing more important to you than music, was the person you were in love with? (Requited or not.) Remember that moment when you could not even explain who you and your friends *were* without referring to this song, or that genre, this artist, that band? Remember being transported—made into something different—by a guitar riff, a line in a song ("and the *click* of high heeled shoes"), a rap lyric ("Straight outta Compton…"), Goodman's clarinet ("the ill woodwind that nobody blows good"), Davis's trumpet, Casal's throbbing cello, Horowitz's dreamy precision —by an insistent bass line, a brilliant "drop" in EDM, by the apparently accidental inevitability of a musical phrase? That is what music is to us. It reaches our core—or maybe creates it.

Music is different. An argument, you can accept or reject, fact-check or analyze. A tune? Not so much. Music seems to flow over, through or behind our mental firewalls. We talk about it touching us "viscerally," as though our viscera, our guts, were a locus for beauty. But music reaches places in our minds, not just our intestines.

Music builds on itself. To those who think that mash-ups and sampling started with YouTube or a DJ's turntables, it might be shocking to find that musicians have been borrowing—*extensively* borrowing, consciously and unconsciously—from each other since music itself began. We don't mean simple copying—the reproduction of an entire song. We mean the borrowing and cultural cross-fertilization that creates more music. Church musicians borrowing from troubadours. The Marseillaise quoted in the 1812 Overture. The African polyrhythms that came to the United States during slavery. The fragment of another tune in a jazz solo. Whether it is the rhythm and blues and country music that built rock and roll, the fusion of blues and gospel that made soul music, or the wall of sound in early rap, the lines of borrowing and cross-fertilization go on and on. Sometimes musical traditions are appropriated without adequate credit or compensation. Sometimes the borrowing brings communities together, creates a shared and more inclusive culture. And that borrowing continues even when it is forbidden; whether by the state, or the church, or the racial segregationist, or the guardians of high culture. It goes on even when the technology of the time seems to make it difficult. In fact, those technologies—from musical notation to the player piano to the tape loop to the sample deck—turn out to be unruly. They often do the opposite of what we expect them to, sometimes to our great benefit.

Music's production systems have changed. The technologies have evolved, of course. (Isn't it remarkable to think that, until about the end of the 19th century, to hear music you either had to play it yourself or hire someone to play it for you? We think ourselves at the bleeding edge of musical technology, but the advent of recorded music is a greater transformation than anything that has happened in our lifetimes.) The *incentive* systems have changed, from the troubadour or the gifted amateur, to the Church composer, the aristocratic patronage system, the rise of music as a commodity for the masses—whether in the form of sheet music, player piano rolls, vinyl, CD, downloads or streams. And with the technologies and the incentive systems, the *law* of music has changed, often for good but sometimes for ill. We now face the irony that as rampant illegal downloading of recorded music goes on, the artistic practice of *making* music has never been so tangled in cumbersome permissions and fees, licenses and collecting societies. Artists should get paid—this book is most emphatically **not** a defense of illegal downloading—but the law should serve creativity, not hinder it.

Music matters. People fight about it—not just the kind of fight when one spouse ludicrously denies the brilliance of Joni Mitchell and the other insists upon it. People fight about music because they think it

---

*The full quotation is "Writing about music is like dancing about architecture." It is popularly attributed to Elvis Costello. He said he does not remember saying it. The difficulty of attribution in a world of borrowing! Someone should write a comic book about it.

has power, that its shape reflects our culture—or changes it—that it strengthens the state or the religion—or undermines it. Name a line that we care about: philosophical, religious, political, racial, cultural, legal. Music is on those battlements, conscripted to hold a line, even when those lines become increasingly…blurred.

This is a "graphic novel," a *comic book*, by two law professors about the history of music, of musical borrowing, from Plato to rap. Obviously, some explanation is needed. We write about innovation and creativity. Ten years ago, disturbed by the way that documentary filmmakers were being hobbled by ludicrous copyright claims over tiny fragments of music or image momentarily caught by their cameras, we wrote a comic book about "fair use" with our late, and much-missed, colleague, Keith Aoki. (For some reason, readers seem to prefer comic books to our law review articles. Go figure.) Our goal was to translate our legal expertise and scholarship into an accessible form for the new generation of digital creators who lacked the high-priced legal advice that established media took for granted. We thought the comic would be read by a few film students. It has been downloaded more than a million times and translated into multiple languages. There was a demand, it seemed.

We thought we were done with comic books. But then we started writing and teaching about musical borrowing—the way that composers and musicians borrow from each other, whether by sampling, quoting, parodying, or building on a genre. We found ourselves disturbed by the same "permissions culture" that we had written about in documentary film. Even the tiniest musical reference brought forth a demand for licensing and payment. Of course, there are lots of occasions when permission *should* be asked and where payment is entirely appropriate: for example, using a fragment of a song in a commercial or taking a substantial chunk of a tune and building a new song on it, not as commentary, but simply as a commercial remix. But this was different. This was the regulation of music at the atomic level. No amount was too small for a property claim, despite the fact that copyright law has many exceptions to allow for insubstantial borrowing and reference. Could one imagine the great musical genres of the past being developed under such a scheme? Jazz? The blues? Soul? Rock and roll? We concluded that it was unlikely. That seemed…worrying.

Our research took us to the history of musical borrowing. Even limiting ourselves for reasons of time and practicality to the Western musical tradition, that history was vast, a scholars' delight, an endless set of puzzles and connections that led us further and further back in time. The research for the book took us years. (Far too many years, in fact.) There are many histories of music that chart the rise and fall of musical movements—classicism to romanticism, or rock to punk. We have benefited from them. But there is another side to musical history. As we worked, we realized that, again and again through history, there had been numerous attempts to police music; to restrict borrowing—for reasons of philosophy, religion, politics, race—again and again, race—and law. And because music affects us so deeply, those fights were *passionate* ones. They still are. The history runs from Plato to *Blurred Lines* and beyond. And to understand the history of musical borrowing, one had to spin the story out still further—into musical technologies (from notation to the sample deck), aesthetics, the incentive systems that got musicians paid, and law's 250-year long struggle to assimilate music. This is that story. It is assuredly not *the* history of music. But it is definitely a part of that history and, we think, a fascinating one. Remember those musical moments that we mentioned earlier? The music that made you, you? You wouldn't have those moments but for this history, this story. We have tried to tell it here. We hope you like it.

James Boyle & Jennifer Jenkins
Durham, NC. 2017

Acknowledgments and Further Reading

This is a book about borrowing. And scholars are borrowers. Massive borrowers, whose only surety is the promise to "pay it forward."

We have benefited from so many sources—colleagues, scholars we have never met, online resources, blogs, books about the Renaissance music scene, or the Mississippi Delta, or classical music or the blues. What follows here is not a complete list of our sources. Instead of offering that here and making the book 400 pages long, we've provided an extensive set of references for the comic online here: https://law.duke.edu/musiccomic/references. But what follows is a good place to get started for the person who is interested more generally in the comic's themes, as well as a heartfelt "thank you" from us to those whose work informed our research.

The History of Western Musical Borrowing

Everyone interested in the history of borrowing in Western music should begin with the work of Professor J. Peter Burkholder. We consulted his work extensively. In particular we relied upon:

- The "Borrowing" section Professor Burkholder wrote for *Grove Music Online* http://www.oxfordmusiconline.com/public/book/omo_gmo (part of Oxford Music Online). Unfortunately, this is behind a paywall. This resource offers exhaustive details about borrowing in Western music through articles that run from medieval monophony and polyphony to Renaissance music, various classical periods, "art music," and jazz.
- Burkholder also compiled with Andreas Giger and David C. Birchler an online resource called "Musical borrowing: an annotated bibliography" (formerly available online at http://www.music.indiana.edu/borrowing/). As of December 2016, that site is offline because of a 2015 cyberattack. We hope to see its return soon.
- J. Peter Burkholder, *All Made of Tunes: Charles Ives and the Uses of Musical Borrowing* (Yale University Press, 1995), a book on borrowing in the work of the American modernist composer Charles Ives.
- Moving beyond borrowing alone, the broader history of Western music is covered in J. Peter Burkholder, Donald Jay Grout and Claude V. Palisca, *A History of Western Music* (Ninth Edition) (W.W. Norton & Co., 2014).

Apart from Professor Burkholder's prodigious *oeuvre*, we found many other works useful. Here are a few that are particularly worthy of note. A fuller listing is in the online reference guide to the comic.

- Honey Meconi, ed., *Early Musical Borrowing* (Routledge, 2004)
- Norman Carrell, *Bach the Borrower* (Allen & Unwin, 1967)
- John T. Winemiller, "Recontextualizing Handel's Borrowing," *The Journal of Musicology* (Autumn 1997)
- David Metzer, *Quotation and Cultural Meaning in Twentieth-Century Music* (Cambridge University Press, 2003)

Law and Musical Borrowing

Despite its fascinating features, music's relationship to copyright—through history—has been a subject that until relatively recently received little scholarly attention. The articles and books noted below changed that. Carroll's series of articles is a magisterial introduction to music copyright's history. Arewa writes sensitively of music, property and cultural appropriation—particularly across racial lines. Boyle illustrates the story of musical borrowing and copyright with a 100-year long history of a protest song written after Hurricane Katrina (told in the "I Got A Mashup—A Song's Tale" section of this comic, pp. 201–222). Vaidhyanathan and McLeod were the first seriously to engage with the cultural and aesthetic effects of restrictive legal regulation on musical borrowing, particularly in rap and hip-hop music. Together with the work of Lessig, their scholarship has defined the field. Greene has written extensively about the intersection of music, copyright, and race. McLeod and DiCola have offered the definitive account of the law and culture of digital sampling. Demers provides a musicologist's perspective on these issues.

- Michael W. Carroll, "Whose Music Is It Anyway?: How We Came to View Musical Expression as a Form of Property," *University of Cincinnati Law Review* (Summer 2004) and "The Struggle for Music Copyright," *Florida Law Review* (September 2005)
- Olufunmilayo B. Arewa, "From J.C. Bach to Hip Hop: Musical Borrowing, Copyright and Cultural Context," *North Carolina Law Review* (January 2006); "Copyright on Catfish Row: Musical Borrowing, *Porgy and Bess*, and Unfair Use," *Rutgers Law Journal* (Winter 2006); "Blues Lives: Promise and Perils of Musical Copyright," *Cardozo Arts and Entertainment Law Journal* (2010)
- James Boyle, *The Public Domain: Enclosing the Commons of the Mind* (Yale University Press, 2008), Chapter 6 "I Got A Mashup." This book is freely available online at http://www.thepublicdomain.org/download/.
- Siva Vaidhyanathan, *Copyrights and Copywrongs: The Rise of Intellectual Property and How It Threatens Creativity* (NYU Press, 2001)
- Kembrew McLeod, *Owning Culture: Authorship, Ownership, and Intellectual Property Law* (P. Lang, 2001)
- Lawrence Lessig, *Remix: Making Art and Commerce Thrive in the Hybrid Economy* (The Penguin Press, 2008); *Free Culture: How Big Media Uses Technology and the Law to Lock Down Culture and Control Creativity* (The Penguin Press, 2004)
- Kevin J. Greene, "Copyright, Culture & Black Music: A Legacy of Unequal Protection," *Hastings Communications & Entertainment Law Journal* (Winter 1999)
- Kembrew McLeod and Peter DiCola, *Creative License: The Law and Culture of Digital Sampling* (Duke University Press, 2011)
- Joanna Demers, *Steal This Music: How Intellectual Property Law Affects Musical Creativity* (University of Georgia Press, 2006)

When it comes to the way that the structure of economic incentives affects music, there is no better resource than:

- Frederic M. Scherer, *Quarter Notes and Bank Notes: The Economics of Music Composition in the Eighteenth and Nineteenth Centuries* (Princeton University Press, 2004). (Professor Scherer judiciously decides not to present the reader with any conclusions about which is superior: music developed under a patronage system, or music written for some form of mass market sale.)

Online Resources

We made extensive and grateful use of an excellent collection of historical documents compiled by the University of Cambridge, "a digital archive of primary sources on copyright from the invention of the printing press (c. 1450) to the Berne Convention (1886) and beyond." You can find some of the documents we refer to in this book, from Petrucci's patents to Orlando di Lasso's printing privileges (filed under the alternate name Orlande de Lassus), in this database.

- *Primary Sources on Copyright History (1450–1900)* http://www.cipil.law.cam.ac.uk/primary-sources-copyright-history-1450-1900

Another extremely useful website is the "Music Copyright Infringement Resource" sponsored by Columbia Law School and the University of Southern California Gould School of Law. There, you can find judicial opinions from over a hundred music copyright cases from 1844 to the present, along with commentary and relevant sheet music and audio files.

- *Music Copyright Infringement Resource* http://mcir.usc.edu/

Those interested in following endless trails of musical borrowing will enjoy the encyclopedic, crowdsourced "Who Sampled" website—you can choose a song and find both the songs it used, and the songs that in turn used it, along with the relevant audio.

- *Whosampled* http://www.whosampled.com/

The Music

The materials cited above—particularly the encyclopedic *Grove Music Online*, Burkholder et al.'s *A History of Western Music*, and Meconi's *Early Musical Borrowing*, provide a wealth of information about Western music throughout history, including Renaissance music and "classical" music from the Baroque, Classical, Romantic, and 20th century periods. Here is a selection of additional resources on the music of Ancient Greece, the Middle Ages, and the Renaissance.

- William A. Johnson, "Musical Evenings in the Early Empire: New Evidence from a Greek Papyrus with Musical Notation," *Journal of Hellenic Studies* (2000). For our discussion of Ancient Greek notation, we are particularly indebted to this article written by a Duke colleague, which casts light on Greek notation using a Roman-era papyrus.
- Thomas J. Mathiesen, *Apollo's Lyre: Greek Music and Music Theory in Antiquity and the Middle Ages* (University of Nebraska Press, 1999)
- Anna Maria Busse Berger and Jesse Rodin, eds., *The Cambridge History of Fifteenth-Century Music* (Cambridge University Press, 2015)
- Richard L. Crocker, *A History of Musical Style* (Revised Edition) (Dover Publications, 1986)
- Richard L. Crocker and David Hiley, eds., *The New Oxford History of Music: Volume II: The Early Middle Ages to 1300* (Second Edition) (Oxford University Press, 1990); Gerald Abraham and Dom Anselm Hughes, eds., *The New Oxford History of Music: Volume III: Ars Nova and the Renaissance 1300–1540* (First Edition) (Oxford University Press, 1960)

Turning to more recent genres and American music, the following resources illuminate everything from how slaves influenced American music and the history of the banjo, to our national anthem, to genres such as jazz, blues, rock and roll, and hip hop. Many of these resources detail the impact of black music and the persistence of racial anxieties in response to new genres.

- Eileen Southern, *The Music of Black Americans: A History* (Third Edition) (W.W. Norton & Co., 1997)
- Laurent Dubois, *The Banjo: America's African Instrument* (Harvard University Press, 2016)
- Brian Ward, *Just My Soul Responding: Rhythm and Blues, Black Consciousness, and Race Relations* (University of California Press, 1998)
- Mark Anthony Neal, *What the Music Said: Black Popular Music and Black Public Culture* (Routledge, 1998)
- Samuel A. Floyd, Jr., *The Power of Black Music: Interpreting Its History from Africa to the United States* (Oxford University Press, 1995)

- Mark Clague, *Star Spangled Songbook* (Star Spangled Music Foundation, 2015) (collecting reuses of the national anthem)
- Ted Gioia, *The History of Jazz* (Second Edition) (Oxford University Press, 2011)
- Paul Berliner, *Thinking in Jazz: The Infinite Art of Improvisation* (University of Chicago Press, 1994)
- Robert Palmer, *Deep Blues: A Musical and Cultural History of the Mississippi Delta* (Penguin Books, 1982)
- Holly George-Warren and Patricia Romanowski, eds., *The Rolling Stone Encyclopedia of Rock & Roll* (Third Edition) (Rolling Stone Press, 2001)
- Paul Friedlander, *Rock and Roll: A Social History* (Westview Press, 1996)
- Glenn C. Altschuler, *All Shook Up: How Rock 'n' Roll Changed America* (Oxford University Press, 2003)
- Paul Miller (a.k.a. DJ Spooky, that Subliminal Kid), ed., *Sound Unbound: Sampling Digital Music and Culture* (MIT Press, 2008)
- Mark Costello and David Foster Wallace, *Signifying Rappers* (First Edition) (Ecco Press, 1990) (yes, that David Foster Wallace)

The People

The comic features a fascinating cast of composers and performers, and the lives of many others informed our research. The sources cited above (especially *Grove Music Online* and *A History of Western Music*) offer biographical sketches of the classical composers we discuss early in the comic. For Stephen Foster, Scott Joplin, George Gershwin, Dizzy Gillespie, Robert Johnson, Chuck Berry, Little Richard, Elvis Presley, Jerry Leiber and Mike Stoller, Ray Charles, and the Beatles, here are selected resources.

- Ken Emerson, *Doo-dah!: Stephen Foster and the Rise of American Popular Culture* (Simon & Schuster, 1997)
- Edward A. Berlin, *King of Ragtime: Scott Joplin and His Era* (First Edition) (Oxford University Press, 1994)
- Howard Pollack, *George Gershwin: His Life and Work* (University of California Press, 2007)
- Robert Wyatt and John Andrew Johnson, eds., *The George Gershwin Reader* (Oxford University Press, 2004)
- Dizzy Gillespie, with Al Fraser, *To Be, or Not...To Bop* (Doubleday Books, 1979)
- Elijah Wald, *Escaping the Delta: Robert Johnson and the Invention of the Blues* (Amistad/HarperCollins, 2004)
- Bruce Pegg, *Brown Eyed Handsome Man: The Life and Hard Times of Chuck Berry* (Routledge, 2002)
- Michael T. Bertrand, *Race, Rock, and Elvis* (University of Illinois Press, 2000)
- Jerry Leiber and Mike Stoller, *Hound Dog: The Leiber & Stoller Autobiography* (Simon & Schuster, 2009)
- Charles White, *The Life And Times Of Little Richard: The Quasar of Rock* (Harmony Books, 1985)
- Michael Lydon, *Ray Charles: Man and Music* (Routledge, 2004)
- Ray Charles and David Ritz, *Brother Ray: Ray Charles' Own Story* (Da Capo Press, 1992)
- Elijah Wald, *How the Beatles Destroyed Rock 'n' Roll: An Alternative History of American Popular Music* (Oxford University Press, 2009)
- Walter Everett, *The Beatles as Musicians: Revolver through the Anthology* (Oxford University Press, 1999)

The Technology

Sources on the earliest "technology" we discuss—notation—are listed earlier. Here are some excellent resources discussing the revolutions wrought by the advent of sound recording technology, radio, and the Internet.

- Mark Katz, *Capturing Sound: How Technology Has Changed Music* (University of California Press, 2004)
- Greg Milner, *Perfecting Sound Forever: An Aural History of Recorded Music* (Farrar, Straus and Giroux, 2009)
- Christopher H. Sterling and John Michael Kittross, *Stay Tuned: A History of American Broadcasting* (Third Edition) (Lawrence Erlbaum Associates, 2001)
- Russell Sanjek, *Pennies from Heaven: The American Popular Music Business in the Twentieth Century* (Updated Edition) (Da Capo Press, 1996) (a comprehensive look at how 20th century technological developments changed the music business)
- Whitney Broussard, "The Promise and Peril of Collective Licensing," *Journal of Intellectual Property Law* (2009) (discussing the ASCAP antitrust consent decree)
- Paul Goldstein, *Copyright's Highway: From Gutenberg to the Celestial Jukebox* (Revised Edition) (Stanford University Press, 2003)
- William W. Fisher III, *Promises to Keep: Technology, Law, and the Future of Entertainment* (Stanford University Press, 2004)
- Yochai Benkler, *The Wealth of Networks: How Social Production Transforms Markets and Freedom* (Yale University Press, 2006)
- Jonathan Zittrain, *The Future of the Internet—And How to Stop It* (Yale University Press, 2008)
- Michael D. Smith and Rahul Telang, *Streaming, Sharing, Stealing: Big Data and the Future of Entertainment* (MIT Press, 2016)
- Matt Novak, "Watching David Bowie Argue With an Interviewer About the Future of the Internet Is Beautiful," available at http://paleofuture.gizmodo.com/watching-david-bowie-argue-with-an-interviewer-about-th-1791017656 (offering highlights from a prescient interview between David Bowie and the BBC, along with a link to the video)

Copyright Law and the Music Business

The Center for the Study of the Public Domain provides many resources on copyright law, all freely available online. In addition, the full text of the 1906 debates covered on pp. 89–91 of the comic is available on Google Books, and the Copyright Office offers useful information circulars covering the minutia of copyright law. A few prominent resources on music licensing and the music business are also included below.

- James Boyle and Jennifer Jenkins, *Intellectual Property: Law & The Information Society: Cases & Materials* (Third Edition, 2016), available at http://web.law.duke.edu/cspd/pdf/IPCasebook2016.pdf
- Keith Aoki, James Boyle, Jennifer Jenkins, *Bound By Law?* (Center for the Study of the Public Domain, 2006), a comic about copyright, fair use, and documentary film, is available at https://web.law.duke.edu/cspd/comics/
- The Center's materials on orphan works are here https://web.law.duke.edu/cspd/orphanworks.html
- The 1906 debates are online in full at https://books.google.com/books?id=m7QvAAAAMAAJ
- The Copyright Office's information circulars are available here https://www.copyright.gov/circs/
- Stanford University offers information about copyright and fair use at http://fairuse.stanford.edu/

- The Future of Music Coalition offers resources on music, law, and technology at https://futureofmusic.org/research
- Al Kohn and Bob Kohn, *Kohn on Music Licensing* (Fourth Edition) (Aspen Publishers, 2009)
- Donald S. Passman, *All You Need to Know About the Music Business* (Ninth Edition) (Simon & Schuster, 2015)
- M. William Krasilovsky and Sidney Shemel (authors), John M. Gross and Jonathan Feinstein (contributors), *This Business of Music: The Definitive Guide to the Business and Legal Issues of the Music Industry* (Tenth Edition) (Watson-Guptill Publications, 2007)

For the rest? Turn to the comic and just…"Pull."

CPSIA information can be obtained
at www.ICGtesting.com
Printed in the USA
LVHW061352251120
672674LV00036B/892